PREFACE

TO A

RELIGIOUS PHILOSOPHY

OF

LIVING

EZRA FRANTZ

Preface
to a
Religious Philosophy
of
LIVING

Pageant Press
New York: New York

To

Verna

Marjorie

Allan

STATEMENT OF AIM

The main object of my manuscript is to make a substantial contribution to the cause of World Peace. I am impatient of the small part that the church, as such, is playing toward the attainment of that goal. It is disappointing that philosophers, per se, seem never to be called on for help.

It is iterated and reiterated that we must recognize that progress is being made; that we must strive to accelerate the tempo of progress.

The manuscript is aimed to instill a faith in a God that did not create a failure when he created man. It is aimed to present man as the link between nature and spirit. That link, if made sufficiently strong, will insure World Peace.

The manuscript begins with a rough outline of how Protestants, Catholics and Jews could get together by taking as a starting point the pure religion of James, the Christian apostle, as described in his epistle. They should take the attitude that the U.N. is taking: "We dare not fail!"

I am hard on the churches who have made forms their masters; on the Jews who rest on laurels of the past; and on philosophers who delight in tearing down what other philosophers have erected. I try hard not to be like that. I try to accept what others have to offer, and work from there. Civilization is a torch that is constantly growing brighter. We dare not scorn the light from the past, nor the light that we hold in our hands. Most of us are blinded by the light of the present.

Here is the incident that actually got me started in the preparation of my manuscript. A clergyman tried to show that Lincoln was a very religious man. He drew up a Lincoln creed which Protestants, Catholics and Jews could accept without reservations. But the clergyman himself subscribes to a creed that excludes a live Lincoln. The point I stress is that the church must learn to be as easy on live liberals as it already is on dead ones.

The heart of my theme is that the important individual, as opposed to group of which we talk so much, is not myself, but my neighbor. We must learn to be jealous not for *our* rights, but for our *neighbors'* rights.

CONTENTS

INTRODUCTION

For years I have been searching for a satisfactory philosophy of religion. I have looked in books; I have explored my own mind. Books on the, or a, philosophy of religion extend little, if at all, beyond general philosophy; or, worse yet, become an apology for the authors' theological views.

I am convinced now that I have been looking for something that does not exist, a *satisfactory* philosophy of religion. A philosophy of religion is religion based on, or explained or justified by, philosophy.

On what is philosophy based? "Pure" philosophy is swallowed up in infinity and in the absolute. It has no foundation that has meaning to us. We mortals must find a foundation other than infinity and absolutism.

I propose a religious philosophy. This is philosophy with religion for a foundation; a philosophy that does not view with detachment.

Philosophy is the quest for a meaning to be found in life. Pure philosophy is but a minor phase of that quest. It is concerned about roots that are left dangling in infinity and the absolute. Pragmatic—or religious—philosophy is concerned about roots that can be probed in familiar territory.

In this book a strenuous effort will be made to draw a sharp line between religion and theology. This sharp line can be more clearly felt than delineated on paper. It will emerge gradually as we dwell on the concept of religion.

An excellent starting point toward a comprehension of this concept should be a consideration of the teachings of James, the Christian apostle.

He said, "Pure religion and undefiled before God and the Father is this, to visit the fatherless and widows in their affliction, and to keep himself unspotted from the world."

I am interested in the first part of his explanation. If we were acquainted with conditions as they existed among the people to whom he wrote, and I am assuming that we do understand them, we would hear

1

James saying that pure religion consists in giving help where help is needed most.

But this is not enough. Such giving can become a mere formality. And formality without the spirit is a form of idolatry. We must try to understand the *spirit* that should prompt us to give help where help is needed most.

This spirit is love for our neighbors. What is love? In this book love will have a restricted meaning. Perhaps every parent at times completely effaces himself in the interest of the child. He is not interested in personal credit. He is not motivated by a sense of duty to the child. He projects himself into the life of the child so completely that he is unmindful of himself. This is love.

We can cultivate this love by persistently projecting our lives into the lives of our neighbors. We thus learn to have a feeling of sympathy toward the aspirations of our neighbors. We gradually begin to sense the joy of self-effacement in the interests of our neighbors.

True love embraces duty so completely that duty loses its identity. There are some who are so obsessed with a sense of duty that they have little room for love. To such people life is a pain; they look to the next world for life's compensations. Such people should concentrate on losing themselves in the *interests* of others. Gradually they will thus come to a balanced view of life; and duty will become a joy rather than a pain. Love, not duty, should point the way.

This religion of love for our neighbors does not deny God. On the contrary, it recognizes this love as being of God. We can best worship God by having respect for His creation, chief of which is man, our neighbor.

Love is a leaven. Why is the whole lump not leavened? For the same reason that the progeny of a pair of flies will not populate the whole earth. Opposing and conflicting forces must be nullified or redirected. But love is the only force that will do it.

Let me suggest this supplement to my definition of a religious philosophy. It is the attempt to give a reasoned conception of man, my neighbor, and my, and the universe's, relation to him.

I am one, my neighbor is many, and I will let the universe take me only as far as I can go without losing contact with my neighbor.

This is deliberately called a preface because it is designed to be but a beginning toward thinking old thoughts along new lines and in new connections. This is probably as much as anyone can do. I have selected a big subject and can hope to do no more than *approach* it from many angles. It is a preface also in the sense that there is no attempt to split hairs in the use of such terms as religion, philosophy, education, etc. It is

2

definitely not meant for philosophical technicians.

Let me inject here the two thoughts that are uppermost in my mind as I write this book; tolerance and World Peace. It is hoped that you will keep them continually in mind as you read on, and in your subsequent meditations.

My thoughts on education are not restricted to the classroom. Whether I write about the classroom or the world outside the classroom, an effort should be made to make the application in both places.

Jesus never spoke about education in the classroom; the education that we receive in school. And yet He was a great Educator. True education is all-pervasive and never-ending. The school lends stress and direction. We are always learning; are we learning the right things? This is a major concern of the school and society.

Our education is influenced more by what we do in life than by what we do in school. The schools reflect life better than life reflects the schools. Even the conservative teacher is slightly bent in the direction of life as it is lived and he follows trends, but too slowly because too reluctantly.

Some teachers, for all practical purposes, believe that the school is more important than society. To such teachers perfect attendance by the pupils is the supreme achievement. To them it is unthinkable that there could be anything outside of school that could be more important than attendance. Such an attitude does away with the need for thinking. Such teachers are thinking too much about the past, when parents often kept children out of school for insufficient reason. Poor attendance was the rule.

Today good attendance is the rule. We teachers today need to learn to place more reliance on the judgment of parents on the question of justifiable absence from school. Such an attitude will tend to make us less complacent about what we are accomplishing in school; and bring us to the realization that the school is not all-important in the acquiring of an education.

Actually the schools dispense little education. Their big chance is in the social studies—human relationships. But few of the teachers succeed in liberating themselves from the shackles of *form*. They give little thought to the life and change that is continually going on within these forms; and they forget that all forms should always be in the plastic stage, responsive to human needs.

Basically, education is a process of continuous change—in the right direction—in our thought patterns; and a corresponding outward change. These changes never reach the perfect stage. And this is what should make life interesting for us to the very end of our days. A child looks for adventure around every corner. In the spirit we can live just as

3

adventurously, if we regard form, technique, and matter as catalysts, and not as ends in themselves. Such living is always in the metamorphic stage, always pressing onward and upward. True education is a spiritual growing to the very end of our mortal existence. It never stops.

This is why I should like to call this a philosophy of *education*. But the word "education" has too restricted a meaning for most people. It is enough to drive people away from reading many a good book. I am therefore substituting the word that comes closest to it in meaning, namely, "living." So as we move along let us think of education as living, and living as education.

I am not interested in starting arguments. I *am* interesting in starting a tide of sustained thinking along the lines of pure religion. The illustrations that I shall use will in general be intended for limited application unless you yourself can justify a wider one. Christians go out of their way to justify every word of Jesus recorded in the New Testament. They should also try to find the truths that He utters in their own experiences. Unbelievers attempt to discredit His words. All I ask is that the reader of this book take a middle ground in passing judgment on what I have to present. Try to get my viewpoint, and then expand to your heart's content. This is the religious and the democratic ideal.

In the course of our deliberations, it will be easy for you to assume that I am placing too much emphasis on the material and too little on the spiritual; unless I make it plain right here that it is always recognized that the only material thing that is worth considering must have a close relationship to a spiritual reality,—and that reality is always assumed if not expressed. Spirituality is reality.

Materialism is never reality, but it can point to reality; or it can be so immersed in spirituality as to be, for all practical purposes, reality. This apparently was Jesus' approach.

There is a continuous stream of articles and books coming out on the general theme that to achieve happiness and peace of mind one must be interested—lose oneself—in the lives and interests of others. This, of course, is true; but it has a too ready-made look. When people read about it and then try to put it into practice, they discover that it is not as simple as it appears.

It is still true that the surest guarantee of a satisfying old age is a *lifetime* of consecration to the welfare of others; and a continuous struggle against selfish impulses.

People try altruism and discover that it does not bring the expected results. The fact of the matter is that their altruism is not altruism at all.

4

Real altruism does not help others for its own personal benefit, but because of its interest in others.

Wealthy people sometimes try this shortcut to happiness. They give away fortunes. I believe they often are about as miserable as ever at the end. They all too often do not lose themselves in those whom they help. They tend to draw too sharp a line between what they give and what they keep. They stay in their own world. This is not altruism.

Altruism is a slow growth. None of us acquire it fully grown. We must have faith to believe that there is growth when none is apparent.

I might almost say that the object of this whole book is to consider many of the innumerable problems that must be faced and solved if we want altruism to permeate our whole existence.

It appears that at least ninety-five percent of the writers who get into print take it for granted that we are living in a most miserable age. I am ready to challenge that attitude. We have spent so much time dwelling on our shortcomings that the crying need of the hour is a judicious viewing of our accomplishments or, perhaps better still, "their" accomplishments and "our" shortcomings.

We need a recital of what "they" are doing for good and then much soul-searching to determine whether "we" have the right to be included with "they."

Our troubles have been the troubles of every age. Technological progress merely highlights the things that have always been humanity's shortcomings. We, as did every preceding age, pine for the resurrection of some mystical and mythical halcyon past when people loved their neighbors more than we do.

We must believe that we have advanced in our human relationships. This belief will give us the faith to carry on with renewed zeal. All capacities and abilities are for good and for evil. But that should not discourage us. We are rational folks. We can and must choose.

As you move from chapter to chapter—sometimes within the chapter—you will be confronted with many repetitions of the same ideas. These repetitions are put there, and left there, deliberately. They are in recognition of the tenacity with which most of us resist new ideas. One exposure is seldom enough.

1. BEGINNINGS

This book is the culmination of the musings of a lifetime. Still I can point to the incident that planted the idea for this book.

About four years ago, in one of the Sunday School lessons, a Protestant pastor set out to show that Lincoln was a very religious man. He combed Lincoln's papers for his sayings on the subject of religion and combined them into a statement that purported to express Lincoln's religious views.

I am a Protestant. I heartily approved of everything that was contained in that statement. A Catholic or a Jew would have approved just as heartily. The statement was confined to things of the spirit. All the symbolism of conflicting theologies was conspicuous by its absence.

This definitely is not meant as an argument against symbolism. But we must be careful that the symbolism that we employ in this book is only that which is acceptable to all three theological groups.

I call them *theological* groups advisedly, because we want to think of them as striving for the same *religious* ends. It is possible to have different theologies and one religion.

There are phases of religion that have special application and significance in connection with certain theologies; but I am interested in the broad and deep central stream that can be embraced by all three groups.

These three groups have made commendable progress in the quest for fields of common religious beliefs. But they have almost reached an impasse on the question of what to do with the fields. There is too much recourse to the uttering of universally accepted platitudes.

Attitudes are basic to techniques. But attitudes can be so played up that techniques become the crying need of the hour. When the three groups get together, let them move on to the techniques that will implement their attitudes.

I suggest a committee of theological and educational leaders from the three theological groups. Like the United Nations, they should persist in spite of heartbreaking differences until they can come to an agreement.

The framers of our Constitution took the attitude, "We dare not fail." They faced apparently insurmountable obstacles. The UN is also setting a lofty example in the face of much deep gloom. Can our theologians afford to toil on a lower level?

I want, on that committee, people who believe in, not apologize for, their creeds; who believe in them so strongly that they are not afraid of what other creeds may do to them; and who are frank about their doubts; who

6

can have respect for the creeds of other people—their neighbors, God's children.

I am thinking of a preacher of high standing in his denomination who became badly confused when he was asked how to treat questions from children about Jonah and the whale. I was so struck by the turmoil and the doubt that came to the surface that I have forgotten his answer, if any. He is a type of person I do not want on that committee.

The first task of this committee would be a religious course of study based on the Old Testament. I am convinced that there are many basic matters on which all three groups can agree.

The next task would call for the services of experts in many fields. It is the task of grading this general course to the age levels of the various groups.

I now propose a task which is much more difficult, but fundamentally most important. It is a course of study based on the Christian New Testament *and* the post-Old Testament writings of the Jews. Such a course would include all the personalities involved in these writings.

A final step is essential to the continued success of this program. It consists of the preparation of a handbook for teachers on pitfalls to be avoided if the three groups are to continue working and striving together toward the good and better life.

If a matter comes up that cannot be brought to a satisfactory end on account of theological difficulties, two courses are available. Sometimes it will be better to stop short. In that case it should be made plain that the theological institutions would rationalize it for their students.

A better way, if the danger signs are discovered in time, is to taper off, not water down, before coming to palpable contradictions.

The story is told of one story houses that were built with stairways leading to the roof. The original specifications had called for two story buildings. A supplementary order canceled the second story with instructions that the first story was to be built according to the original blueprints.

This illustration should be kept in mind as the grain of salt that we must apply when we say that we must stop short instead of watering down. We must not start issues that cannot be brought to a satisfactory conclusion. It can also mean that we may initiate lines of thought or action that the pupil, or some other institution, will carry through.

What attitudes should be stressed in these religious courses? The following is merely suggestive, not exhaustive: helpfulness, unselfishness, selflessness, learning from others, humility. In fact, the chapters that follow should furnish an excellent outline of things that can be accomplished, provided proper consideration is given to the degree of maturity of the pupils.

Such a course of religious instruction would condition the minds of the pupils to thinking in terms of the common interests and aspirations of all peoples.

I have read many books and articles on the efforts that these groups have made when they got together. These efforts always stopped short of the most fundamental issue involved. It is the question of what the combined groups will do with Jesus of Nazareth. I am convinced that no real progress will be made until this question is faced. And it can be faced successfully if we believe that we are living in One World.

I just read a book on science, philosophy and religion, written by men who are supposed to be experts in their respective fields. The result was pitiful. They tried to get together and did not even make a beginning. They did not succeed because they stayed away from what should have the heart of the discussion, Jesus of Nazareth.

It is possible for Christians and Jews to get together on a life and teachings of Jesus that is in complete harmony with Jewish belief and at the same time does not dilute essential Christian faith. Jewish authors have repeatedly demonstrated this. They can eliminate those things that are in conflict with Christian theology and still have enough left to give us pure religion. Substitute the name "religious living" for Christian living and the Jews could accept most of the Christian program.

It would be disastrous for the various theological creeds to suddenly drop their forms and beliefs. We can believe that all sects are aiming for the same pure religion without believing that they should come together now. It is the much that they have in common now that is the concern of this book.

Christian theologians generally say that the salvation of the world depends on the world's acceptance of Christianity. But they do not say it when they sit down with Jewish theologians. They are inconsistent. What is the middle ground?

In the middle ground we must recognize a difference between the *name* of Jesus and the *spirit* of Jesus. Let a Christian describe the spirit of Jesus to a Jew without calling Jesus by name and the Jew will probably say, "Why, that is the spirit of Judaism!"

If the Jew similarly described the spirit of his theology, the Christian would exclaim, "Why, that is the spirit of Christianity!"

It is possible for a Jew to come closer to the heart of Jesus' message, than one who is hemmed in by Christian formalism. Similarly, a Christian

8

can find a spirit in the Old Testament that escapes the formalistic Jew.

There are very few sayings of Jesus, as recorded in the New Testament, that the Jew cannot accept, provided he is allowed to place his own construction on them. And isn't that what we Christians also do? Our various constructions are very much conditioned by our respective theological heritages.

S. L. Frank in *God With Us* oversimplifies the problem of how the theologies of the world are to be evaluated. He suggests considering the original leaders, like Moses, Jesus, Mohammed, Buddha, etc., and what they stood for. A much better criterion is, "What do the theologies stand for today?"

But the question of what we stand for is not enough. We must *do* what we stand for. For instance, if we Christians in America were to say to a caste theologian, "We believe in the brotherhood of men," he would reply, "Why don't you practice it?"

It is not enough just to *believe* that pure religion is love for one's neighbor. It is in the practice that no group has attained it. The values of the theologies lie in the contributions that they make to this pure religion.

2. SETTING

I have presented the bare outlines of a long-range program, on which all three groups can work, on the assumption that in the foreseeable future, the three groups will continue their separate existences. It is further based on the assumption that our ultimate goals tend to be one.

The main object is to make the pupils — and ourselves — conscious of our many common religious interests. The work of the church and synagogue should be to show their followers what peculiar contributions their respective followers can make to the common cause.

The chapters that follow are all aimed at contributing to an attitude that will bring us ever closer to the ultimate goal of pure religion.

There are many books in which the authors try to view the theologies as from a distance, and — it must be said — they generally do it with a superior air. The result is something with an artificial flavor. The superior air can hardly be prevented when we do not set down our own convictions.

Let us consider what Woodward tried to do in *Humanity's Greatest Need*. His quest was the golden thread that runs through all the enduring theologies. He stressed tolerance, conformity, the search for happiness, etc. He quotes Jesus copiously, but there emerges a very one-sided picture of Jesus. Too much stress is placed on the eternal fitness of things and none on the temporal unfitness of many things. The admonition is to bear injustices with fortitude because pretty soon everything will be righted.

Jesus' caustic remarks about human exploiters are all omitted. There is no hint that we should strive to make the eternal fitness of things a goal of our everyday existence.

What Woodward found had no resemblance to a golden thread. At best it was a faded line. It lacked life. It had the artificial flavor because he viewed with a detachment that was not ardent.

When a speaker from another denomination speaks in my church, he may follow any one of three lines: he may ignore denominational differences, he may try to gloss them over, or he may talk enthusiastically about his own denomination without being derogatory of the others. I prefer the last type. I believe we nearly all like that type of person. I propose to be the enthusiastic exponent of the Protestant angle.

I, a Protestant, intend to plunge into the Protestant stream, and stay there; or rather, move along with it. Always staying on the inside is perhaps worse than detachment. The ideal condition is the ability to go in and out without getting lost.

Every theology has, I believe, a phase that at least *points* toward universality. That shall be my aim. Closer analysis will probably always show that this pointing toward universality has its origin in the *core* of all theologies.

In addition, I shall generally try to concern myself only with those things in my stream that are also found in the Catholic and the Judaistic streams.

This will not be easy, but the stakes will be worth the effort. The question of similarity will often be a question of personal opinion. Dissimilarities that point to similarities will also be considered.

The Religions of Democracy by a Jewish, a Catholic, and a Protestant writer is mostly concerned about the *peculiarities* of the respective theologies. I came away from it a firmer adherent of Protestantism than ever before. I have no doubt that Catholic and Jewish readers had similar experiences about their own faiths.

So if I stray away from the strait path that I have laid out and dwell overmuch on the *peculiarities* of Protestantism, the other faiths need have

10

little fear that I will tamper with their basic beliefs.

The reader must not make the mistake of looking here for an elaborate outline for religious instruction. There is no such outline. But the reader will, consciously or unconsciously, form such an outline to fit his interests, capacity, outlook, and scope. This must be an elastic outline to change with subjective and objective changes. The teacher's hardest task will not be to teach religion but to acquire it. The teacher who has religion will teach it, unless he is peculiarly inept with his techniques.

3. ANIMATED DICTIONARY OF WORDS AND PHRASES

One of the greatest sources of misunderstanding between people is the lack of agreement as to the meanings applied to words and phrases. My effort here is to *restrict* the meanings of words and phrases to the meanings I give to them when I use them in this book.

I have already so restricted the meanings of love, philosophy, and religion.

Think of this chapter as being a *preface* to an animated dictionary of words and phrases.

ASCENDED OR DESCENDED: Up or Down?

I shall make every effort to change our ways of thinking in the use of these words. We are *ascended* from the past. Our heritage is handed *up* to us. If any of us claim kinship with the monkey, let us say at least that we are ascended from him.

I firmly believe that these changes would be tremendously uplifting spiritually. They would help to counteract the natural tendency to regard the world as gradually growing worse.

CHURCH:

By church I shall always mean the physical organization of believers, especially that part of the organization that is vocal, and determines policies. It is administered by men who have the common human tendency to err.

COLD WAR — COLD PEACE:

In the spirit of Omar Bradley, let us give the name "cold war" a different complexion. Let us call it the "cold peace." The people from all sides are pursuing the paths that they think will bring us closer to World Peace. And the people are more powerful than a handful of evil-minded men. Without the people's wholehearted cooperation, the cold peace can not be warmed up.

CONSERVATIVE, REACTIONARY, RADICAL, LIBERAL, IDEALIST, VISIONARY:

The conservative does not see the need for change; or, seeing it, considers the cost of change too great.

The reactionary, unlike the conservative, is not satisfied to stand still. He wants to go back.

The radical sees the need for change but does not sufficiently consider the cost.

The liberal sees the need for change, but also has a fairly clear idea of the cost. He makes changes slowly but surely.

The idealist is the projection of the liberal into the future.

The visionary gives too little thought to the road that must be traveled. He has much in common with the radical. Both may become cynical and conservative in the end.

Liberals can be put into three classes: (a) those who pull their own load in the upward movement; (b) those who need a litte urging but not so much as to be classed as conservative; (c) those who pull more than their own load.

Does radicalism mean starting at the roots and working up? Or does it mean tearing out the roots? The second is the meaning that I accept, or else I should have to coin a new word to describe that kind of person.

EDUCATED:

For simplicity's sake I am generally going to employ this word in the sense in which it is generally understood. In this sense, a man's education is measured by the amount of time he has spent in the institutions of learning. The context will make it plain when I mean true education.

HEAD AND HEART:

The head reasons; the heart feels. It is in these senses that I shall always endeavor to use these two words. The heart can often *sense* factors contributing to a condition that the head cannot clearly delineate. Its promptings dare not be ignored.

Our emotions are from the heart. Perhaps it would be better to say that they are channeled through the heart. They have at least two sources — natural and spiritual. They are very much conditioned by the activities of the head. They may be good or bad.

12

OUR HERITAGE:

Our heritage will always be thought of as being the product of good and evil. If this were not so, there would hardly be any need for improving it. It must be recognized that part of our heritage is predominantly evil. Our task here is to change its character, diminish its baleful aspects, or eliminate it entirely. The only excuse for not eliminating it entirely is that it refuses to be eliminated, or that the consequences would be worse than the original condition.

INDIVIDUAL, IMPORTANCE OF:

When I write about the importance of the individual I always mean my neighbor, not myself.

NEIGHBOR:

The word neighbor is used to include all in whom we have an interest. Some of us can truthfully call the whole world our neighbor. Children all start with a small sphere of interest and gradually enlarge it. This sphere can also contract. In fact, some of us have no neighbors. This definition will enable us to use the word neighbor without going into labored detail each time.

THE RELIGIOUS APPROACH:

This is my pet expression. It is used repeatedly, perhaps to the point of palling. But it will not be palling to those of us who are most keenly alive to the need for the attitude that is implied in the expression. It is based on the assumption that an ounce of proper start is worth more than a pound of the patchwork that must be resorted to if the wrong start is made.

The religious approach must be ever with us, not just at the beginning. It must be applied to all new angles that are constantly rearing their heads as we grope for a solution to a problem. These new angles sometimes become major problems, the solution of which calls for the *religious approach*.

SKEPTICISM VS. CYNICISM:

In my vocabulary, skeptic and its derivatives are always used in a good sense, cynic in an evil sense. Skepticism is being interested primarily in looking for good points about a problem; cynicism is looking for bad features. My skeptic wants to believe; my cynic wants to doubt. My skeptic wants to be sure that his foundation is solid. My cynic wants to show that there is no foundation.

SIN AND EVIL:

Sin is conscious wrong-doing. Evil merely indicates that a proper function has not yet been found.

SPECIAL PRIVILEGE:

Special privilege is thought of only as some unfair advantage *that can be corrected,* or could have been prevented. It is not something that belongs to just the few. We are all the possessors, in varying degrees, of special privileges. Most laws are aimed at wiping out these special privileges.

By special privilege we should mean something that is shared by a few, or by many, who are not entitled to it more than others. We tend to confuse special privileges with special needs and rights. Privilege is deserved; special privilege not. Therefore special privilege should not be made to mean the same as privilege.

THEOLOGY:

Theology is a study of God; religion is a study of His creation and our relation to it. Theology too often divides people; religion unites them. A recognition of these distinctions calls for a substitution of "theology" and its derivatives for "religion" and its derivatives in many places where normally the latter would be used.

4. OUR HERITAGE—SOMETHING FOR NOTHING

A proper evaluation of the current scene has been the crying need of every age. It is the inability to evaluate properly that largely accounts for the painfully slow climb of civilization. It is so difficult because it involves a delicate balancing of spiritual and material values; and because it involves us and our selfish interests. A keener insight into the nature of our heritage will enable us better to evaluate this ever-present current scene.

There is a sense in which we never get something for nothing. It seems to be more practical, however, to regard our whole heritage, good or evil, as being something for nothing.

Perhaps the prime prerequisite to the religious approach is a thorough appreciation of our heritage and our relation to it. One who is keenly aware of the dynamic nature of his heritage can hardly help loving his neighbor, for he recognizes that it was neighborly people of the past who made his heritage dynamic.

Much of our heritage represents rights that past generations have wrested from special privilege groups. Most of us who recognize this fact cannot see that the same struggle is now going on. Even those of us who are keenly aware of this everlasting struggle are not at all agreed as to the salient points of this struggle. Life is complex.

Life was also complex for our forefathers. Issues were never as clear-cut as they appear to us when we study history. Historians are not too much to blame for this condition of our thinking. Since we cannot feel the pulse beats of the many live issues that beset our forefathers, it is necessary for historians to simplify them, and give them a clarity that they did not possess. Simplification is necessary; but when does it become over-simplification?

Over-simplification consists in not giving the proper weight to all factors. None of us can do that, so we are all over-simplifiers. It is one of those things in which we cannot attain perfection; we can merely approach it.

We must be ever alert to this danger. Most speakers do not see it. A speaker should have more in reserve than he gives to the audience. It is impossible to present all the factors involved in a discussion, but the speaker should be conscious of these factors. If he is not, then he is not a man of sound judgment. He has sound, but not judgment.

The over-simplifier has that smug, complacent look that goes with the belief that he has given all factors the proper weight, and therefore has come to the proper conclusion. And the gullible audience generally nods assent. That lean, hungry look that portrays the man who is always probing for new revelation is absent from the countenance of the average speaker.

It is over-simplifying to say that we always achieve rights by wresting them from others. It often happens that the rights won by one group become the heritage of all at nobody's expense. This world of ours would be a static world if it were not so. The immediate or apparent effect often is at the expense of others, but ultimately it is for the general good.

The forward-looking man has spent a great deal of time looking back. Thomas Jefferson is a good example. He got much of his theory of inalienable rights from a study of ancient Saxon customs. Let us not make the mistake of thinking that the Declaration of Independence issued from a source that was all religious. One of its main sources was the theory of natural rights, which certainly was not religious in the sense here used.

15

We have a tendency to think of the customs of the day as being divinely ordained; as issuing from a divine source that has no regard for human needs. Jefferson showed how the customs of contemporary England were the result of gradual accretions to the Saxon customs. And, of course, he convinced those only who were looking for light.

This was his springboard for launching into the future. He looked to the past for proof that all customs are in constant flux. The rate of change in the forms of democracy should keep pace with changing circumstances. Actually it is nearly always behind.

Our thankfulness for our heritage must not blind us to the fact that part of it is unmitigated evil. It is a dead weight when we receive it. Our duty is to discard it or put it to new use. Conservative thinkers, in particular, are prone to consider our heritage as being all good.

Some of our heritage was originally good; but we put it in cold storage instead of nurturing it and it has now become evil. After all, the question of good and evil, as applied to our heritage, is the question of the function that our heritage performs today.

Dirt is matter out of place. Evil is good out of place. Every effort must be made to root out evil so long as it remains evil; that is, so long as its legitimate function is not found.

We teachers have an especial responsibility to make our charges see their heritage *as such*. Books are an indispensable help. But it is not there that the heritage is found. Books contain only directions for finding it in the pulsating life all around us; and in the more distant forces that affect the pulsating life about us.

It is a special task of teachers to see to it that, as the pupils gradually grow more mature, they will begin to accept their heritage as a growing, expanding thing. They must get some insight into the satisfactions that accompany or follow the sense of having helped their neighbors up a trifle. But more important is the feeling of having helped to change the rules of the game to give *their neighbors* a more nearly even break.

If, by pure chance, someone gets a much better break than another and I have a chance later to do something that tends to equalize matters, it is my duty to do it. The only excuse for letting inequities exist is the inability to do anything about them; or, rather, an inability to correct them without introducing greater problems.

Those who talk most glibly about the blessings of poverty have never experienced it themselves. Those who like to say that in this land of ours everyone gets what he deserves, nearly always got more than their share of something for nothing.

Can anyone, as an instance, look at a heterogeneous group of children and still believe that we have achieved equal opportunity for all? The pinch of economic inequality is written in the clothes they wear and even more in their faces. This is part of our heritage that still needs a great deal of adjusting.

I once listened in while a keen, alert, well-preserved old man dwelt on one theme: "We never get something for nothing." I did not listen long. It soon became very tiring. This man had gone through college because his parents had had plenty of money. A large part of the success that he enjoyed was due to the start that his parents had given him. He made good use of the something-for-nothing that he received. His big mistake was in not recognizing it for what it was. He is a proud man. He did not receive graciously.

I know a poor man who inherited a low mentality, a poor physique, and poverty from his parents. He has a wife much like himself and several children whom he cannot support properly. They both have genial dispositions which apparently they did not inherit.

His parents are now old, penniless, and homeless. Most of those who know him think it is awful that he does not support them instead of allowing them to live on a government dole.

Compare this man with the well-to-do man previously mentioned. This well-to-do man received much from his parents while they lived and received more when they died. The poor man received comparatively nothing and is expected to show his gratitude for the lot that has been thrust upon him by supporting his parents until they die. Was Jesus voicing an ideal or did he merely recognize a cold, bitter, cruel fact when he said: "To them that have shall be given, and from them that have not shall be taken what little they have"?

Here is a sequel to the account of the poor man mentioned above. Recently his father died. Most of those who had contact with him joked about the matter. They wondered how many days he would take off to settle the nonexistent estate.

It is probably still true that most of us like to step on those who are down and pat the back of those who don't need it.

It is still true that we get out of life about what we put into it. But it is equally true that we can also make it possible for others to *put more* into life, and so get more out of it.

"It is more blessed to give than to receive." True, but we adults, in particular, need instruction in the art of receiving graciously. Here we can learn from children. How can we best repay such aid? By passing it on to someone else who, we hope, will receive our aid graciously. There is too much back scratching and horse trading in our giving and receiving.

The idea that help should be passed on oftener than reciprocated should be thoroughly implanted in the hearts of the pupils. Many practical applications will readily suggest themselves.

It is questionable whether anyone can give graciously who has not learned to receive graciously. If we accept graciously, we shall make every effort not to arrogate to ourselves credit for what has been handed up to us.

I know a lady who is very helpful. She is constantly giving things away. She gives to the charitable organizations. She will not receive anything from anybody; yet she is very insistent that others accept graciously whatever she has to offer them. Her help is in the spirit of those who take loving care of the animals. She thinks she is very humble. Actually she is very proud. The idea of receiving graciously *and* passing on graciously is a stranger to her.

We are not yet sufficiently sold on the idea of a free college education for all who can profit by it. We need to clarify our thinking on this subject. Our cloudy thinking on impartiality has made something of a mess of the high school situation.

There is too much thinking that since high school is free, then all should go to it for the same length of time. It does mean that the high school should offer that which cannot be better offered elsewhere or at a later time. It means that every pupil should go until the law of diminishing returns begins to operate *for him*. And it should be free, to impress on the pupil that since he has freely received, he should freely give. It fosters the idea of "passing on" instead of reciprocating. The same argument can be advanced for a free college education.

So long as people acquire an education and training at great personal sacrifice, they tend to feel that they are entitled to take it out of the public later on. Giving tends to induce giving.

The gap in pay between skilled and unskilled labor is being narrowed. This is as it should be. It should be kept in mind when we advocate the free preparation of the child for the thing for which he is best fitted.

Several years ago I taught a Sunday School lesson on covetousness. All the commentators on the lesson wrote about the covetous poor. They apparently completely overlooked the fact that when Jesus talked about covetousness, he used the covetous rich as an example. For what is covetousness but a consuming desire to amass more and more for oneself without any

18

regard as to how much good it will do and without any regard for others? Professors of religion have great need for reappraising Jesus' teachings on covetousness.

Covetous people are in the embalming business. They arrogate to their own *abuse* things that should be *used* by others. They overlook many necessary details when they think of heritage as being passed up to the next generation. Those details are found in our daily lives. They consist in passing over to our contemporaries instead of embalming for the future. This embalming process is insidious, slow moving, and tends to embalm the embalmer.

The preceding paragraph reveals nature in the raw. When I shifted to covetous people, I unwittingly shifted from "we" to "they." I should have kept the "we." We are all guilty, although there is a great difference as to degree; and it makes a great deal of difference whether this covetousness is a minor tugging force, or whether it is the dominant theme in our lives.

Much of the sense of futility and frustration that often besets us is the result of doing not enough of a creative nature with our heritage as it flows past us. We must not weary of doing the things that will benefit others more than us. We must have faith, if we have not yet experienced it, that such altruistic service has compensations that do not appear on the surface.

The children's game of "Pass it on" can be given great significance by us adults in dealing with children. A row of upright dominoes can serve a similar purpose. Life should *tend* to be like that. "Don't repay; pass it on."

We must be careful when we reciprocate that we are not just feeding our egos, that we are not engaged in old-fashioned horse trading. This is just a further argument for passing on to others in preference to reciprocating. It is a reflection of our own low opinion of the motives of the giver when we insist on repaying in full. Naturally, this does not apply to business transactions.

We must be careful not to carry this thought to the point of ruling out mutual helpfulness. It merely rules out repayment when no real need exists, and when obviously greater needs rear their heads elsewhere.

For me to enlarge on this thought for your benefit would tend to obviate the obvious. It would merely muddy the stream with my own pet ideas. It would be cluttering up an attitude with pet techniques of my own that in many cases would not clarify the thought for you.

19

"By their fruits ye shall know them." Many parents like to talk about how they brought up their children. It generally is a recital of how they repressed them and piled on burdens, instead of "passing on." They gave too little thought to the question of how their methods worked. If their children did not turn out well, they take the attitude that they did what they could for them. Actually, in many cases, they took what they could from them. The covetous person does not pass it on.

Some parasites are of our own making. Many of them are part of our heritage. All rich people who do nothing to justify their existence are parasites. All of us who do not pass on to others at least as much as has been passed on to us are parasites. This statement, of course, assumes that there is reasonable ability to pass on as much as has been received.

This generation is today clothing and feeding a multitude of people because their fathers, or grandfathers, or great-grandfathers had enough initiative, business sense, hard work, saving habits, or crookedness in their system to pile up a reserve that is still pyramiding for the benefit of the parasites that *descended* from them. Whether they enjoy the fruits of graft or of industry, they are parasites. The only way for them to wipe out the deficit is to pass on to the next generation, and share with their neighbors— not in dollars and cents, but in service to humanity—what they received, with interest.

Inherited wealth will someday be passé. Future generations will undoubtedly be surprised that we could not see the injustice of our present system. In the world of sports, we would not think of giving the son of wealthy parents a head start. Yet that is what we are doing in the economic world. Justice demands that all be given an equal chance to exploit their capacities.

The question of parasites and what to do about them is closely related to the question of special privilege. The solution of this problem is the continuing task of all generations.

It is very difficult for parasites who were born that way, to recognize their true status of abject dependence on the workers of the world. Even those who acquire their parasitic status gradually are often oblivious of the insidious change that is remaking their lives.

Somewhere I read about a lady who began to suspect that money was disappearing from her cash box. She started keeping track and discovered that twenty-five cents disappeared every day. One day she removed all the change and substituted a five-dollar bill. The next day she found four dollars and seventy-five cents in the box. The maid had persisted in this

20

wrong so long that she began to regard it as a right.

This story illustrates why so many wrongs that we inherited from the past are now considered right. If a wrong is perpetrated often enough, it gradually begins to be viewed as a right.

About three years ago I came across *The Liberal Tradition* by Orton. My first reaction to the title was that it was contradictory. "Tradition" conveys the idea of being handed up whole, without question. "Liberal" is forever examining things to see if they fit into the contemporaneous pattern.

Despite my misgivings about the title of the book, I read it. As the author let the pageant of history pass in review, I found myself in almost complete agreement with his liberal interpretations—until we came to the present scene. Then he seemed to become completely ossified.

Consistency, *as popularly conceived,* is practically one with conservatism. Consistency advocates want us to do it as Jefferson did it, without regard to changed conditions and improved techniques. Such an attitude, if not born of selfishness, is an example of lazy thinking.

This is the kind of consistency that Orton practiced in evaluating the current scene. He made many references to Herbert Hoover and Franklin D. Roosevelt. Every reference to Hoover was to show how liberal he was. Every reference to Roosevelt was to show how illiberal he was. If all his references about Roosevelt were true, I would call Roosevelt a nihilist.

I believe that even Roosevelt haters will agree with me that there is something faulty in the reasoning of a man who finds all the virtues in one man and all the vices in the other.

James Robinson in *The Mind in the Making* aptly states that we must learn to substitute purpose for tradition in evaluating the current scene. All tradition, if followed back to its source, will be found to have its roots in purpose. It must find a purpose in the present, and gradually take new root here.

The regulations that Moses laid down took account of conditions then existing. Jesus evaluated the scene in terms of conditions that then existed. Anyone who takes the attitude that there are some inviolable *external* criteria that hold in all ages and under all conditions is substituting the letter for the spirit. Anyone who takes the attitude that every word, phrase and sentence in the New Testament is literally true for all ages is substituting the letter for the spirit. "The letter killeth, but the spirit maketh alive."

The early church was almost immediately faced with the question whether a Gentile could become a Christian without first becoming a Jewish proselyte. Paul said yes. Peter said no. Peter was undoubtedly originally supported by the other apostles who had been with Jesus. Paul won them

21

over. The *spirit* constrained them to change.

They had not taken their initial stand as a result of their association with Jesus, but in spite of it. It was simply a case of heritage having a stronger initial pull than two or three years' association with Jesus. Heritage is powerful, but the spirit *can be* more powerful.

Paul was fortunate in that for him, in this case, heritage and spirit pulled in the same direction.

This brings out the difficulty so many excellent evaluaters of history have in evaluating the current scene. They cannot detach themselves sufficiently to give an unbiased verdict. They are completely immersed in one school of thought without being aware of it. They are too much addicted to trying to prove things by citing *incontroverted facts*. Too little consideration is given to the spirit that produced the facts and whether the facts fit the case. Conservatives tend to give too much weight to facts; thus overlooking the progressive spirit that brought the facts into being and that the facts may be hollow because the spirit has departed.

Many of us who hail the Magna Carta as a great heritage breathe in the atmosphere that the Magna Carta condemns; and we are not aware of any inconsistency.

The spirit which the Magna Carta condemns has new lodgings today; but it is not so secure as it once was. Progress is being made.

Consistency, properly applied, can be a jewel. If by consistency we mean keeping in mind the main objective or the direction in which we are heading, then the religious attitude is all for it.

The professors of religion must assume their share of the responsibility for this irreligious attitude. Their attitudes are often so uncompromising that their slavish followers quickly smother any new thought that they may harbor.

Is the liberal attitude religious? It certainly is. Is the conservative attitude irreligious? At its best it certainly is not the highest type of religion. It is, consciously or unconsciously, covetousness. But let us look into this more deeply. There are many other factors that help to make the conservative the man that he is.

Nature is part of our heritage. It really merits, and has, a chapter of its own, and since it impinges itself on almost every subject that is considered, only enough is presented here to keep thoughts on nature in the forefront.

Nature conditions our heritage and our reaction to it.

Education in its earliest stages follows the natural bent of trying to *preserve* the past for the future. Savages are notoriously afraid of thinking

22

new thoughts and of changing the routine that has been handed up from the past—and savages are very natural. Savages are very conservative.

Children are also conservative. They are still close to nature. They are the pawns of nature until, and to the extent that, the spirit conditions the nature within them.

If they appear radical to us, it is because their ways are new to us, despite the fact that we once were children. Give a child a problem in which a literal application of a rule plainly will result in injustice, and he will almost invariably suggest the literal application, provided he himself will not suffer the injustice. Even here he will often still ask for a literal application. Children are great believers in adhering to patterns that have been bequeathed to them. They are conservatives until, if ever, education makes them otherwise.

As I look back over my life, I marvel at how conservative I was as a child and as a young man. Try this on your own life. You will be surprised, unless you are still conservative.

Perhaps all persons are conservative in the formative stage. In their immaturity, their greatest need is to learn to conform. They remain conservative and become selfish if they do not recognize that with increasing maturity they should become conformers-plus.

How can this view be reconciled with the accepted fact that young voters are more liberal than old voters? It is a matter of perspective. Compared with petrified conservatives, they are liberal and radical indeed. Compared with a green and growing, but comparatively old, liberal, they are conservative indeed.

Radicalism is the result of a lack of respect for the laws of growth—for our heritage. It is a growing of, or an effort to grow, new roots when the old roots would be best. It fails to recognize that even if new roots are necessary, the old roots must remain until the new roots will have become self-sufficient. Most of what is called "liberalism" in young voters is, in truth, radicalism. True liberalism is a growth, and there is no growth without roots.

Some people try to over-simplify the problem of the relative merits of the old and the new. They try to solve it by rejecting all that is old and accepting all that is new, without regard to purpose.

Some teachers try to show their modernity by belittling the old-fashioned habit of screwing school desks to the floor. After a lifetime of thinking on the subject, I still do not know what is wrong with screwing the seats to the floor. The question should be settled by the practical method of determining which best serves the teacher's purpose.

23

The French Revolutionists were radical; Jefferson was liberal. The radicals did not recognize the need for an adjustment of ideals to local roots. Jefferson laid great stress on this need. Radicalism that insists on a slavish adherence to its tenets is heading toward conservatism. This explains the basic conservatism of children.

We have in the American Revolutionary period examples of my point that conservatives and radicals are closer to each other than either of them is to the liberals. Patrick Henry and Samuel Adams are the arch radicals that have been handed up to us. Since they had little root, they gradually became conservative. Both were slaves to form. It might be added here that the conservative makes form the master of the spirit that created it. That form may be old or new.

The picture becomes more encouraging when we recognize that none of us is one hundred percent liberal or one hundred percent conservative. Both forces are still striving within all of us.

Quantitatively speaking, even the liberal is more conservative than liberal. But his thought and creative activities center on the plus part of conformer-plus. He is ever looking for a chance to conform, in order to free himself for more exploring in new fields.

When the first magazine of condensed articles came out, many "intellectuals" bemoaned the introduction of this predigested material. They simply would not recognize that the average reader just does not have the time to sift all the magazines to get at the cream.

The same cry went up when the first book club was organized. The alarmists still cry that this amounts to regimentation of our thinking. They say that it robs us of the power of initiative. They forget that if we want to advance we must make the initiative of today automatic for tomorrow. This clears the way for initiative in new enterprises.

If my estimate of the current situation is correct, then the most rabid Lincoln worshipers are the conservatives. On the contemporary scene are public servants with the heart of Lincoln. The conservatives hate them and love Lincoln. They recognize progress that has been made, but progress in the making eludes them.

In the field of theology the same consistent inconsistency is found. Professors of religion set up standards of salvation that exclude most liberals of the present; then get up in their pulpits to praise similar liberals of the past. They judge dead liberals by their fruits. They find it very difficult to give proper credit for the fruits of the present. Their treatment of Lincoln, past and present, is a good example of this. Theology loves the past, which it has not seen, more than the present, which it sees. It

24

needs religion.

Jefferson got treatment from the theologians that was more bitter than that which they later applied to Lincoln. Because he attacked abuses connected with the church, he was called atheistic and anti-religious. They were careful to ascribe everything he did to base motives. Name calling was one of their specialties. They were very careful not to consider all the evidence. They lacked the religious approach.

Today's clergy are not to be blamed for the sins of the clergy of the past, but it is a fair question to ask whether they are not living in a climate of theological opinion that harbors much intolerance. Groups as a whole change slowly.

Conservatives praise the liberals of the past. They hail them as people after their own heart, because their liberal ideas have now become standard practice. They hail them for the form from which the spirit has fled. Liberals follow the *spirit* to its new lodgings.

Let us go back to the Old Testament for an illustration. Conservatives of today laud David the liberal—yes, radical—and condemn good, solid, conservative Saul. This is why well-meaning Saul has a warm spot in my heart. He has so few friends today!

One way to study *our* past as a nation is to study those nations who are not as far advanced as we are. There we can often find phases of development that we have passed.

When we hear about the horrible things that are going on in Russia, it will help to clear the atmosphere if we remember that all governments and peoples passed through similar stages. Future historians will probably marvel at the speed with which Russia made the transition. Russia has much inertia to battle.

Eisenhower, in *Crusade in Europe,* shows clearly how the Russians have not yet acquired the respect for the individual personality that we deem so important. When we see this in Russia we should give thanks that our forebears once also nurtured this lack of respect, and overcame it for our benefit. But they did not overcome it completely, and we have not yet overcome it completely; there is still much room for growth.

I still recall the words of some of the officers in the United States Army of 1917. In general their words ran about as follows: "Men, we are not interested in your morals. All we are interested in is that you keep your bodies in fighting trim." There is lack of respect for personality for you!

It is essential that we consider the problem of our heritage from all possible angles, including the problem of the kind of heritage we are going to hand to the next generation.

25

We can get a good idea as to what we should do with our heritage by considering what our forefathers did with theirs. They received their heritage graciously, improved and enlarged it by use, and passed it on to us, with interest. This simple explanation overlooks the fact that they also diminished the balefulness of their evil heritage. It also overlooks the fact that these modifications have always been spotty. It is merely a statement of general trend.

That part of our life which has become routine for us is perhaps all heritage. Inherent in it are routines of the past that have been swallowed up in improved routine. It harbors and nurtures the roots of the activities in which we find ourselves. Our contribution is the modification we are giving to this routine. If we try to preserve this routine as grandfather handed it up to us, then our contribution is nothing; we are holding back.

When we say that we do not want to hand to our grandchildren the kind of heritage that grandfather handed up to us, we are not necessarily criticizing grandfather. We are merely recognizing our heritage as a growing and expanding thing.

Much of this something-for-nothing that we receive is vital, vibrant. In our hands it can become a dead weight. It can be a millstone about our necks. Our heritage requires exercise to endure. In its exercise we are contributing our share, or part of it, toward the upbuilding of the kingdom.

This whole turmoil called life can be looked upon as our heritage. At least it harbors our heritage. We must make the adjustments that are needed to give it purpose for ourselves, for our neighbors, and for the next generation.

Much hope for the world lies in the fact that in the long run the general public tends to sense the motives that actuate our leaders, whether they be theological, political, social, economic, etc. The public will follow those who appear to have the right motives even though it does not fully understand their program.

It can probably safely be said that the vast majority of Jefferson's followers did not understand clearly what he was fighting for. But they had a keen sense that he was fighting for the underprivileged. And their sense did not betray them.

What are we bequeathing to the next generation when we make provision for the old age of those who are now working? One thing is certain. This generation cannot support the workers of its own generation who will be retired the next generation. We are doing little more than deciding who shall support whom in the future. In this connection let it be remembered that this is what past generations have done for us. By paying social security taxes, we are reducing the government's debt and thus easing the tax load that the next generation will carry. Certainly the next generation will raise the food and make the things that will be bought by those, then retired, with money furnished to them by that generation. Similarly the debt that we are bequeathing to the next generation will be paid by the next generation to itself.

The problem of the nation planning for the future has many points of dissimilarity with that of an individual planning for the future. An individual who has saved for the future will be able to buy from others. The nation must buy from itself.

The two preceding paragraphs perhaps explain better than anything else why conservatives are so conservative. They do not recognize clearly enough that there are many basic points of difference between the ideals of a group as a whole and those that the individuals within the group must of necessity hold for themselves.

If they do see the differences in aims, they too often put their Marxist thinking caps on and say that one or the other of the "irreconcilables" must go. They do not explore sufficiently the vast possibilities that lie in co-operative competition. This thought will be developed more fully later. A keen sense of the implications of play will unlock many compartments in our thinking that would otherwise remain forever closed. Teachers please copy! And more about play later.

Those of the next generation who do not get this vision will praise the liberals of the present and the conservatives in their midst. They will denounce the conservatives of the present and the liberals in their midst. Yet in spite of it all, progress will continue to be made.

Man produces so that *he* can consume. Is that all? Who looks after those who are not in a position to produce? Let George do it.

The Georges among us are building up a goodly heritage to pass up to the next generation.

Let us say that man produces so that he *and others* may consume for the purpose of producing still more.

Let us consider here a sense in which all, including children and old people, can be producers. Children are producers when they are building their lives for future usefulness. We adults are consumers when we draw inspiration from their unflagging, upward drive.

Old folks can be great producers with their example of the rewards of a life well spent; by demonstrating for us that spiritual growth need never stop.

Children, adolescents, young men and women, middle-aged men and women, old people,—all should be workers of the world, producing so that they can consume for the purpose of producing still more.

It might help if we visualized our heritage as a tree with branches that die when their period of usefulness is over; with branches that become sturdier to carry heavier loads; with new branches shooting out from other branches or from the main trunk to take care of new human needs.

Our heritage is the sacrifice of the past generations for us. Yes, they even sacrificed for the evil part of our heritage. It is an evidence of faith. We shall do well if we do not regard our own contribution to the present and future as being sacrifice, but rather as being payment, with interest, to the future for favors from the past. The credit for the advance goes to the divine spark. No real sacrificers think of their own contributions as being sacrifice.

But the message from the divine spark never comes to us whole. It is very much conditioned by the human channels through which it must pass. Two persons can listen to the same spirit and record different answers. Their hearing apparatus is very much conditioned by their heritage. This accounts for the many cases of open conflict between two persons who both claim that they are guided by the spirit within. More about this later.

When we see a loved one lying in a casket, do we really see him? No, we visualize him. We are looking at his former abiding place, or anchoring point, or point of reference.

He is in the air we breathe, in the thoughts we think, in our aspirations, in our faith. Perhaps the most graphic illustration of this thought can be found in a consideration of the wave of a spiritual something that swept the earth at the news of Franklin D. Roosevelt's death. There is a spiritual heritage.

In fact, our basic heritage is a spirit. Form and material substance are merely handmaids to wait on the spirit.

This could be the last chapter in this book if we could see our heritage clearly, especially that part of which we are a part. But that is impossible; even the best among us harbor but a dim outline of it.

So we must grope along and consider some of the many things that stand in the way; and come to decisions—often tentative—that will bring us ever closer to our goal. Those of us who really get started find the scenery along the way very beautiful.

5. PROJECTION AND INTROSPECTION

I am always going to use introspection in a good sense. I shall reserve introversion for describing an unfavorable dwelling within.

When I am alone with my thoughts regarding my duties to my neighbor, I am engaged in introspection. When these thoughts tend to dwell on my neighbor's duties to me, then I am engaged in introversion. Introversion is selfish. Introspection at least *tries* to be unselfish.

It is not unusual to hear a "glad-hander" is referred to as an extrovert. Often he is a pathetic introvert desperately seeking to cover up his inner feelings. I have discovered that among the people who have that "don't care" air there are many who are really very unsure of themselves.

On the other hand, we often think of the person who is often alone with his thoughts as an introvert. Actually, extroverts find their own company more cheerful than do introverts.

The basic difficulty lies in a confusion between introspection and introversion. Introversion can be called inverse projection. The introvert generally tries to overcome that feeling of frustration and futility by penetrating still more deeply within himself.

This can make the introvert's case appear hopeless until we realize that none of us are one hundred percent introvert or extrovert. Both introversion and extroversion are continually contending within all of us.

I know of a case where a psychiatrist told a troubled man to expose his worries to the light of day, not to keep them buried. The man took that to mean that he was to pour his troubles into the ears of all with whom he came in contact. But he is doing more than that. He is manufacturing miseries to pour into other people's ears. His attitude now is, "See how much I suffer!" and his suffering grows apace. This is inverse projection.

We must rise above the tendency to make mountains out of molehills. We must learn to reach across the molehills—if we do not cross them— and extend the hand of fellowship to those on the other side.

We get rid of woes by transforming them. If we toss them to the other side of the molehills, they are like the cat that came back. And the other side is contaminated. Fortunately, the same thing is true of the good that we do.

For the vision to grasp this, we need the third dimension that only the spirit can give.

"They all do it," is the attitude of the cynic. Not only do we apply it to ourselves; we include our friends. When a friend asks advice about a project, we too often suggest a selfish course of conduct because "they all do it." The ills of the world are blamed on "them," not on "us."

We do not have enough of that rare combination of projection and introspection that enables us to tap our inner potentials for altruistic service.

Introspection is an act—a mental act. Introversion is a more or less chronic condition.

Projection and introspection are interdependent. Neither is complete without the other. This will become very apparent as we move along.

Projection is primarily a matter of the heart, not head. Here the head is definitely the handmaid of the heart. Projection is not merely cold analysis, but warm feeling for something outside ourselves.

The best groundwork for this warm feeling is a highly objectified capacity for introspection. This does not mean that the warm feelings within are to be discounted. Rather, they are the most important things to be studied. But every effort must be made not to consider these inner feelings more important than the inner feelings of my neighbors; and to use them to gauge my neighbors' feelings. Keen introspection and self-analysis are the groundwork of projection. It is a job that is never completed. Projection must begin bit by bit. The groundwork is helped by this projection.

In this self-analysis I must be harder on myself than on others. After all, I am on guard against myself. My neighbor cannot similarly guard himself against my scrutiny because he does not know when and where he is being analyzed. My big concern should be my duties, not my neighbor's duties. After all, my neighbor will draw his greatest inspiration from seeing me buckle down to *my* tasks.

Here are some practical illustrations of the workings of self-scrutiny. When I was a young man, I was told that I always put the worst possible construction on the motives that prompted others to do things. That remark has stayed with me all through the years and has done me a great deal of good. I also recall that the man who made the remark was a very unstable character. We can learn from all kinds of people.

At another time I was told that I had an extraordinary capacity for making insulting remarks. That remark has always stayed with me and still serves as a check on my tongue, even though I have never been convinced that I was quite as guilty as charged.

An occasional jolting remark can leave lasting benefits. I am convinced that I have made occasional jolting remarks to some of my pupils that they will always remember to their benefit. And I am basing my conclusion on the effect such occasional remarks have had on my own life. But it must be emphasized that their worth lies in their rarity, and truth. It also affects those who are not addressed directly. We learn from observing others.

We have all heard the expression, "I know how you feel." This is projection from a background of introspection.

Love, as I have defined it, is fed by projection. I used parental affection as being the most nearly perfect type of love. But there is much parental affection that is not love, but selfishness. It seeks to sink the children's interests into the parents' interests.

This suggests a further limitation on my definition of projection. This warm feeling for something outside myself must have for its purpose the enlargement of this something outside myself for its own sake, not for mine. Parents please copy.

We teachers often imagine that we are projecting ourselves into the life of the pupil when we are merely looking at him or through him or past him. Our *insight* lacks depth. When he creates a disturbance, mental or physical, we generally think of immediate causes, to the exclusion of underlying factors.

We adults must project ourselves more fully into the lives of children and into our own childhood days; and we should make it very plain to them that we sympathize with them in their strivings without necessarily approving of all that they do.

It is not easy to have a sympathetic interest in other people's hopes when we feel that their hopes are leading them along the wrong trail. But it can be done and it must be done. If we feel that our way of life is best, then the lives we live will make a much stronger impression on them than the words we say.

I have heard teachers say to their pupils, "Think of the feelings of others," when they seemed to have no regard whatever for the feelings of their own pupils. Knowing other people's *duties* is not projection.

Do we realize that the problem of child discipline is ninety percent a problem of adult self-discipline? The child's capacity for imitation has not been sufficiently utilized here. We should set the example of being more interested in doing good than in condemning the bad in others. There is such a thing as crowding out the bad with good deeds. And the motive for the good deeds must not be too far-fetched or too abstract.

My experience with teachers who take in-service training leads me to the conclusion that when they go to class as students they cheat more, as a class, than the pupils to whom they try to teach ethical value. I have often conveyed this bit of information, or opinion, to my pupils, and I am firmly convinced that the total effect on them was definitely good. I always try to impress on them that as adults they will tend to continue the bad habits they are forming as youngsters; and that they will also tend to set up

31

standards of conduct for the younger generation that they themselves do not live up to. In other words, unless they are very careful, they will also become poor projectors.

Children have the right to know that in some respects they are superior to their elders and that we realize it. I have often had occasion to teach habits, or break them, to pupils when some teachers possessed them more glaringly than the pupils. I remind them that they are still young and are still conditioned to taking correction; that when they grow up they may become fossilized like so many adults.

What should be my attitude when I catch my own child in a wrong act or with a wrong attitude? I should be as tolerant at least as I expect my neighbor to be toward his children. Convincing children that they have committed great sins seldom helps and often does permanent harm. It is a great help if children can see that we feel with them in their predicaments. It is generally enough for them to know that we do not approve of a certain line of conduct, provided they are convinced that we have a proper attitude toward them. This is just another way of saying, provided we have projected ourselves into their lives. We must realize that a child's life is full of fears, many more than we adults can realize. It is a great help to the child if he can feel that there is one who feels with him as he is constantly trying to adjust himself to ever-changing conditions.

The average teacher and parent pictures the average child as a rebel in need of confinement. It is against this unjust confinement that the child rebels. He is trying desperately hard to be like us adults, and his adult teacher is setting such a poor example.

What often happens to children by the time they reach the upper grades in school? By this time, they are often boiling over with indignation over real and imaginary past and present injustices inflicted upon them by their physical superiors. They often take it out on anyone who happens to come along. They are *almost* as unreasonable as those who inflicted punishment on them were when they were children.

The hope for the future lies in the "almost" in the preceding sentence. Somehow children as a group manage to turn out a little better than did their parents. And their children will turn out a little better than they. More projection will speed the process.

I feel that the time has come to revise our picture of justice as being blind. It once served a useful purpose. It was a guard against measuring retribution inversely by the amount of pull that the criminal had. But it placed the emphasis on the crime, not the criminal.

Let us remove the blindfold and redirect attention to the criminal.

32

After all, that is what we are doing already. All that is necessary is to bring the picture up to date. It seems hardly necessary to add that now our concern is about what the criminal is, and not what pull he has.

Special privilege rears its ugly head particularly in the field of social justice, but perhaps it can better be understood in connection with projection.

Special privilege can be likened to a dark glass that is more a mirror than a glass to see through. When I look at my neighbor, I must look through this glass. It is there; I did not put it there. Unless I am very careful I will see only my own image in that glass. However, with practice I can condition myself to disregard the reflection in the glass and to that extent see through it more clearly.

When I look at my neighbor, it is very difficult for me to see wherein special privilege has given me an advantage for which I deserve no credit. The difficulty becomes an impossibility when I do not even try to see clearly.

Anyone can make windows of his mirrors of special privilege if he begins with sufficient humility and retains it. Then he can really project himself into his neighbor's heart and begin to read it.

What are vested interests? They are groups of people who have acquired unfair control over something. When we consider this problem, we nearly always stop before it hits us. If we did not stop so soon, we could see ourselves as also having our fingers in some pies.

Vested interests have the peculiar faculty of gratefully accepting a boost without acknowledging it as a boost, and then howling over the danger of spoiling the underprivileged by giving them a long overdue boost. Vested interests are very much concerned about the danger of spoiling people by helping them.

We are often unconsciously selfish. We are brought up in, and live in, a climate of opinion that is weighted in our favor. It requires strenuous projection to overcome this handicap.

Those of us who are favored above others must learn to project ourselves more and more into the lives of the less favored among us.

The truly religious person, it has been said, has windows, not mirrors. He does even more than reflect the views of his neighbors. He *absorbs* them for the contribution they can make to his spiritual storehouse. The resulting fusion can open many a window, for himself and others, that did not exist before, or give a clearer view than was before possible. Loving our neighbors is excellent for the windows of our souls. The completely selfish soul is a soul without windows. A soul without windows is dead, being alone.

The religious person is never alone. He always harbors thoughts of his

33

neighbor's weal. These thoughts, God's thoughts, are ever his companion.

The selfish person wants things for himself alone. Too often he succeeds only too well. He is alone—alone with his thoughts on how to get more things for himself alone. The vicious circle.

What happens when my neighbor is the possessor of the special privilege? The glass is still there, and the vision is not perfect, but it is now less a mirror and more a glass to see through. The glass turns out to be, to some extent, a one-way mirror.

Physical facts can hardly be denied through this glass. It is the intangibles that are reflected. And they are the most important and most real things. I imagine I am reading my neighbor's motives when I am reading my own. I am blind to the "something-for-nothing" that perhaps has made me superior to my neighbor.

The problem of racial tolerance is largely a problem of special privilege and how we are going to use it. It is particularly true of the Jewish problem that the "vices" of the Jews would be considered virtues if the accusers possessed them.

Let us try to be a little more practical with this problem of projecting ourselves into the lives of our neighbors. With what should we be concerned? We should ask ourselves such practical questions as: Does he have all the comforts of home? If not, whose fault is it? Is he getting a fair break in the present economic set-up? What can be done to get him a better break? Enough thinking along this line by enough people would do a world of good.

It is easy to say that this is placing too much emphasis on material things; that the spiritual element is missing. The spiritual element is found in *our* interest in the material welfare of *others*. And the others are very prone to catch the spirit from us.

Perhaps I have created the impression that I am against seeing the low motives behind my neighbor's actions. I am not, but I am against those who fail to recognize their own low motives for what they really are. Their introspection apparatus is faulty.

Yes, I will go even farther and say that sometimes I should do something about my neighbor's shortcomings; but it must rest on the same ground of introspection.

This second phase has been ignored because our natures will see to it that it is not neglected. It is enough to mention here that it is recognized that others have duties similar to ours.

These few paragraphs are injected here merely for the purpose of recognizing the whole picture. The important point here is to recognize our

34

natural tendency to look into our mirrors of special privilege and imagine that we are projecting ourselves into the World of Other People.

Tolerance is a handmaid of projection. Tolerance does not imply agreement. In fact, there is no need for tolerance where there is agreement. Tolerance is more than forbearance in things that matter little. It is forbearance in matters that to us mean much.

Tolerance implies more respect for personality than for the issues that divide personalities. It also recognizes that, no matter how deeply we feel, the other person may still be right. And it recognizes that we cannot force opinions on others. Tolerance does not make martyrs.

Children are perhaps our greatest army of martyrs. Martyrs are born of intolerance, and we as a rule are most intolerant of those who have the least power to assert their rights.

Intolerance results from improper projection. It also can result from a gradual accretion of prejudices which in turn are the result of our efforts to protect our special privileges. Intolerance, being an accretion of the ages, is generally not recognized as such. When we are intolerant, we are contributing to the martyrdom of others. If I, in self-pity, feel that I am a martyr to a cause, I must at least carefully consider whether perhaps I may be contributing to the martyrdom of others.

Underneath our misgivings about Russia is the subconscious feeling that tolerance means assimilation. It means granting to others the right to live their lives within their own selected spheres. This, of course, must be modified in those cases where spheres overlap. Tolerance need not lead to amalgamation.

Taking the religious attitude toward Russia does not mean that we believe Russia has a superior form of government. Russia has much to learn about the art of government and much of it must be learned in the school of bitter experience. It is not merely a question of what the government will do to the people. The people's reaction is also important. In this connection it is well to remember that the Russians are not people, but peoples.

The case study of tolerance is excellent. But it is not fundamental. The fundamentals begin at home. Tolerance, like charity, begins at home. Children who learn true tolerance in the home have won more than half the battle.

This is not to decry case study and the improving of techniques. The onward march of civilization is largely dependent on this. It is to emphasize the greater need to get down to fundamental virtues, or attitudes.

We must have a thorough understanding of the "yes, buter" if we are to make real progress along the road to tolerance.

If we talk about the natural tendency of people of all periods of history

35

to think of their period as being the worst yet, the "yes, buter" will reply, "Yes, but our period is really the worst."

If we cite examples of intolerance, he will reply, "Yes, but . . . ," and then he will proceed to show how the cases that involve his personal interests are different from the other cases.

Others will say, "Yes, but why should I give in when I know I am right and the other is wrong." The best rejoinder is that the two classes of people that are most certain that they are right are the ignorant and the holders of special privilege.

I have no desire to place parents on an eminence above teachers. Everyone will agree, on reflection, that the requirements for becoming a teacher are much stricter than the requirements for becoming a parent, Nevertheless, we teachers must recognize that circumstances often make a parent's judgment superior to our own.

Parents generally understand the inner thoughts and desires of children better than do teachers. Too often the study of child psychology does not bridge the gap between the child mind and the teachers'. Too often the teachers see in the youngsters lined up in front of them only brats bent on mischief. And too often the brats manage to live down to the teachers' estimate of them. Too few teachers are good projectors.

It might help matters considerably if the newspapers of the country would carry this headline: "Teacher Charges Pupil with Serious Crime." Under the caption, among other things, should be this statement: "The teacher pointed the finger of scorn at the pupil and screamed, 'You have a low I. Q. and I am going to punish you for it!'" The punishment would be left to the imagination.

Leaving out the dramatic license, this is what is happening in our classrooms every day. This, of course, is not true of every classroom. Some teachers have succeeded in projecting themselves to the extent of having a fair understanding of the pupils' limitations.

People who see dire things when they go through the motions of projecting, are often like the backwoodsman who looked into a mirror for the first time. Terror-stricken, he rushed home and panted, "Mirandy, I have just seen the awfullest thing!"

It is not to be assumed for an instant that teachers are worse offenders in this than parents. In addition to the lack of formal training, the parents have an unwholesome desire and demand for their own children to attain a position beyond their limitations. Parents must steel themselves to the urgent need for the heart to listen to the head when they project themselves into their children's inner sanctums.

My reference above to the screaming teacher prompts me to state here that there are not as many yelling teachers as one would judge from listening to the pupils' accounts of what happens in the classroom. I believe all teachers know that there are always some pupils who characterize every bit of reproof that comes from the lips of the teacher as yelling. Parents can easily discount this if they will but stop just an instant and consider how they themselves like to exaggerate.

This is being written during the Christmas season. What a pleasure many of us get in bringing happiness to others! We shall be able to say that the millenium is here when the majority of us can get the same glowing satisfaction out of doing the things that will make the special joys of the Christmastide a permanent and universal possession.

Many cruel persons have periods of excessive hospitality. They are hospitable only when they can well afford it. They use it as a cover for the many cruel things that they perpetrate. And many of us are often taken in by the ruse. Some of us who see through it, openly or secretly admire them and wish that we could be like them. Perhaps we are. Eternal vigilance is the price of altruism.

For what is altruism but the ability to project myself into something outside myself; "losing" my life in that project? I am not thinking of martyrdom, although it is recognized that martyrdom cannot always be ruled out. This service can take many forms. It can consist in lending a hand, or in taking the lead in agitation for a worthy goal.

Let us not delude ourselves into thinking that we can discharge this obligation by merely joining a service club. We must be keenly aware of the fact that the help which does not include the helper is pharisaic. It is so easy for us, in such groups, to assume lofty attitudes that have very insecure foundations. We are in danger of forgetting that group strength must depend on individual strength.

Projection emphasizes the point that the trees are more important than the woods. Trees are fundamental to the woods. The reverse is not true. This is not gainsaying the importance of the woods. When economic royalists think of economic problems, they think of executives and factories. The workers are just a blur to them.

Glenn Frank, in 1931, took a look into the future and gave us a picture of the future that today seems startlingly real. He described the kind of leadership that would emerge. When that leadership apparently did emerge, he could not recognize his own brain child. Frank proved better at portraying the woods than in recognizing the trees that made the woods.

All the illustrations so far have had for the two principals myself or

37

ourselves, and others. We always had to take into consideration our natural tendency to be too lenient toward ourselves. Therefore, it had to do almost entirely with our duties to others, not their duties to us.

Let us now take a more detached view. Let us eliminate ourselves as the principals. Let us view, as from the sidelines, our public officials and the public. Let us consider each group in turn as projector.

The public official must project himself, as much as possible, into the lives of those who are affected by his functions. Naturally he has duties that are not directly connected with the welfare of all the people; but he must perform his routine duties with an eye on the ultimate objective, the individual personality.

The general public must think of the government as being always cognizant of the problems of the individual personalities that comprise it. The public is the government that is interested in the public. This is deliberately made confusing because it is innately confusing. Let us rest it here with the observation that if our democracy is to survive, then we must become better projectors than we have been thus far. And we become better projectors only as we begin to recognize that life is complex indeed.

Consider this problem. A rabbit is 50 jumps ahead of a dog. A rabbit jumps 4 times while a dog jumps 3; but a dog leaps as far in 2 jumps as a rabbit does in 3. How many jumps does the dog make to catch the rabbit?

The object of this problem is not to get you to sit down and try to solve it. Rather it is to illustrate the point that life is much more complex than this problem.

The problem has factors that are presumed to be constant. In life they are not constant and they are much more numerous. It should illustrate the danger inherent in trying to solve a life problem by cold logic. Logic is not psycho-logical if all the factors are presented; and it is not logic if some of the factors are omitted.

A teacher friend of mine told me that I look on one "side" of a question while he looks on both "sides." Well, there are four "sides" to a problem. A problem has length, breadth, depth, and circumstances. Someone will say that a problem should be made large enough to include circumstances within the other three limits. The answer is that we do not want to be too ambitious. There is also the vastly more important fact that the newly admitted circumstances are conditioned by circumstances outside the new limits.

Some day all strikes will be outlawed. That day must wait for improved techniques and a better knowledge and weighing of the factors involved. More intensive projecting by all three sides will speed the time.

It seems hardly necessary to enumerate the three most obvious sides to

38

a labor dispute. The third side, of course, is the public. That problem is flat indeed that has only two sides! This thinking about projecting ourselves into the lives of others can be very narrowing if we do not recognize that still others are involved in whatever passes between us. Even in projection life is complex.

After we have projected ourselves into the interests of others, let us look around from that vantage point. There the vision is clearer. Many of the mirrors of special privilege have been left behind and things are beginning to emerge in something resembling their true light.

We must be careful not to project ourselves too far — in distance and in time, past and future. The spreading out into these three directions should be gradual. True projection pays special attention to how *I* am involved in my neighbor's problems. False projection is concerned with how *others* are involved in my neighbor's predicaments. It is for this reason that projection which goes far afield is often false.

A good illustration is the pre-Civil War Abolitionist movement in the North. These northern people projected themselves into the lives of the poor slaves way down South. They were concerned about what *others* had done to these slaves. They were not aware that they, too, were contributing to the problem. They could or would not see that many of their neighbors were worse off than the slaves. At home, the projection was nil because the solution of the problems of their next door neighbors would call for some contribution from them.

Here is a typical way of staying "away from home" in making applications. It is a bare outline of a speech that I heard.

The subject was, "Meet the Common Man." The speaker made it plain at the beginning that he meant the down-trodden common man of Asia. He also made it equally plain that the problem was not here in America where democracy is in operation.

But he said that he had acquired his sympathy for the common man because as a boy and young man he had been one of them. He had been exploited here in America.

Throughout his discourse on Asia, I was impatient for him to come back home to make the application here at home. When he did come back, he moved back to Abraham Lincoln, uttered a few platitudes, and stopped.

He should have brought it up to date. The exploitation to which he referred has not ended here in America. Among his hearers were many exploiters who did not make the application at all.

The questioning that followed made it plain that those who moved and lived in the climate of opinion that gives comfort to the exploiters had not been touched by the main theme of the address.

Yes, he referred to us as a privileged, therefore exploiting, nation. This was easy to take because there were so many shoulders to bear the onus.

The foregoing will perhaps help to explain my irritation when all kinds of people sing the praises of Lincoln, the Common Man. Too many of them do not recognize him when they come face to face with a Lincoln in the flesh.

Lincoln was against exploiters. It is so easy for exploiters to view exploiters of another age, or another country, or even another section of their country, with a superior air. At the worst they think of themselves as benevolent despots.

Some time ago I listened to a speaker on the subject of the economic, social and political problems of England. Among the audience were representatives of many shades of opinion regarding our own problems as a nation. They all apparently took in and accepted everything the speaker handed out to them. I think his presentation was fair; and we have a mania for fairness when we have no personal stake in the matter.

Now everything that the speaker said could have been said of us as a nation, the only difference being one of degree. But the reaction of some of the audience would have been violent indeed! Personal stakes would have swallowed up the mania for fairness.

"It had to be." This statement often exposes the fatalist. It is generally used as an excuse for our complacency about our own responsibilities. "The Civil War had to be fought." What did it settle? Slavery would have been eliminated without the war. No one knows what the status of the Negro would be today if there had been no Civil War; but most people believe that he would be better off than he is.

It did not speed up the economic growth of the South. It raised a bogey man that will take a long time to die out in the South. It is an illustration of what can happen when one section of the country is too much concerned about the sins of another section and too little about its own. It was the result of an irreligious attitude. It did not have to be. It made too free a use of the word "we."

We must be careful that we do not make too free a use of the word "we." For instance, we are perhaps all agreed, at least in theory, that we should be harder on ourselves than on others. Then to illustrate what "we" must do, the Northerner says to the Southerner, "We must practice racial tolerance," (meaning "you.") Nobody should be included in the "we" without his consent. We must get adjusted to the fact that *basically* "we" must mean "I" — and those who *choose* to be included in "I." Too few people mean "I" when they say "we."

40

This is not an apology for slavery. It is an argument against biting off more than we can chew. It is an argument for cleaning up our own backyard before contemplating our neighbors' backyards.

The abolitionist movement had started in the South. When the North took over, the southern abolitionists threw up their guard, and war gradually became inevitable. Today we are paying the penalty of an accumulation of sins of the past. This is not meant as a cover for the many sins we ourselves are committing.

William Lloyd Garrison is to my mind an illustration of misguided zeal in other people's affairs. Garrison thought that a change in *form* was the big objective. He thought that the Emancipation Proclamation accomplished in one stroke all the things he had been fighting for.

And yet a change in the form can be a great impetus to the achievement of a goal. As an instance, in India the untouchable class has been eliminated. This is a great forward step; but it is just the beginning, not the end.

Would we want a Garrison in this atomic age, a man who looks into his neighbor's backyard and sees what is wrong with it; and thinks he has the remedy; a man who thinks that evolution never works; that progress depends on revolution?

The answer to the Abolitionist of the pre-Civil War period is the condition of the Negro and the South today. We should also consider that Jesus lived in an age of exploitation and slavery, but he never took the attitude that it could be eliminated by one big external change.

Nevertheless, the South must learn that if they do not want others to remind them of their duties, it is up to them to think more about their own duties. This does not completely preclude outside interference, but it does give that inner balance that we all crave, but too often are not willing to earn.

In projecting, let us be careful not to project our *troubles* into some distant place that cannot answer back. Pure religion has no place for a scapegoat. We must also be careful that we do not project ourselves too deeply into our own selves. Here we can easily become lost—and very selfish.

The Jews of Jesus' time spent a great deal of time blaming the distant Roman government for their troubles. Jesus would have nothing to do with that attitude. The average citizen today places too much blame on our lawmakers. In both cases housecleaning should begin in the community, with the focus on ourselves.

Where does that well-known feeling of frustration and sense of futility come from? It is born of self-interest. There is too little projection. Childless couples are especially prone to this feeling. Their projection into each other's lives is too narrowing. They will not, in general, voluntarily assume their

41

share of the responsibility for building up the rising generation. Parents are different from them in that they have these responsibilities thrust upon them. The most appropriate appellation for *such* childless couples is "parasite."

Occasionally a speaker comes forward with the statement that if the world had enough neighborly people performing the little acts of charity, then there would be no World Peace problem.

Ernie Pyle thought that our national framers of the international Good Neighbor Policy should have studied the good neighbors of the midwestern rural neighborhoods. I believe they did, and found them wanting. The seat of pre-war isolationism was just such neighborhoods. Their circles were too exclusive. They had not the proper feeling of kinship toward those outside their circle. In general, they hated foreigners. They made their starting point their stopping point.

Projection recognizes no stopping point except as a temporary expedient to allow time to cultivate the field behind and at hand.

I shall venture the statement that in the days when martyrs were burned at the stake, many of those who participated in the ceremonies would have been classed as neighborly people. Neighborliness can easily become a rite instead of being prompted by love. But even when it is sincere, it seldom encompasses a whole problem. Let us remind ourselves continually that "little acts of charity" have worth only if they contribute to an *expanding* way of life.

When we see a nation partly opening its arms to the displaced persons of the world, we are prone to say that if it opened its arms wider, then the whole problem would be solved; and we are prone to add that in this way the whole problem of over-population in all parts of the world could thus be solved.

Let us take a case that is by no means extreme. What would happen if we formed a policy of admitting a million Europeans a year to our country? Europe is admittedly over-populated, but at the end of each year, Europe's population would be greater than it was at the beginning of the year when it still had its million.

One of the basic requirements for world amity is a recognition on the part of all nations that those countries that are over-populated must solve the problems within their own borders.

This is not meant to rule out giving sanctuary to displaced persons. It is not meant to rule out a reasonable immigration policy. It is merely meant to rule out immigration as the cure for over-population. And it is meant as a graphic illustration of the fact that the complete mastering of any problem is seldom as simple as it appears on the surface; and that in addition to Good

Samaritans we must have people who are willing to engage in the hardest of all tasks—thinking.

So let us think more on this problem of displaced persons. What would have happened if the nations of the world had immediately and enthusiastically opened their arms to the displaced persons? The displaced persons would undoubtedly have been almost immediately replaced by a million more "displaced" persons. This is definitely not meant as an excuse for the slowness with which the problems of the genuinely displaced persons was attacked.

One's vocation should be a projection. Since this is a life-long project, it affords a good illustration of counting the cost before plunging in. Because of the amount of preparation, there is no turning back without an expensive revamping of the base of operations. A poor base of operations means poor projection.

This is just another way of saying that great consideration must be given to the prospective material reward, because that will have a direct bearing on one's usefulness. There is the further consideration that work that is not sufficiently remunerated is not sufficiently appreciated, and therefore not sufficiently effective.

This is projection into the future. It is never easy. All long range problems are projections into the future. To cite one instance, future historians will probably regard the issues in the present Russian-Greek problems as having been clearly delineated from the beginning. They will overlook the fact that from the profusion of issues, only a few will have survived and been passed on to them. The issues that remain for them make it comparatively easy for *them* to pass judgment. Straining out the other issues was no easy task and involved unpredictable extraneous issues. They will think that our problems were much simpler than theirs are.

It is the essence of pure religion and of democracy to get the other person's viewpoint. Therefore, projection will be continually assumed when we shall consider religion and democracy as separate subjects.

6. RELIGION

My definition of pure religion in the introduction was just a beginning. In this chapter there will be just a continuation. In the main it will be a looking at the religious attitude from many viewpoints; and applying the religious attitude to many case studies. Every effort will be made not to make

43

techniques appear more important than attitudes. At the same time, it must be stressed that attitudes that are not implemented by technique die a slow death. The church's great shortcoming is substituting form for technique.

The religious attitude and approach cannot be clearly defined, outlined, or delimited; but we can point out many attitudes and approaches and say, "These are religious."

In this chapter much thought will also be given those things that *parade* under the banner of religion. They will generally be unfavorable things, because the truly religious things draw attention away from themselves.

There is much talk these days about the preëminence of spiritual values. There is too little on how these values are to be realized. The best way for us humans to realize them is through a keen interest in the *material* well-being of our neighbors. We must think of these material conditions as harboring the spirit.

Here is an address on the mysteries of the Near East. The question the speaker seriously raised — and did not answer — was: "Has our vaunted Western civilization made us any happier than are these Near Easterners?"

First he took up the Great Pyramid. The pyramid does not look impressive from a distance. It is only as one looks to the top from the bottom that one is duly impressed. Even then, unless he is put on his guard, his guess on facts and figures about the pyramid will be a minor fraction of the whole.

The speaker thinks that we should gaze on this vast engineering feat of long ago with awe and admiration and ask ourselves whether we have progressed so much after all.

He made no mention of the vast lack of respect for personality that went into the building of that pyramid! He made no mention of the fact that all this energy went into the building of *one tomb!*

He referred to the Egyptians' apparent ability to stand more pain than we can stand. He used as an illustration an old man who emerged from a neighborhood quarrel with a badly battered head. This man refused an anaesthetic. He was probably afraid of it.

This incident helps to illustrate some of the inner turmoil that often hides behind a pleasant exterior. We do not hit our neighbors with clubs because we love them. The speaker had said that these neighborhood brawls were common. The people are not as happy as the speaker thinks.

He referred to the Egyptians' apparently greater resistance to infection. He mentioned that an Egyptian will wash a wound with gutter water and the wound will not become infected. He assumed, without proof, that if an American did the same thing he would probably not fare so well. I believe he would fare just as well. Our great precautions are a guard against the occasional

44

infection. I believe that if the speaker had followed this up a little longer he would have discovered that occasionally an Egyptian's wound also becomes infected.

A person without facts and figures at his disposal would have assumed from the speech that the average Egyptian is healthier and lives longer than the average American.

He referred to the dervishes who apparently are able for a few hours to transport their spirits into the next world. He assumed that these dervishes at least occasionally achieve a bliss that is forever denied us. They get their occasional glimpses of heaven by looking away from the world.

When Jesus suffered most keenly, his thoughts were on suffering humanity. He did not achieve heaven by directing his attention elsewhere. Heaven slowly enveloped him as he went about maintaining his interest in humanity.

The early Christians retained much of the other-worldly philosophy. They had their eyes turned toward the next world, more than toward their neighbors in distress. In this respect, the light is still in the process of dawning on us. We are slowly learning that heaven is not primarily a place we go to, but something that gradually envelops us as we are engaged in altruistic service. Or we might say that heaven is a direction.

There are many people today who insist that it is the hope of life after death that makes people religious. Granting that this may be true of the hope as a basic urge, we must be careful that our religion does not make it the goal. The goal of religion must still be the welfare of my neighbor.

Anything that will not build up faith and hope in things this side of the grave will not build up a faith in life after death. But faith in the afterlife is an inevitable byproduct of pure religion.

We have too many people who believe, or profess to believe, in life after death, but who have no faith in the life before death. They appear to picture themselves as being in the world but not of the world. They are temporarily in the world's grip, but their arms are outstretched and pointing *away from* the world.

How different is this picture from that of the person whose arms are outstretched *toward* the world! Such a person is ready to lend a hand and do his bit to bring more of heaven to earth. This person is also in the world but not of the world, but in a different sense.

Too many people of all ages look for something outside themselves to bring them happiness. Some people place prime confidence in medicines to keep them in health. Some people depend on panaceas — things outside themselves — to solve their fundamental problems of individual and social adjustment. They are alike in mistaking helps — sometimes great helps — for fundamentals.

Psychiatrists never cure anybody; but they can make it easier for the patient to cure himself. Medicines do not cure, but they can be a great help in setting the stage for the body to cure itself. Social scientists can merely set the stage to make it easier for the individual members of the community to find their mission in life, which is salvation. Happiness and a feeling of well-being in general flows from the sense of having ourselves contributed something to a cause.

The speaker made the mistake that is so often made. He jumped from the extreme of poverty to the other extreme of special privilege, and back again. The golden mean was ignored. Religion strives for this golden mean.

Jesus — and others — came into the world to fight this oriental resignation toward the inevitability of the extremes of this world. If we absorb his spirit, we will not wonder whether we have dropped behind the oriental. Those of us who see no signs of progress have ourselves contributed too little toward the movement.

Let us grant that Western civilization exalts material satisfactions; and that Eastern civilization exalts spiritual values. But let us not too readily conclude that Eastern people have achieved a higher spiritual level. To say so would deny that the material and the spiritual tend to move up together. The leaven in all materially progressive groups is provided by those in the groups who give thought to the material welfare of their neighbors.

In Jesus' discourses and activities, the spiritual and material are so intermingled that it is difficult to tell where one begins and the other ends. We too should not make undue efforts to separate them. They often are inseparable.

When foreigners visit this country, nearly all of them are impressed by the courtesy and genuine considerateness shown by those who are placed in positions of authority. They notice it more than we do because it is something that they did not find where they came from. We are demonstrating that the material and the spiritual tend to rise together. There is plenty of evidence that our great material prosperity has raised us to a higher spiritual level than has been attained by the less favored nations.

It should be remembered that the Eastern philosophers who exalt spiritual values, generally have more than their share of the material things that are presumed to be so meaningless. Their thoughts often did not dwell on the blessings of poverty until after they had emerged from that state.

Many of the Chinese proverbs that have such a lofty ring were formulated by those who always had a backlog of abundant material possessions. Few of the proverbs are imbued with the crusading spirit that is found in Jesus' sayings.

It appears to be a fair evaluation of the Eastern philosophy to say that it exalts spiritual values — for the other fellow; and keeps the less important material comforts for itself.

Jesus told the rich young ruler to sell all that he had and give to the poor only after he had insisted that he had always kept all the commandments and recognized that he still lacked something. The man was owned by his own property. Jesus never told anybody to take all that somebody else had and give to the poor. We spend too much time on evils over which we have no control. If we insist on worrying, let us worry about the things *we* can correct, until we start correcting them. This is just another way of saying that we are too much concerned about evil and not enough about sin.

The church's prime short range objective is to make its members conscious of evil that can be corrected, particularly the evil in their own hearts. Consolation is an end product. To be real it must come from within. The church must recognize that it cannot manufacture consolation and then dispense it. Its members must deserve it to get it. The church's job is to show them how they can deserve it.

Here is an interesting experiment. Consider the reactions of certain people when you mention a project that involves them. They think instantly in terms of how their rights are being infringed. Others just as quickly think in terms of how they can help further the project, and then they plunge in. One has the irreligious, the other has the religious, approach.

Professors of religion delight in saying, "This is going to hurt!" The congregation braces itself for the shock only to discover that it didn't hurt at all. The barbs were directed at those who were out of earshot. Jesus directed most of his barbs at those who could hear him. He made it plain that they had to do something besides say, "Yes, I believe," to earn salvation.

Lip service has worth only in so far as it portrays its counterpart in belief and action. Professors of religion lay too much emphasis on lip service. Lip service can hide as well as lay bare. They assume too readily that those who are sitting in front of them are by that act to be counted among the elect. They have withering words of scorn for those who are not there to listen to them.

Yes, professors of religion spend too much time telling their own flock how good they are, compared to those outside their own fold. This leads to an intolerant attitude in all secular matters as well as in matters theological.

This intolerant attitude strongly suggests a lack of faith in our own stand. It rejects the idea of learning from other viewpoints. Jesus was always ready to consider other viewpoints. He was willing to learn from those outside his fold.

So the church will survive because underlying the gropings of the professors of religion is the essential truth and worth of Jesus' message.

The religious approach is based on faith. This faith is based on a belief that God possesses and dispenses all the virtues — ultimately, if not now. Those of us who use the religious approach will try to speed the day when all these things will be fulfilled.

Faith can be built up by the knowledge that our efforts can bring results outside ourselves. Faith is built up by the knowledge that we can do something to correct evils. Faith does not say, "Why doesn't somebody do something?" It does it.

A labor leader looked the president of a large Protestant denomination in the eye and said, "You people of the church take too small an interest in the laboring man." The reply was, "We are guilty, as charged." The object here is not to raise the question of church-labor relations. It is rather to point to an act of real humility on the part of a churchman that is remarkable only because it is so rare.

Let us assume that every Christian theologian were asked the question, "In what does the hope of the world lie today?"

The most common reply would undoubtedly be, "In the Redeeming Love of Jesus."

The capital letters have the effect of putting Redeeming Love at arm's length. The statement is nearly always accompanied by the implication, "Now, if others had this Redeeming Love as I have it, then there would be no problem of World Peace."

There are a few theologians who have translated this Redeeming Love into love for neighbor. *Their* answers would probably have something to do with what this Redeeming Love looks like in action. They recognize most keenly that saying does not guarantee doing and practicing.

What would be the result if the first type of theologian were pinned down to practical illustrations of Redeeming Love at work? Many of the answers would have to do with reaching *down* and helping those who are wallowing in their devil-inspired lusts. They would be too ready to assume that those who have mastered their carnal appetites are the possessors of this Redeeming Love. They lack vision.

There is a strong tendency to consider Jesus' Golden Rule — and the Ten Commandments — as exemplifying the highest form of spirituality. The flaw in the Golden Rule is that it is not easy to determine what I should like others to do to me if our positions were reversed. I believe that Jesus placed

48

the law of love above the Golden Rule. Love makes others, not myself, the criterion. Again, the difference is one of emphasis only, but it is a vital difference.

Racial, class and caste intolerance perhaps best illustrates what is still the world's greatest shortcoming: the feeling that we can best boost ourselves by hindering others. Many of us are not yet ready to grant others the same chance that we have had, have, or feel that we should have.

"We best help ourselves by helping others," has more foundation in fact than most of us appreciate. Here, by all means, we dare not overlook the spiritual phase of the reward. The main criterion is not the material reward, but the nature of the addition to our spiritual storehouse.

Every material thing and action has a spiritual measure. That is why there is might in the widow's mite. There is also might in the strong man's *might* — if it is devoted to selfless service.

The strong man must be strong for his neighbor. Thus only will he liberate his inner potentials that can find expression only in selfless service.

It matters not whether he is strong because he is lined up with the strong, or whether he is strong in his own strength — the obligation is the same. Others must also be made strong. We rise together, not against each other. "If I rise, you too shall rise." This is the spirit of Christianity. It is also the spirit of Judaism; and of all religions worthy of the name.

As a nation we are numbered among the strong. Let us use our strength in service to other nations. Let us learn to take our thoughts off Number One when we minister to others.

We do not work for democracy, or World Peace, or religion. Rather religion and democracy constrain us to work for our neighbors. World Peace will steal on us unawares if enough of us world citizens are dedicated to this task.

The goal is a *sense* — of rising with others to newer heights and broader horizons.

Living religion is essentially auto-functional — its greatest impact is on the life of the one who *believes* in it.

Religion recognizes that rooting out selfishness is a task that is never completed; that the best technique is to guard against translating selfish thoughts into selfish acts. Acts *tend* to mold our thinking.

On a world scale, we must nurture a national passion for guaranteeing justice for the other nations. The first step in this nurturing process is to see to it that it is functioning in our own national life.

Legislators will have a passion for looking for the good in the program of the opposing party, and then supporting it unless or until they are prepared to offer something better.

The nation that is seeking to avert catastrophe by forgetting the rights of other nations is heading for a fall. Are we such a nation? The answer is still in the making.

We all recognize the barrenness of the life that places all the emphasis on material possessions. The church can be just as barren by placing the emphasis on the letter. "The letter killeth, but the spirit maketh alive." Let it not be recorded of our theological organizations that the letter kept them apart when the spirit was crying for unity.

We impute cynicism to those outside the theological groups. Perhaps the most incurable cynics are found within the groups. For what is cynicism but a refusal, often through fear, to give proper consideration to all the evidence? Too many of us are fearful of entertaining a new thought. We are afraid that others may associate an "ism" with our name. Many Christians will not try to get at the heart of other theologies. They are afraid. They are afraid that a recognition of worth in other faiths implies a lack of faith in their own faith. They are afraid!

Once in a Sunday School class I gave a rough outline of the procedure that was followed in picking the books of the New Testament. An old member of the class told me afterward that he had gone to church all his life and this was the first time he had ever heard anything about it. Why did he have to be kept in the dark?

He said that he had often wondered about such subjects. . . . He might have added that he never raised the question for fear of having his faith called in question. "Faith" can cover — yes, engender — a multitude of doubts.

Professors of religion presume the privilege of making statements without bothering about substantiating evidence. They abuse the word faith. It is a word that is made to create doubt. If a man raises a question, they are too quick to say that he lacks faith.

Professors of religion are generally experts in the art of attributing base motives to those who do not think as they do. They are better at calling names than they are in disposing of charges. This is generally the cover of those who do not believe in social justice for all.

The question of Sunday movies was recently a hot issue in my community. A clergyman said, "We want to keep this town clean." The implication was very plain: That those who favor Sunday movies do not want to keep this town clean.

Many clergymen are very cynical in their attitude toward the workaday world. In their own thinking they have not achieved a proper integration of

50

the spiritual and the material. Cynicism is the end product of a one-sided development.

The church in general nurtures this cynicism. The wholesale staying away from the church by a large segment of the people is in part an inarticulate protest against this cynical attitude. The irony of it all is that this cynicism — fear — is classed as faith. Oh faith! What crimes are still being perpetrated in thy name!

Those professors of religion who take the attitude that their theology is the only true theology seldom approach their own Bible with an open mind. They use it only to bolster them in their pet convictions. Here at least they could profit from the scientific attitude.

An honest confession is good for the soul, and professors of religion have great need for starting on themselves. They must recognize the fact that no mortal is possessed of the whole truth and that we all can learn from others.

Efforts of the theologians to get together are not accompanied by enough confession of sin. We Christians, as an example, must honestly ask ourselves, "What do we stand for that the Jews do not stand for?" And we should answer the question in the light of pure religion as we Christians define it.

A speaker said, "What Russia needs is a few carefully planned funerals." I noticed that one who chortled most gleefully was a minister of the gospel. Hitler believed in carefully planned funerals.

Plainly this speaker overlooked the fact that such talk plays into the hands of the lawless element. It is the hoary attitude that those who "know" they are right should take the law into their own hands.

The religious attitude is not to jump at conclusions. It is forever striving to see all sides and circumstances of a problem. It does not presume to have all the answers. It tries to get over the attitude that whatever is, is right.

Why has the church so long, in the light of her access to Jesus' teachings, persecuted and even put to death those whose beliefs they did not like? One reason undoubtedly is the subconscious feeling we all have that every power for good has its equally powerful adversary. This attitude is contrary to the religious attitude that all things work together for good to them that love God.

Another reason is the attitude that there is just one right way. This attitude would not be so bad if it were not accompanied by the conviction that my way is the right way. No one's way is the right way. We are all groping for the right way.

Then there is the very common conservative feeling that whatever is handed up from the past in the way of the established institutions should not be questioned by individuals. This is regarded as being equivalent to arguing about God's designs. It is basically the old argument that whatever is, is right.

Finally, there is the well-known feeling that if a large group of people is gathered together, and of one mind, then they must be right. Mob psychology is mistaken for divine guidance.

In passing judgment on new projects there is too great a tendency, if we are opposed, to think too much in terms of what they did not accomplish. If we are favorably disposed, we ascribe to them results that probably have other causes.

Whether we are for or against a project, we should always strive to think in terms of what it will accomplish that is not accomplished by the discarded measure. Consideration must also be given to its shortcomings.

Much thought must be given to this problem because of the average person's inability to weigh all factors impartially. The field of politics is probably the best illustration of where we are so sadly lacking. There are still too many legislators more interested in the welfare of their party than of the nation.

The church, too, must come around to the attitude that the *religious* element in a project must also be judged by its fruits.

The church says that the church-supported colleges graduate men and women with nobler qualities than are found in the graduates of other colleges. John Dewey would say, "Where is the tangible evidence?" This is practically one with Jesus' stand that "by their fruits ye shall know them."

This stand does not make the material the measure of the spiritual. It is more an indicator.

I am going rather deeply into the travails of the professors of religion, because if we educators are to introduce religion into the schools, we must have a rather clear conception of what we mean by religion. And we must look to the churches and synagogues to see what there is worthwhile that we can assimilate.

The vices are stressed because the contrary virtues can be easily envisaged. And I am writing, not as from the outside, but as from the inside. When we view our insides, we should be much concerned about our shortcomings.

Lewis Browne is an excellent guide for those Christians who want to take a look at their theology as a judicious outsider sees it. All of us must do this occasionally if we are not to be encrusted with theological tradition.

I have repeatedly discovered that many of those who are classed as atheists in the public mind have a very sympathetic interest in the Jesus whom they see adventuring through the four Gospels of the New Testament. Even in Jesus' adventurings in the *spirit,* they often follow him with more facility than does a formalistic Christian.

But we dare never forget that it was formalism that assured the perpetuation of the Christian church. Without the tradition for preserving the earliest available records of Christianity in their original form, it is doubtful whether the spirit of Jesus would shine as clearly today as we can still see it shining in the New Testament. However much we adventure in the spirit today, we must still occasionally return to this original source for our bearings. But it cannot be emphasized too strongly that the adventuring must be in the world in which we live, not in a dead past. In the words of Lincoln, "The dogmas of the quiet past are inadequate to the stormy present."

Jesus' religion of love was so far ahead of the times that it was necessary to erect a rather fixed structure within which it could get its bearings. But this expanding love refuses to be restricted when it is ready to reach out into new fields. We are now in that period. The new fields are beginning to embrace the whole world.

The question of divine inspiration should be primarily one of whether we are inspired as we read, and in our subsequent meditations. Scripture is inspired for those who draw inspiration from it. In this world in which nothing is perfect, it is proper to regard as being divinely inspired that which is the best available at the time. This question of availability must consider both the tools that are available and the spiritual status of the people and age for which a message was intended.

The church is too much exercised by the fear that if the average Christian is taught to regard the forms of religion for what they really are, he will lose faith. The church itself does not have sufficient faith to make a deep probe of the faith of its own members.

Let us consider our flag as a symbol, or form. Few of us regard it as being more than a piece of cloth. The plus value is found in *our* hearts, minds, and lives. What a help it would be if we regarded the symbolism and formalism of religion in the same light!

The church is still in the position in which the schools found themselves fifty years ago. The schools were then priding themselves that the students were acquiring things without bothering to substantiate their beliefs by cold analysis. The schools then were possessed by the "almighty" attitude that the church still assumes.

In this respect, the school still has a long way to go. The church has not yet started. The church is still glibly assuming that its members hold certain beliefs without attempting to find out what they really believe.

There are few clergymen with sufficient faith and background to successfully conduct a forum on theology among their church members in which the members are encouraged to bring into the open their inmost beliefs, without fear of losing caste as a result.

The church should take the attitude that it is no more inconsistent to carry on its rolls those that openly express doubt than to go ahead with the knowledge that they have many members who are submerging their doubts.

Instead of setting up a complete faith as a prerequisite for joining the church, the church should think of faith as something that is gradually acquired within the fold.

Forms have the meanings that *we* give to them. If other theological groups have forms that are different from ours, our concern should not be to quarrel with their forms, but rather to consider the spirit that those forms are meant to portray. There is too much dependence on the mind and not enough on the spirit-lighted heart.

The French revolutionists of the eighteenth century, our Abolitionists, and Woodrow Wilson, did not preserve a proper balance between technique and attitude. They gave too much weight to technique. They assumed that if people were given the *form* of democracy they would perforce use it to good advantage. We Americans as a group made the same mistake about Germany after the first World War. We must guard against being doctrinaires.

Jesus knew that a change in form, as a permanent cure, was meaningless if it was not accompanied by a change of heart. The struggle upward has been a slow, tortuous one, but it has been the only way. Too few Christians can see clearly enough through their theologies to see in Jesus' death on the cross the same kind of sacrifice that is continually being made to bring the spiritual kingdom to more hearts and in ever-increasing measure.

This is not an argument against forms and formality, but it is an argument for knowing them for what they are. It is an argument for changing the form to take care of the growing spirit. It is also an argument against setting up forms before the spirits are ready to occupy them.

There was a time when the church made it impossible for a man who placed the emphasis on the things of the spirit — as against form — to stay within the fold. That is no longer necessary. For that reason I do not have much patience with those intellectuals who scorn the forms and formality of the church to the extent of remaining on the outside. They have not given sufficient thought to Jesus' statement that "in my Father's house are many mansions."

Let us see how a consideration of conscience and the thing that we Christians call the Holy Spirit can bolster us in the stand we are taking — in this volume — on pure religion.

Religion recognizes the important role that conscience plays as a prodder. It flogs us mercilessly if we loiter along the way. It is much concerned about what our neighbors think of our thoughts, ideas, ideals, and actions. Conscience urges us to be morally correct. It urges us to conform. In its initial stages it is based on fear of neighbor. We, in practice, believe it is more important to conform to the demands of an intolerant neighbor than of a tolerant God; because we consider the demands not intrinsically important.

We should think much on the fact that none of us seems to worry about what God thinks of our beliefs. Even King David had a conscience that existed very much in this initial stage. After he had committed a heinous crime, he did not seem to worry as long as he thought that his neighbors did not know. He does not appear to have given a thought to the fact that God knew all the time. He did not confess his sins to *God* until after his *neighbor* had found him out. We tend to find God's law in our neighbors' sense of propriety.

But there comes a time when conscience is concerned about more than the question of what our neighbors think of us. It begins to lose itself in our neighbors' interests. The Holy Spirit is making an entrance. *Fear of* neighbors is being replaced by *love for* neighbor. Neighbor is still the criterion, but in a different way. "The voice of the people" — my neighbors— "is" still "the voice of God."

Note the analogy found in the history of the ancient Hebrews. At first they were actuated by fear of God; later by love for God.

Does authoritarian religion tend to substitute fear of God for fear of neighbor? Quite the reverse. The authority in authoritarian religion is of men, not of God. David seems to have subscribed to an authoritarian religion and we know what it did not do to him. The conscience that is not permeated by the Holy Spirit is primarily concerned with the fear of being *caught*.

So we tend to find God's laws in our neighbors' needs. Sin is transgression against these laws—against God's creation, chief of which is man, my neighbor.

And this brings us to a consideration of religion and morality. Some will say that my religion is high morality. It is true that if morality goes far enough it becomes religion. All good things tend to become one as they move in the direction of the absolute good.

I have defined religion. The true religionist in interested in the fortunes, and misfortunes, of his neighbor. In morality, the emphasis is on conforming to the laws of man. The religious emphasis is on the effort to see our neighbor as God sees him. The religionist is interested in his neighbor's world.

55

Moralists often have that superior, other-worldly look. Most of those of us who in the vernacular are called *very religious* people are in reality merely being morally correct. We conform to the mores of the group.

The morally correct man does not have to consider his neighbor's welfare. In other words, he does not have to love his neighbor. He conforms to custom. He does the things that are good for him in a shortsighted sort of way. He does not necessarily have vision. He may be very covetous. His value is probably neutral. Nevertheless, it is probably correct to say that he has at least a touch of the religious approach. But he is guided too much by conscience, and too little by the Holy Spirit.

I have just been reading about a meeting of Protestant, Catholic, and Jewish leaders in the interest of a "common morality." I looked in vain for any evidence of coming to grips with reality. They have a greater need for a *common religion*.

After all, morality is a conforming to accepted standards, or the accepted standards themselves. Morality is a form, or a subscription to a form. We need to come to grips with the religion that helps to create these norms. No norms will be permanently satisfactory. They must change with the widening horizons that religion is constantly opening up.

The crying need is a get-together on religion, not morality. Morality is the end product.

Our role is more than a conforming to standards. It is taking an active interest in the needs of our neighbors. It is respecting the viewpoints of our neighbors. It is putting our neighbors first and ourselves second.

Making Jesus the center of these discussions is also to impress on Christians that their teachings on human relationships are not beyond the apprehension and practice of our Jewish brothers. The Jews have no figure in history that we Christians will not accept as a basis for discussion.

"How firm a foundation!" Every one of us craves the sense of resting on a firm foundation. Those of us who lack this sense should carefully check our lives to see if they are not self-centered. Forthwith they should become neighbor-centered. The natural instinct is to wrap our arms around all the material things of life and hold on tight. Nature does not realize that matter disintegrates from disuse.

It also disintegrates from use, but here the transformation is into something nobler than itself.

This foundation must be firm, and supple, and plastic—not solid, immovable—it must change with my neighbor and his needs.

We should have faith in a God that possesses all the absolute virtues. We should also have faith that these virtues are helping us to slowly transform the world. Instead, too many of us are beset with a sense of impending doom. This attitude is the result of not giving sufficient weight to the things of the spirit.

God speed the day when most of us will substitute for this sense of impending doom a sense of the eternal fitness of things!

Man-made rules are not absolute; and many "absolute" rules turn out, if we go back far enough, to be man-made for a particular set of circumstances that existed at that time.

What is more inspiring than the belief that man has helped to shape our religion? It helps us feel that we are playing our part now in remolding our religious beliefs to conform to new conditions; and in trying to mold conditions into a more religious pattern, an elastic pattern. There is perhaps nothing more inspiring than to trace the persistence of an idea through centuries, or even millenia, despite the faltering human channels that it must follow.

H. G. Wells apparently does not like the Pauline influence on the New Testament. He should remember that if it had not been the Pauline influence then it would have been some other influence. It appears that the Pauline influence was the best possible for the times. But we Christians will do well to evaluate Paul's teachings on flesh and spirit in the light of the nineteen hundred years of experience that we have had since he wrote. The same holds true concerning the works of most of the other writers of the epistles of the New Testament.

Let us consider his teachings about placing God's judgment above our own. Who is to pass judgment on what are God's judgments? We, or some other persons who must rely on their own judgment or that of still others.

If we are able to trace these judgments to their original source, we generally find a man who was very much interested in his neighbors' welfare. This is about as close as we can come to an apprehension of God's judgment—plus the common experience of the most enlightened among us as to what are the most satisfying things in life. We just cannot get away from our neighbors' welfare!

In fact, it is not too much to say that, practically, there is no absolute or divine rule except that all rules must be gauged to the needs, aspirations, and shortcomings of my neighbor. For example, we observe Sunday or the Sabbath, not because God needs it, but because we need it.

The early Christian church was much concerned about the vulgar revelry that the masses engaged in at New Year's time, which was also supposed to be the shortest day of the year. And it did something about it. It set that period aside for celebrating the birth of Jesus. It directed the people's exuberance into a new channel. And it worked. The celebration is not marred today by the knowledge that we do not know at what time of the year Jesus was born. Verily, Christmas was made for us Christians.

The ever-present conservative push toward formalism is another reason for stressing the importance of the individual. We should be continually asking ourselves, "What are the needs of the individual?" If we do not stress the individual, my neighbor, we will stress form, or our own needs.

> *"Momentous to himself as I to me*
> *Hath each man been that woman ever bore;*
> *Once in a lightning flash of sympathy*
> *I felt this truth, an instant, and no more."*
>
> —William Watson

The task of religion is to make this lightning flash a glowing, constantly growing, flame.

Is it wrong to stand up for one's rights? Is it wrong to praise one's self? Is it wrong to talk about one's accomplishments? Is it wrong to talk about one's qualifiications for a job? It certainly is not. The person who can do so with objectivity is seldom resented. Great care must be exercised, of course, that other people's toes are not being stepped on.

Many of us are too selfish to fight for our own rights. We are afraid of the stigma of selfishness that will be applied to us by some. We slink in the shadows and hope that someone will come along and fight our battles for us. When the battle is nearly won, we often come into the open and join the fray with the smug attitude that we are helping the other fellow. Yes, it often takes courage to stand up for one's rights. The weak among us as a result hide and let the strong appear selfish.

The religious attitude is the strong attitude. It is the attitude that I can give my neighbor all that is coming to him, including the right to think for himself, and still make my way. Jefferson is perhaps the best national example for this religious attitude. He applied it in his daily life and in his thinking.

The dairy industry was not thinking of its neighbors, unless it had a very narrow conception of the word neighbor, when it succeeded for years in almost strangulating the oleomargarine industry.

Is rugged individualism religious? I like a rugged individual who tries to outdo his neighbor under rules that are fair; who applauds when his neighbor outdoes him; who is a hard loser in the sense that he is always striving; who is a good loser in the sense that he does not feel disgraced if his neighbor outdoes him; who recognizes that rewards are not always just.

Jesus knew when to retreat. He often ran away from his enemies. Many of us are too cowardly to retreat. We are afraid to face the stigma of coward-ice that may be applied to us.

Jesus knew when to speak up and when to hold his tongue. There is considerable truth in the statement that there is a time for everything.

Which should conform first, my environment or I? My duty is first to conform to my environment unless I have special reasons not to. Having conformed, or partially conformed, I shall then be in a strategic position to work on my environment. Unwillingness to conform is evidence that I am attaching too much importance to myself. It means that I have too much faith in my natural rights.

The task of religion is to place the emphasis where nature is lacking. Religion teaches us to think about our neighbors' welfare; nature sees to it that we give ourselves the proper recognition. Religion teaches us to con-sider no task impossible until we have probed all the possibilities in the light of our capacities; nature sees to it that we expect the same of our neighbors.

But religion also takes part in the tasks that nature assumes so willingly. In the process it often transforms nature, at least as far as a particular in-dividual is concerned.

There are two bases on which disputes are often settled. One is recourse to hard and fast rules. The emphasis is on the letter. The other is based on common sense. Here the emphasis is on the spirit. Which line do children generally follow? The one that best serves their interests. What about adults? The same. It should be noted here that this problem is treated from a differ-ent angle in one of the other chapters.

In both cases, the reasoning should be on the basis of what is best for the other party to the dispute. The children's cases can be more readily settled because their candor affords us a more realistic approach to the problem.

There is candor in humility. Children have both. Unless they are com-pletely spoiled, they ask as from one who is higher than they. We adults can learn much from this attitude if we are alert to the modifications required. It must not betray too much blind selfishness. It must not be used in spite.

If everybody were altruistic, would all our own rights be taken care of by others? No, simply because others cannot see and feel our hopes and fears, and needs, as we ourselves understand them.

Even civil courts would still be needed because there would still be differences of opinion that are not self-centered.

Glenn Frank in *Thunder and Dawn* aptly brings out that, with primitive man, religion was part of his whole existence. As human inventiveness took over many fields that had been the province of the gods, religion began to be thought of as a thing apart. We must recapture the primitive man's conception of religion as a thing of his whole being. But when we add that this new religion must be a thing of the spirit, we must never forget that the spiritual cannot be separated from the material. We must remember that the material's prominence is due to the fact that it feeds the spiritual.

"The time is coming when people will not worship God in this mountain or in Jersualem. God is a spirit, and they that worship him will worship him in spirit and in truth."

Here Jesus seems to visualize a time in the future when God will be so much a part of our whole workaday existence that it will no longer be necessary to go to a particular place to worship God.

If this was what he had in mind, we should be careful to note that in the absence of such an ideal state of affairs, he continued to go to the temple and synagogue to worship. In looking to the future, we dare not tear ourselves loose from the present. But we must work on the present and strive to make it conform as nearly as possible to the ideal.

The spirit of God is everywhere; in our jobs or callings, in our recreation, in our dealings one with another. All jobs can be made holy. The job of religion is to try to make forms and formality unnecessary; and at the same time work on new forms so long as they can be made to serve spiritual ends. In fact, no matter what our calling, every effort must be made to make our jobs unnecessary—to release our energies for new projects. This is the lifeblood of progress.

Lately there has been a tendency to contrast the pay of teachers with that of garbage collectors .Only a person with an irreligious approach could suggest such a contrast. The contrast should have been on the basis of the different amounts of preparation required by different callings. There should be no looking down on those who do the lowly chores. There would be less need for garbage collectors if we superior persons had cleaner habits.

Is teaching or preaching a holier calling than the other jobs and professions? I doubt it. I believe that our legislators, collectively, are possessed of more pure religion than our professors of religion and theology. Perhaps pure religion is forced on them by the power, through the ballot, of the common people. At least they have it.

Robert Penn Warren in *All the King's Men* poses many problems, the solution of which calls for the religious approach.

The frank, steady gaze of those who have given their evil deeds a veneer of respectability paints a true picture of the Pharisee in all of us.

Such a man helps to explain Bilboism and its followers. Their line seems to be that the main difference between them and their predecessors is that they lack the veneer.

This is not to imply that they have the answer. The solution is to make things look respectable without veneer because they are respectable at the core. We teachers must continually wrestle with the question as to whether *our* respectability is just a veneer.

Teachers often say that they are hanging on to teaching, in spite of poor pay, because they love it and the kiddies. I doubt it. The great majority of us are hanging on because it is the best we can do under the circumstances. These are the circumstances.

Our investment is in preparation for teaching. It is not a simple thing to change horses in midstream. There is the further drawback that the teacher retirement system is divorced from the federal social security system. A change would mean a start from scratch in building up social security, and in working up in the new field. This is adventuring into the field of utility; and the religious spirit is all for it.

The religious spirit finds beauty in utility. This is a flat concept if we do not recognize that in its essence, utility is all spirit. The beauty can best be found in *place* utility; putting things and services where they will do the most good, even if it means giving things from me to you, or to others.

The *practice* of religion is the full-time job of everybody. It is not enough for the sociologists, economists, historians, etc., to outline the skeleton within which we must operate. They must all have a keen awareness of their responsibility in working on the human heart.

The problem of the economic know-how is essentially a religious problem. It is a very complex problem; and anyone who does not have the religious attitude can find many *facts* to substantiate his stand, whatever it is. He eliminates the facts that are inimical to his short-range welfare and interests.

Recently I read an article by an apologist for the capitalists in which he suggests that we go back to Adam Smith. He apparently does not know that in Adam Smith's scheme of things, there were no vested interests in the manufacturing field as we know them today.

It is distressing to note that the part of Adam Smith that has made the keenest impression on us is his statement that the sum total of all our selfish pursuits adds up to the best interests of the state, or group as a whole.

About the only truth in this statement is that selfish humanity manages to move in a generally upward direction; and that selfish action is generally better than no action. These concessions must be made if we are to believe that all things work together for good to them that love God. But some

61

things work better than others. One of religion's jobs is to seek and point out these better ways.

Rohrlich's *Education, Politics, and Transformation of Culture* demonstrates that this self-interest theory still has a strong hold in high places as well as in low.

His article agitated me more than any other. The most disturbing thing to me was that it did not seem to agitate any of the other members of the committee of scientists, theologians, and philosophers.

I believe that next to Ecclesiastes, it is the most cynical thing I ever read. The fact that it was written by a research analyst makes it all the more cynical.

He does not believe that the world's problems will be solved by altruism, because there are not enough altruistic people. He sounds the tocsin with an appeal to *enlightened* self-interest.

What has failed, altruism or enlightened self-interest? There probably never has been a time when the majority of the people did not claim to be guided by enlightened self-interest. Really altruistic people make no such claims for themselves. They realize that there is no such thing as enlightened self-interest. This realization spurs them toward the goal of pure religion.

Enlightened self-interest does not work because it focuses attention on self. Attention must be focused on the other fellow.

It might be well to state here, for the benefit of those who still favor enlightened self-interest as a motivating force, that it is recognized that a very *logical* case can built up for it. But *psychologically* it will not stand.

Self-interest has been tried and found wanting. Enlightened self-interest does not exist. That leaves altruism, or the love of pure religion. Pure religion can redeem the world, and will redeem the world if enough of us say so, and mean it.

In justice to Adam Smith, it must be stated that he by implication set his plea for the selfish strivings of *all* against the selfish strivings of the *few*. So his contribution was a forward step for his age.

Religion is a way of life. It is a way of getting along with my neighbor *and with myself*. Religion is an expanding way of life. It is also an intensive way of life. It is living.

The religious way of life is open to all. Profound mental penetration is not essential. A moron can be religious. It is difficult to see how he would qualify for Walter Lippmann's "high religion." In a sense he may be better off than a philosopher. He, perhaps, has the special privilege of not being weighted down spiritually by the many special privileges that may be the lot of the philosopher.

The Unecso says, "No people possesses superiority by reason of Divine gift." This is a bitter pill for many theological leaders to swallow. They think it is contrary to the teachings of Jesus to say that God reveals himself to others besides us Christians.

Many Christians are genuinely torn between their obligations to think of their world neighbors as brothers and therefore, equals, and their belief that only Christians will be saved. It may help them to acquire a workable philosophy if they try to reconstruct the conditions under which Paul worked. Paul probably did not come in contact with any group of thinkers with a program that approached his in idealism. Therefore, the only program that he could visualize was Jesus' program. Jesus himself often contradicted himself. They were only surface contradictions; for if we consider the circumstances under which they were made, the inconsistencies disappear.

The apostles themselves argued and changed their minds in the light of new circumstances. So we must recognize that God can impart His will to man under many guises and circumstances, *and still does.*

We Christians regard Jesus as the great example. Not argument about what we must do, but example, is the great convincer. People are very much interested in the question of whether a theory will work. The religious person is always conscious of the need for thinking in terms of what effect his words and actions will have on those who may copy from him. This he does without being self-conscious in the accepted sense of the term.

Professors of Christianity sometimes try to follow in the footsteps of Jesus by drawing lessons from the contemporary scene, as he so often did. But they are not interested in the welfare of the individual members of their flock, as was Jesus. Rather they are interested in getting their people to conform to a mold that often is outmoded.

Respect breeds respect. If a parent has respect for his child and his neighbor, his child and his neighbor tend to have respect for him and for society. The reverse is also true. Have you ever noticed that when you do your neighbor a good turn, he often responds with something more than you gave him?

There is much about Jesus, the example, that Jews can accept. We have had people throughout all history who gave up their lives that others might live. Jesus started with people as he found them. An excellent example. Jesus did not believe in turning the world upside down. He believed in gradual external change in pace with a change of heart.

Jesus may be considered the perfect reform pattern. He considered himself an insider. He tried to reform the religious life of his people by trying to convince the theological leaders of his day that there was need for change. He did not succeed. But we must not make the mistake of thinking that such a method never succeeds. The possibility should always be explored. Whether it succeeds depends largely upon the attitude of the ones who must be convinced, and the justness of the reform movement.

When it started becoming plain that reform from within probably would not succeed, then only did He call the twelve to be his constant disciples and companions. They were to be the nucleus of a separate movement, if such a movement should prove necessary. In the meantime, Jesus kept on striving to reform from within.

This is the pattern that has been followed repeatedly by genuine reformers—and will continue to be the pattern. We have a right to question the genuineness of the reformer who is very anxious to start a separate movement. He does not recognize the difficulty of establishing an entirely new blueprint for his followers, and much less the fact that this blueprint must be set in the minds of his followers, who harbor other blueprints that are slow to fade.

We have just read about the aftermath to the purging of old guard politicians by some enterprising ex-service men in one of our states. It develops that they do not have enough preparation to carry out the task they assigned themselves.

Was the total long-range effect good or bad? Undoubtedly good. If the old guard again regains control, it is very unlikely that they will ever again stoop as low as they did in the past. History is full of ill-timed reform movements that nevertheless proved more beneficial than harmful.

Sir Stafford Cripps, who writes much on Christian democracy, says that if even a small segment of the church taught and acted Christianity as Jesus did, then there would be a major upheaval within the church. He may be right. But we must face the question whether this changed attitude had not better come about gradually, so as not to do too much violence to our understandable inertia. We must learn to bend without breaking. Jesus was perhaps more of a bender than we are prone to realize. He started with life as he found it. He appeared revolutionary only to those who were themselves unbending.

Religious progress is slow progress. It is slow because it builds people up to help themselves by giving new impetus and direction to their dynamic natures. Basically it depends on the accord of many minds. These minds, like all mass, change slowly. One leader, great though he may be, will not greatly affect the direction of their thinking unless they are poised on a great divide and must choose between opposites.

64

Jesus himself, with his followers, did not transform his own little land of Palestine. It is easy to see how non-Christians can imagine that they are drawing lessons from the fact that the geographic cradle of Christianity is to this day such a hotbed of strife.

The religious person does not weary in well-doing. He follows through. He works as hard at the end as at the beginning, perhaps harder because he has the habit of gradually transforming work into play. He does not lose faith if his work is not appreciated or if the apparent results do not seem to justify the effort. He will be right even when surface indications seem to say that it pays to be wrong.

Jesus suggested *voluntary revolution* within our own hearts. He recognized that for society as a whole, the process must be *evolutionary;* that the examples are set by the comparatively few men of faith who will not be weary in well-doing.

But sometimes we are forced into a revolution against our will. All revolutions that have been justified by posterity were those that were brought on by the exercise of force by the oppressors. Rehoboam of old furnishes a good example of this.

There must be wholehearted cooperation in any revolutionary movement. There must be a careful consideration of the cost—but not too careful. Revolution must be more than a plowing under of those that are now at the top. The victors must be willing to turn the other cheek, go the extra mile, etc. The subjugation of women is a vestige of the reign of brute force as king. Religion makes it possible for two to live in harmony without an apparent master.

I believe that we are agreed that one of the objects of religious education is to learn to substitute evolution for revolution. It is true that Thomas Jefferson, the evolutionist by nature, accepted revolution as the lesser of two evils. But his revolution was different from William Lloyd Garrison's. He fought for separation from tyranny without.

Compared with revolution, evolution is conservative. It tries to make full use of its heritage. It has much in common with the conservation of natural resources that is stressed so much in school. It is too bad that we do not have a more apt name for those who go by the name of conservative in the public mind. Religionists are the true conservatives.

James's definition of pure religion is adequate if all that it implies is distinctly understood. This, however, can hardly be expected. We must take it apart.

Would it be wrong to give our conception of pure religion a wider scope? Would it be wrong to say that pure religion is helping others, graci-

65

ously accepting their help, *and* learning from them? Learning implies moving in the direction of the truth. "You shall know the truth, and the truth shall make you free."

It is all right as far as it goes, to say that in the light of the Eternal, men are all equally low; but it does not view my neighbor as I see him. We must judge him by the lights that God gave *us*. We must learn to judge men by standards that have meaning in our workaday world. We are not all alike in the use we make of our gifts. And we don't all receive the same gifts.

Nevertheless, we must make an effort to see our neighbors as God sees them. To God, our neighbors are as important as we are. We must recognize the fact that, while God's design is perfect, no mortal can fully grasp it. Inspiration is recognized as a gradual unfolding. We all, to the end of our days, but see through a glass darkly.

We must recognize that our neighbors perhaps have a keener grasp of God's plan than we. No religious organization has an exclusive private wire to the mind of God. But in deep humility they all can contribute.

We must recognize our natural selfishness, which becomes sin only as we consciously allow it to mold our lives. Knowledge makes sin. It also can make life worth living.

We must recognize that when we speak of democracy as recognizing the importance of the individual, we mean not ourselves, but our neighbors. This emphasis is necessary to properly subdue our selfish impulses. It is this phase of democracy that Communists do not seem to grasp.

We must be committed to the principle of giving help where help is needed. This is basic. An interest in the material well-being of *others* is one of the highest forms of spirituality. For us Christians to reject this thesis comes dangerously close to rejecting Jesus.

Helping people help themselves, rather than direct aid, in the long run is easier on the helper and the one helped. This is particularly true when the help is in the form of giving. Direct giving has a tendency to build up in the giver an unhealthy ego. It tends to give him a false sense of superiority. Is it not true that much of our giving is accompanied by a false sense of superiority over those whom we help? Too seldom do we think of it as an overdue righting of inequalities.

"He that humbleth himself shall be exalted." Many of us think that this means saying something derogatory about ourselves in the hope that others will disagree with us. True humility *feels* the lowliness that it gives voice to. It is gratified when a *genuine* voice tells it that it is not as low as it thinks it is, but it does not fish for these compliments.

One of the basic requirements of the religious approach is a recognition of limitations. It is because of our limitations that we try to see through the eyes of God. We must recognize the limitations that our selfish natures impose on us. It is literally true that of our own natural selves we cannot project our lives into the lives of our neighbors.

True humility recognizes the individual's strong points. In fact, it is from the vantage point of these strong points that we can really see our overall lowliness. The hypocrites view their humility from the low points. True humility consists in working our way to *our* top, and then recognizing that—temporarily, at least, and without help—this is as far as we can go.

There are theological groups who deliberately put obstacles in their own paths and urge the same on their neighbors. Their object is to make themselves humble. Too often it has the opposite effect. It is much more humbling to go as far as we can, until we reach obstacles that are not self-imposed; obstacles that are not sought out by us, but which must be surmounted if we are to achieve our objectives.

Henry C. Link cites the case of the man who faced the problem of whether to convert from coal to oil in his home. He decided against it because his boy was supposed to need the discipline that furnace cleaning was supposed to give him. It is questionable whether "made" work ever accomplished that purpose. The world is so full of things which need doing that no time should be wasted doing the things that don't need to be done.

We should take the attitude that life offers so many difficulties that we have no right to add to them, except for the purpose of achieving worthwhile goals. Civilization's progress is dependent on our ability to make difficult things easy; to free our energies for higher goals.

Is it ever right to do the things that do not need doing? Yes, for pleasure; but then it is not work, but play or recreation. It should hardly be necessary to state that doing a thing solely for the practice it gives the doer does not come under the ban. But even here we should be on the alert to substitute an externally worth-while task.

"Cast thy bread upon the waters" has been given a too materialistic treatment. Some people give as to a lottery. Their only projection is into their own selfish selves. They must learn that the gift without the giver is bare. They must also take the attitude that in giving they are dispensing justice more than charity. Giving, on my part, should be for services rendered by others to me, or by the recipient to others, or in the spirit that the recipient is more entitled to it than I.

Giving as to a lottery often ends up in cynicism. Such a giver has no interest in the welfare of others and gradually comes to the attitude that others are like him. There is at least one authentic case of a gambler who gave one-tenth of his winnings to charity because he thought that it improved his luck.

Too many professors of religion say that if we give a tenth of our income to the church or charity, it will come back to us in a material way, with interest. There is no altruism in giving that is done in this spirit. Those who give in this spirit are trying to buy happiness. Happiness can never be bought. It must be earned.

Saying that giving comes back to us in spiritual values is quite a different story. We have gone too far in stressing the material values—for ourselves—of Christianity. If we subscribe to this materialistic conception, then we are going to drop out of the race as soon as we are convinced that our gifts are not coming back to us in a material way.

The question of extra pay for extra work is up now for discussion among the local teachers. Those who are opposed to extra pay take the high-minded stand that they should not expect remuneration for "every little thing that they do." Nobody will quarrel with that.

A better way of putting it would be that we should not be quick to refrain from doing something simply because there is no money in it. On the other hand, those who have the responsibility should pay each one, as nearly as possible, according to his deserts.

A few years ago we collected tin cans in our local school to help the war effort. A handful of pupils collected more than the other hundreds of pupils combined. The school was paid for these cans. I was for giving some of this money to the outstanding collectors. I was out-voted. The majority said that patriotic effort should not be rewarded. They made the mistake of thinking that rewarding the pupils would set the pupils' minds on the reward, not on helping their country. It is passing strange how we are willing and anxious to force ideals on children that we ourselves reject in practice.

We must disabuse our minds of the idea that there is a material reward for every neighborly act. We must be keenly conscious of the many blessings we enjoy that are the gift of the generations of neighborly people who went before. We can partially repay them by making our contribution to the welfare of our neighbors and of the coming generations.

The religious attitude toward giving and compensation can be summarized as follows: We do not lose what we give. Help to others tends to be self-help. Help is looked upon as justice, not charity. Helping others is contagious. The material and the spiritual are so interlocked that they cannot be treated separately. We generally reach the spiritual through the material.

I should like to ignore the devil completely; but he has such a hold on many of us—at least on our imaginations—that he must be given some consideration.

I am going to steer clear of all theoretical and theological discussions concerning the question of the reality of the devil. I shall merely concern myself with the question of how belief in the devil affects the average person.

I once listened to a sermon on the devil and evil. Evil and the devil were pictured as being diametrically opposed to all the forces for good. I spoke with several who had listened to the sermon. Not one of them had identified the devil with his own natural self. Every one of them had made the devil and evil the scapegoat for his own natural shortcomings.

They seemed to take the view that every time they tried to do good, some force for evil—outside themselves—tried to thwart them. That is what they got out of the sermon. The doctrine about the devil and evil did not "take" as it is supposed to theoretically and theologically.

So from a purely practical point of view we should start concentrating on our own natural selves, and call it nothing but that. Then real progress will be made, because the kernel will no longer be lost in a maze of theological disputation.

The book of Job is the best known epic on the subject, "Why does God permit evil?"

It does not answer the question because the problem is unanswerable. We can talk about the good that can come out of evil; about greater good because of evil, but we are not coming to grips with the fundamental issues involved.

There is, of course, a more immediate question: Does God sometimes permit greater evil to be visited on the heads of the righteous than on the unrighteous?

"Job's friends" said no. Most of us are agreed that Job's friends were wrong; but in the application of our theory, we too often take the attitude that they were right. We are too prone to say that those who work the hardest go the farthest. There would be no room for reformers and liberals if this were always so. We too conveniently forget the many people who work hard and get nowhere, and many who fold their arms and go places. We go too far with the acknowledged fact that *in general* those who work hard go farther than those who don't.

Some day perhaps we Christians will take Jesus at his word when he gives us his opinion of the rich; when he finds the rich more covetous than the poor. And we Americans will be on our guard against the dangers inherent in the fact of our being the richest nation.

Our lofty position as a nation is not a fair measure of our worth. It is a measure that is not fair to other nations. By the same token we must recognize that our official station in life is often a poor index of our real worth. Special privilege plays too important a role.

Wives, as a class, are addicted to the habit of expecting too much of their husbands. They make it plain that if their husbands had more initiative they would occupy a higher niche in life. At the same time they are so afraid their husbands will to the wrong thing that they rob them of the very initiative they want them to have. But it must be recognized that their role of watcher is much harder on the nervous system than the husband's role of doer.

Too often their attitude is that they should fold their arms while their husbands set the pot of gold at their feet. This is not denying that husbands, like all other mortals, should have more creative initiative. It is, however, reminding wives that they should concentrate on the part they themselves should play; not other people's duties, but their own.

Too many wives have the idea that the positions their husbands hold in society are true indexes of their worth. They seem to be blind to the large part that heritage, inheritance, luck, and downright dishonesty plays in determining a man's position in life. In other words, they place too much emphasis on the material aspects of life.

All the higher positions in life that wives feel should be filled by their husbands are in most cases filled by husbands whose wives feel that if their husbands would exercise more initiative they would occupy a still higher niche. There just are not enough high positions to go around.

But it is still true that a dynamic member of society will find enough to do, although it may not give him the social and economic eminence that his wife thinks he should have.

Wives in particular must come to recognize this. Their first duty is consideration of the part they, not their husbands, must play if there is to be wholehearted teamwork. Wives have a peculiar mixture of confidence and lack of faith in their husbands.

It is said of Dr. Wiley, of "Pure Food and Drug Act" fame, that he once ruefully commented that he believed every informed person in the United States—except his wife—recognized him as an expert in child feeding.

Bachelors have certain advantages. They are not held back, as married men often are. But let it not be overlooked that there are many other factors that are holding bachelors back.

The religious attitude has little sympathy with the Horatio Alger type of thinking. It does not measure success as the world generally does. It measures success in the light of how well the individual is discharging the obligations that he feels are his lot.

Let us work overtime to judge people for what they *are in the light of their talents.* Let us get over the attitude that this world is peopled with a few successes and a multitude of failures. We should not judge as a failure a person who does a job that needs doing. Let him be his own judge on the question of whether he is living up to his talents.

Who are the people who judge others in the light of their worldly success and social position? They generally are those who want to go back to a past of simpler living; but they do not want to engage in simple living now, or any other time.

At present our thoughts are on a cancer cure and preventive. Why does God not give us the formula? I do not presume to know the answer; but I do know that if He gave us the formula, we would immediately, like the covetous rich, look to God for another formula. Certainly God's seeming indifference points to the primacy of things of the spirit and of the transitoriness of the material world.

Religion is not disheartened by God's seeming indifference to human suffering. It recognizes that this indifference can lead us to search for more abiding values. It recognizes a challenge from God to roll up our sleeves. It recognizes that in a very real way, God wants us to work out our own salvation with the aid of the divine spark.

We must recognize that this transitory world is the workshop in which we mortals must build and shape our spiritual lives. This is the workshop in which Jesus labored. Religion makes better use of this workshop than does philosophy.

Religion teaches us to bear the apparent inevitabilities of life, always recognizing that many of these apparent inevitabilities turn out to be myths.

Death is so inevitable and permanent! If we lose a hand, or a leg, or an eye, the loss is also so permanent. These things make us believe in a future that has the compensations we lack in this life. But it is no excuse for not correcting things that can be corrected. Economic and social injustices need not remain so.

What is the basis for the fact that self-denial and sacrifice often have their ensuing compensations? It is because of the suppressed potentials

71

within us that are clamoring for release. Many of these will forever remain dormant because the path to their release is never opened.

The religious approach calls for the seemingly radical view that it is easier to build up than to tear down. Is it not a fact that most people are forever fearful that we are making no progress? And still we progress. Few of us can view the present as impartially as we do the past. But this is necessary if we want to put our finger on what *is* progress and what is *not* progress.

In spite of our fears, our selfish natures still push up and, sometimes in spite of ourselves, push others along with us. It is the religious among us who give a semblance of unity to these forces.

"Eat, drink, and be merry, for tomorrow you die." "Never mind tomorrow; it's a lovely day today." These two attitudes savor too much of whistling in the dark. They are for enjoyment with fingers crossed.

The proper attitude is that enjoyment today—genuine enjoyment—is the best guarantee for enjoyment tomorrow. "Expect the best, and be prepared for the worst" can be an attitude with nothing phoney about it.

"Sufficient unto the day is the evil thereof." Are we sure we know what this means? It means, among other things, that miserable is the man who has nothing to accomplish for the day. Providing for tomorrow does not mean solving all of tomorrow's problems. It does mean solving as many problems as possible to make room for new fields of conquest.

It is because of lack of vision that most of us find work very boring. One of the factors that keeps us working is that we find idleness still more boring. Many of us work at a furious pace just to escape from something. Rather, we should work because of our immersion in a project.

What is temperance? It is using in moderation those things that give the highest returns when used in moderation; and *completely abstaining* from those things that are harmful in any degree.

Let us get away from the attitude that it is all right to do the harmful things in a moderate degree. There is no moderate degree for harmful things.

What is prudence? It is a careful consideration of the cost and probable results. This is a very simple statement of a very complicated problem. MacCallister suggests that perhaps Plato did not criticize the state because he wanted to die a natural death. But perhaps his prudence was based on the consideration that there is no use in tearing down if you have nothing better to rear in its place. What Plato had, existed in his mind only and was not ready for rearing—and perhaps never will be.

In figuring the cost of various kinds of action, sight is often lost of the possibility that the cost of *inaction* may be even greater. The man who seeks

72

security in the amassing of much of this world's goods is living more dangerously than the man who is offering his life.

"*Live* dangerously" is an imperative slogan for today. The only alterna-
tive is to *vegetate* dangerously. There is danger in action and in inaction.
But let us live dangerously for a higher goal than Nietzsche's will to power;
let ours be the will to service. This is the opposite of the life of the animals.
It is the life of saints; losing our lives to find them. It emphasizes that
religion was made for man, not man for religion. Religion is a tool.

Let it be noted here that the life of animals is excellent—for animals.
Our consciences do not allow us to be satisfied with such an existence. Unfortunately, our consciences are not as good in pointing out the better way.

Religion rejects those naturalists who think that we, who have the spark
of divinity within ourselves, can learn from nature, which lacks that spark.
This does not rule out the study of the workings of nature for the purpose
of harnessing it and bending it to our use.

Religion also rejects all shades of anarchism, because at its best anarchism
is live and *let* live. To be religious it must be live and *help* live.

Both naturalists and anarchists ignore the divine spark within us which
could correct the evils of the institutions they condemn.

"Be natural." An animal is natural. "Being natural" plainly means
something else. We are "being natural" when we have allowed our natural
impulses to be so permeated by the spirit that it is "natural" for us to do
the right thing.

Sports and play have much in common with religion. They all feed and
clothe the spirit. The "practical" man often finds little or nothing in any
of them. He does not fully appreciate that man does not live by bread
alone.

Glenn Frank's chapter on the church and war is the most provocative
of all, because the reader will agree or disagree violently with many of the
points that he makes.

He says that in time of war, the church should steer clear of committing
itself in favor of war. But it should not ostracize members who take a stand.

I agree, but for reasons that are different from his. The religious attitude is to concentrate on the things that need doing most. The promotion
of war spirit does not need the church's help. Therefore, the church should
not help promote it.

Let us consider what the church might have done at the beginning of
the last war. A pastoral letter could have made the following plain:

War is an evil. It feeds the ego of the nation engaged in it. It needs no
help from the church. Men are so willing and able to stand up for their

73

rights that they need no encouragement from the church on that score.

Within the walls of the church, the war will not be discussed. In the church we should think primarily of others. We should not pray for victory for our armed forces. We should pray that the right may prevail. We should pray for the welfare of all, and that we may be in the right.

In time of peace, the church all too seldom speaks out against social injustice. In time of war, it all too often fosters the war spirit. It is too quick to do the thing that, it thinks, will attract the multitude to it. But the church is wrong; the multitude keenly senses this inconsistency.

Why is it considered all right to knock politicians in church and not the business interests? It is because we are surrounded by the business male-factors and lack the perspective to see them in a true light. It is safe, how-ever, to attack the politicians at the state capital or at Washington. The church ignores root causes too much.

Many of you will probably draw the conclusion that I am trying to sell Christianity to the Jew. Rather, I am trying to show how much we have in common. Pure religion, as defined by us Christians, is not incom-patible with Jewish teachings. In a sense, I *am* trying to sell Christianity to the Jews. But it is also true that I am trying to sell Judaism to the Chris-tians; and I am trying to absorb it.

The religious attitude is to make a study of the many "isms" to find points, or areas, of agreement. Such areas are generally easy to find. A con-sideration of pure religion is somewhat like a group of strangers getting together, comparing notes, and excitedly discovering that they are related.

"A house divided against itself cannot stand." This is a religious, a democratic, and a totalitarian starting point. The interesting thing is how the three groups try to solve it.

The religious stand can at least partly be explained by the statement that "in my Father's house are many mansions." Live, let live, and help live. Diversity does not necessarily make for antagonism. This is also the democratic stand.

The totalitarians say "that which does not contribute to the general aim shall be modified or eliminated." The members are thrown out of character.

What is the implication of all this? It should teach us tolerance. It should make it easier for us to accept those outside our fold as brothers—real, equal brothers.

S. L. Frank ended up by trying, unconsciously, to confine his *religious* philosophy within the bounds of his *theology*. He became guilty of a form of idolatry. On sober thought, we are perhaps agreed that all idol worship

74

begins, or began, with worship of a spirit. When the spirit refuses to remain within material confines, we continue to worship the material object.

In this sense conservatism is idolatry. Yes, idol worship is still very prevalent. We are all guilty.

Is our religion rooted in our theology, or is our theology rooted in our religion? Do we find God in creation, or do we find creation in God? The second question should suggest the answer to the first.

All the theologies of the world must conceive themselves as being human but crude attempts to approximate the pure religion that should be the fountain of all our theologies. The physical representations of our respective faiths must be regarded as anchoring points for our humanly precarious beliefs. They must have their roots in the central core of pure religion.

Every spirit must have a form if it is to be recognizable to us mortals. But this form must be the spirit's roosting place, not a fence to encompass it. Every spirit outreaches its form.

Primarily, what is it that causes theology to separate people from others who harbor another theology? It is largely questions of physical fact concerning their respective theologies. As soon as we begin generally to realize that all physical facts are at best a very crude representation of a spiritual reality, just that soon will the apparently opposing theologies begin to see eye to eye.

Many readers of this volume will undoubtedly say, "How is this different from utopian schemes of the past?" It is different in that it sets up no external pattern. It looks for the good in capitalism, socialism, authoritarianism, communism, and every other "ism." It accepts the present and its institutions as the starting point. Most utopian philosophies are based on a belief in the inherent goodness of the human heart. The religious philosophy recognizes the inherent evil in the human heart. The Tree of the Knowledge of good and of evil is a fruitful subject for contemplation.

Therefore, it sets itself the task of regenerating this evil heart. And its followers start on their own hearts. They rely mostly on contagion for the effect it will have on other hearts. They do not rely on Gandhi's passive resistance. They are positive.

They believe in fighting for their own rights after they have been scrupulously careful that the rights of others have been considered. This phase of religion is almost ignored by Jesus, simply because people are naturally so adept in looking out for "Number One" that they need no urging. The few who feel it their duty to completely ignore the rights of "Number One" need to have impressed on them that it is their duty to fight for their own rights.

75

It is a thing of the spirit to work for the welfare of all within reach, provided there is a constant widening of the sphere of inclusiveness. It is a thing of the flesh to work for ourselves or to work to constrict the sphere of inclusiveness.

When we say, "The job is too big for us," we are forgetting that as we widen the sphere we are not just admitting new charges. We are also admitting new helpers, actual and potential. It is a thing of the spirit to go about doing good.

All these things are efforts to adjust ourselves to the world in which we live and to adjust it to our legitimate needs. These are things we must constantly keep in mind, whether our role as educators is in the classroom or in life.

A short time ago I had the unique experience of sitting in the social rooms of a Protestant church and listening to a Jewish rabbi of the Reform wing expound on "What the Jew Believes." He was an enthusiastic advocate of his own theology without being in any way derogatory of the others. When talking about the Christians, he had the tone of an *insider*. In fact, he appears to have achieved that enviable condition of being able to find many congenial spots inside any theology.

He looks forward to the one religion which is the quest of this book. I feel certain that everyone who was present felt that it was good to have been there. While they were there at least, they had that sense of the oneness of pure religion.

His address follows in full:

WHAT THE JEW BELIEVES by Rabbi Baruch Braunstein

The Jew's faith and the writings upon which it is based have become bone and sinew of the world's cultural and spiritual treasures. Accordingly, the Jew's beliefs are often taken for granted. Dr. Lyman Abbott, the great Christian preacher of a former day, sums up the elements of Jewish belief which have become universal property:

"It is Israel who brought us the message that God is our Father. It is Israel who, in bringing us the divine law, has laid the foundation of liberty. It is Israel who had the first free institutions the world ever saw. It is Israel who brought us our Bible, our prophets, our Apostles. When sometimes our own un-Christian prejudices flame out against the Jewish people, let us remember that all we have and all we are we owe, under God, to what Judaism has given us."

This is a generalized statement, and for our purposes we shall be more detailed and specific. Jewish beliefs are encompassed within Judaism, the religion of the Jew. Being a religion, it has for its primary function the generic function of all religion—deriving from the original meaning of *religare,* to relate, to bind together. Religion is the linking up of the self with the infinite, of the individual with the world about him. It is an imperative for living if a man wants to understand his world and make necessary adjustments to it. To paraphrase Matthew Arnold, religion is the impulse for self-perfection, but it is also the instrument for perfecting the world.

While all religion has the same basic urge, religions differ due to the simple but impelling reason that individuals differ, as well as groups of individuals, one from another. Whether it would be a drab and uninviting world if everybody and everything were alike, might constitute an interesting academic debate. The argument would be pointless, though, in the light of nature's accomplished fact that there is both differentiation and variety in all nature, organic and inorganic. Because people differ, they have differing approaches to the common and urgent problems all men face, although their solutions are in the end found to be about the same. Thus in religion, that most personal and intimate relationship, there are many roads to God travelled by different people, but the amazing thing is that all roads lead to the same God. The Jew believes that no single road is the main highway, and all others secondary, leading to God. To put it in another way: the Jew believes that no one faith has a copyright on God and enjoys monopoly of Him. Nor is there one chosen people whose direction alone must be followed for man's salvation. No one people can claim that they alone enjoy the effulgence of God's spirit to the exclusion of all other people. The tolerance of Judaism's position of the other man's religion finds expression in our Sabbath Eve Prayer, from our Prayer Book, which is a repository of the faith and ideals of the Jew:

> "Almighty and merciful God, Thou has called Israel to Thy service and found him worthy to bear witness unto Thy truth among the peoples of the earth. Give us grace to fulfill this mission with zeal tempered by wisdom and *guided by regard for other men's faiths.*"
> (Italics Dr. Braunstein's.)

The Jew believes that all men are created equal, and the spirit of our Declaration of Independence, of which this statement is a part, shows clearly its Hebraic influences. The Jewish concept of equality of man is a religious concept, conveyed in the rabbinic commentary on the Scriptural verse that "the Lord God formed man of the dust of the earth." This dust, the rabbis want us to understand, came not from any single spot on earth. Rather,

God assembled dust from all four corners of the earth, and beat and pounded the particles together, and from this dust, taken from all the directions of the compass, God made man. This story aims at deterring any man from saying: "I am better than you; I come from the north, or the south, or the east or the west parts of the world; that part which is better than any other!" A profound truth lies in this homey tale, which expresses in poetic imagery and legend the deep scientific truth that the bodies of all men are basically the same, created or deriving from the same original matter. It also adds telling detail to the basic law upon which our country was founded: all men are created equal. All of us are compounded from the same dust. Let no man say he is better than another!

We have been talking about God the Creator, and in the magnificent story of creation, written by a superb literary artist, you notice that God is used in the singular form. We do indeed take many things for granted, as though the great ideas we inherited were born without pain and travail. Here is a capital example of human striving over millenia, ending in the dawning upon man's mind of the idea of the one God. Up to that hour of triumphant dawning and birth of this great idea, men worshipped gods, representatives of all forces in nature which needed to be appeased. Slowly, very slowly, out of the ascent of man toward the light of truth, emerged the idea of one force and power in the universe, creator and responsible for all in it; and the artist, who chiseled that magnificent story of the Hebrew language, worked with the one-God idea as his most effective tool.

The Jew believes in one God. Through Jewish believers this idea pervades uncounted millions of men by way of Christianity and Islam. Judaism, then, is a one-God religion, called monotheism. It represents a great advance and a victory over the forces of paganism, and the Jew is reminded of this signal victory three times daily in his prayers, when he repeats: "Hear, O, Israel, The Lord Our God, The Lord is One." It is a rallying cry, a call to battle made by the Deuteronomic writer to continue the struggle. For an idea that represents an advance over men's thinking needs to be watched constantly. Hear, hearken, listen; never forget it—our God is one! Some Jews may not know much more about their faith than this passage, but this they know, even in the original Hebrew. It is the holiest affirmation of each Jew for his God. Its sacred character may be judged by the fact that it is the Jew's last words, breathed out when his soul leaves him.

This great and dramatic affirmation is both a description and a characterization of the God the Jew believes in. It is also a description and characterization of our world and the people who inhabit it. God, the Creator, brought order out of chaos; from many and discordant forces. He achieved unity in the world and made it one. *The created always carries something of the character of the creator.* If God is one, the world He brought into being partakes of His nature—indivisible unity and oneness. Here we touch one of the functions of religion: it proclaims and prefigures what science discovers later on. Religion operates on mystic intuitions. Centuries afterwards science confirms these intuitions, these "leaps of faith." We talk about the one-world idea, convinced as we are it must be achieved or mankind will perish. Well, this is the extension into the world of the Jew's central belief in the one God—Creator, Ruler of the world, and Father of all men. The broad outlines of man's approach to the world are religion's concern; filling in these outlines with detail is the concern of science. This cooperative relationship explains why Judaism has never had a serious problem with the discoveries of science. In Judaism, religion and science both represent the gradual unfolding of man's mind in his quest and search after certainty and security in the world—in his quest for God.

Judaism has suffered no convulsions from the discoveries of science because Judaism believes in progressive revelation. We say that with man's growth and development he is able to push back the mysteries and bring light to more and more areas hitherto obscured by darkness. God remains the same, however. He has not changed. Only man's understanding of Him changes. This is the verdict of both Judaism and men on the scientific frontiers—Einstein, Jeans, Eddington, et al—who admit that as they push back the mysteries of the world and of creation they come closer to God. Judaism refuses to believe that God spoke only once to certain men in a given generation, and that since that time He has shut Himself off from all men. Within the Scripture itself there are varying, and advancing, ideas of the God concept, showing that within this document covering only about 1,000 years there is the process of growth and change. We are not afraid to call it by its new name: evolution. In Exodus we read of the name God applies to Himself. Moses asks God Who sends him upon the perilous mission of freeing the enslaved Hebrews.

Moses: "Who shall I say has sent me? What is His Name?"

God: "I AM THAT I AM."

Translated literally, these three Hebrew words mean: "I will become what I will become." The emphasis is upon becoming, growth, change, development—in the ways men see and understand God. The Prayer Book puts the Jewish belief in progressive revelation in this way:

> "O Lord, open our eyes that we may see and welcome all truth, whether shining from the annals of ancient revelations or reaching us through the seers of our own time; for Thou hidest not Thy light

from any generation of Thy children that yearn for Thee and seek Thy guidance."

Up to this point, we have indicated four beliefs held by the Jew: (1) All men seeking God have the right to travel their own road to Him, yet all roads lead to God. (2) God created man equal. (3) God is one; He is the world's Planner, Architect and Creator, and His unity gives the world the character of unity and our only hope for a united mankind. (4) The Jew believes in the concept of progressive revelation, which brings assurance that each generation can and does push back the curtains, bringing us closer to God.

Judaism is also a series of adjustments man makes in order to live with himself, with others about him, and with the world which is always much with us. What has Judaism to say about these basic relationships, remembering religion's function is to bind up, to link men together?

As to man's relation to himself: Judaism does not deny the tremendous potency and reality of the individual, of the self. The command, "Love thy neighbor as thyself," has deep truth, the full recognition of which has come with modern psychology's emphasis upon the driving power of the self. For example, Judaism maintains there is no sin in the satisfactions of the body because there is nothing inherently sinful about the body. Indeed, the body is the dwelling place of the spirit of God, the temple of the soul, which must be zealously guarded from contamination. Judaism recognizes self as the beginning of all things. The self is, in fact, the first thing human beings notice about the world. Only as they grow and develop do they begin to make adjustments to outside elements, to other people, and then to the world. This attitude was expressed by the eminent Rabbi Hillel (the author of the Golden Rule negatively stated): "If I am not for myself, who will be for me?" Myself, me, the self are emphasized here. Does this sound too egocentric and self-centered to be a basic article of faith? It is if you stop there. Judaism says: Begin with the self, but move on from there. If you stop with self, you have only pagan hedonism. No full and satisfying life can result. Judaism says: Extend the love you have for yourself, lavish the care you do upon yourself to others, treat them as you treat yourself—no whit differently—that is religion, the relationship that must be established and maintained in a world in which all are brothers. Is this why Paul said: "The whole Law is fully expressed in this one sentence: 'Love thy neighbor as thyself' "?

Self is never enough. Therefore, the same Rabbi Hillel taught: "If I am not for myself, who will be for me?" and immediately added: "But when I am only for myself, what am I?" Of course the self is important, but

80

steel yourself against making it all-important. For God made man no angel to be or feel exalted; He made him a little lower than the angels. If man maintains this position, he can translate into reality Hillel's great maxim: "What is hateful unto thee, do not unto thy neighbor." Again, the weighing element is *self,* but religion demands the extension of self beyond the narrow pale of self into broad relations with others.

Judaism believes this relationship is capable of achievement because we are dealing with man. Man, the Jew believes, is, at his core and center, decent and good, and has great potentialities for good. Man is an ethical being because he has a fragment of the divine in his being. As our Prayer reads:

"The soul which Thou hast given unto me came pure from Thee. Thou has formed it, Thou hast created it, Thou hast breathed it into me . . ."

Man's soul is originally pure, issuing from the source of purity which is God. Judaism has struggled against the proposition that man is evil, incorrigibly evil. The Jew places his faith in man as one of his cardinal beliefs. In the face of the history of the Jew, it takes a lot of courage and an infinite amount of faith in human beings to retain his belief in the essential goodness and decency of man. But that is the Jew's belief—faith in man, which, adhered to long enough, will bring out the divine in man.

The Jew also believes that there follows from this faith in the essential goodness of man the belief in the essential goodness of the world. Here, again, Judaism runs counter to other theological conceptions of this world as a vale of tears, a vestibule leading only to the better life beyond this world. It eschews the notion that life in this world must be endured and tolerated—not enjoyed—because of the greater and better world that beckons beyond. Judaism is realistic, not escapist. It countenances no flights into other-worldliness. It denies the world is essentially and also incorrigibly evil. It sings in high rapture with the Psalmist: "The earth is full of the *goodness* of the Lord." It proclaims with Isaiah who beheld visions of angels singing: "The whole earth is full of (God's) *glory.*"

No flight from reality is countenanced by Judaism. Part of that reality is the free admission that although this is a hard, harsh, and even ugly world, our task as men is to change its face, and it can be done, if we will it and work at it hard and long enough. Judaism believes the world is still unfinished. God left it that way so that we can act as God's partners in completing it.

The completion of the job is to make, or remake, the world in God's image, teaching men to live in imitation of God. For this is the consummation of all man's striving: to make the world a Kingdom of Heaven. This is the end and the purpose of all our striving and work. Each in our personal and small ways must help usher in the Messianic Time which will bring with it peace on earth, brotherhood among men and the recognition of the Fatherhood of one God. For this consummation, the Jew devoutly prays:

"May the time not be distant, O God, when Thy Name shall be worshipped in all the earth, when unbelief shall disappear and error be no more. Fervently we pray that the day may come when all men shall invoke Thy Name, when corruption and evil shall give way to purity and goodness, when superstition shall no longer enslave the mind, nor idolatry blind the eye; when all who dwell on earth shall know that to Thee alone every knee must bend and every tongue give homage. O may all, created in Thine image, recognize that they are brethren, so that, one in spirit and one in fellowship, they may be forever united before Thee. Then shall Thy kingdom be established on earth and the word of Thine ancient seer be fulfilled: The Lord will reign forever and ever."

This is the consummation of the world, the Jew believes. But of man's end and consummation Judaism does not reveal any such wealth of detail. Judaism is more concerned with the destiny of the world than with the destiny of any one man. Thus the edge is taken off too much concern with and for our own personal selves. Judaism has singularly few blue-prints of eternity or of the hereafter, proving it has no overwhelming concern about it. Not that the Jew is uninterested. It is rather that he places his complete faith and trust in God to do what He considers best for man. Have faith in Him, the Jew insists. "The Lord is mine, I shall not fear" runs a line from one of the great hymns of the Synagogue. Perhaps, also, there is no great and pressing concern in Judaism about the hereafter because that would take man away from that which ought be his main preoccupation: this world, and the now. The Jew believes he ought not worry about heaven beyond. That is God's concern. Rather he ought to concentrate on trying to make a heaven on earth. Our task is in the present, not in the future, for each tomorrow is built up out of todays. Our task is not in some distant world, dimly conceived and faintly adumbrated. Not in the hereafter, but here is our task, for how we live in that *there* depends upon how we have lived *here,* and helped others to live. Man's task, the Jew believes, is to make a heaven on earth, and transform human nature from its lowest to its noblest.

82

These beliefs flow from the undergirding conceptions of Judaism: the oneness and uniqueness of God and of the world He created. Monotheism, blended with justice and tempered with compassion—ethical monotheism—will one day, the Jew believes, transfigure men and the world of men. The world is not perfect, but the blue-print for its perfection is in man's heart. These beliefs, the Jew maintains, while not yet realized, are fully realizable. He has held fast to his beliefs in the perfectibility of man and of the world, despite scorn and rebuffs. They have been more than beliefs—they have been the Jew's ideals, and as the Jew lives by them he partakes of some of their quality of deathlessness and eternity.

What kind of a person has been moulded out of these beliefs? What are his hallmarks, his distinguishing characteristics? Often the world takes the Jew too much for granted, as it has also taken Judaism, its message and teaching too much for granted. Who, then, is the Jew, the carrier and hopeful examplar of these beliefs? What have they made of him? Count Tolstoy, who attempted to translate the realities of the Christian experience to his unhappy land and people, answers the question: What is the Jew?

"The Jew is that sacred being who has brought down from heaven the everlasting fire, and has illumined with it the entire world. He is the religious source, spring and fountain out of which all the rest of the peoples have drawn their beliefs and religions. The Jew is the pioneer of liberty. . . . The Jew is the pioneer of civilization. . . . The Jew is the emblem of civil and religious tolerance. 'Love the stranger and the sojourner,' Moses taught, 'because you have been strangers in the land of Egypt.' And this was said in those remote and savage times when the principal ambition of the races and nations consisted in crushing and enslaving one another. The Jew is the emblem of eternity. The Jew is as everlasting as eternity itself."

This address is presented in full in an effort to demonstrate what can be done to find more footing that is common to Christianity and Judaism. My comments are not to be taken as an *answer* to his address. An answer savors too much of contention. Rather they should be regarded as an enlargement—an effort to find common footing that is suggested *to me* by his address. That common footing is found by exploring contradictions to determine whether they are apparent or real.

To begin with, I find fault with two stands that he takes. One is that he seems to ascribe omniscience to Hillel, a Jew who was born about seventy-five years before Jesus. He refers to Hillel's insistence on the importance of the self. What he said seems to amount to this: that the best way to build up others is to build up ourselves. This appears to be of the same cloth as the "enlightened" self-interest of a century ago that has been found so wanting *in practice*. The average heart, naturally selfish, cannot overcome the handicap of placing self before neighbor. And it cannot overcome the handicap of making "self the weighing element." The world is full of very selfish people who imagine that they are making themselves the weighing element. There is a dark film between their eyes and themselves that few can penetrate. But the film tends to disappear when they make their neighbors the weighing element.

I also object to what he says is the Judaistic stand that man is essentially good; that each man has within himself "a fragment of the divine." Now no Christian will object to the statement about the fragment of divinity. In fact I heard a Methodist speaker use the same argument that our Jewish friend used.

The basic trouble is that we are not agreed on the answer to the question, "What is Man?" Is he that divine fragment, or is he a bundle of natural impulses? If he is the divine fragment, then we can carry the idea to the point where Man is God. I do not object to this as a speculative theory, but I do object that it does not point in the direction of bringing Heaven to Earth. While we are theorizing about the average man, he keeps on being guided mostly by his *natural* bent.

So I insist that a *practical* program calls for regarding man as being naturally sinful, or evil—that is, selfish. The fragment of divinity grows only to the extent that we project our lives into the lives and interests of others.

Now I am perfectly aware that my Jewish friend *himself in his own life* places the emphasis on projection as having precedence over self-improvement. That is because he practices more than he preaches. Preaching must be brought in line with good practice. It must get away from the theories for which practice is not *yet* ready. In *practice* we are not yet ready for the theory that places self before neighbor.

Let us enlarge on this by considering, respectively, the conditions under which Hillel and Jesus lived. Hillel and his followers lived in Babylon and vicinity. They were a minority group. They did not sense the evil of placing self first.

The Jews among whom Jesus lived were a dominant group. It is true that they lived under a Roman overlordship, but they had a great deal of local autonomy. Jesus saw what placing self first did to one who had the upper hand. In the case of a minority group, it might tend to lift them to a higher plane; but if practiced by the dominant group, it tends to be self-destructive. The dominant group tries to become still more dominant; it slowly pushes the less favored in the group into the camp of the oppressed.

Jesus was a great psychologist. His teachings were geared to the capacity of the human mind to grasp and assimilate. He was fully aware of how this mind's reasoning is clouded by the natural strivings within. He realized that in aiming *for* a target we often must not aim *at* the target. He also realized that by aiming at self we are often drawn into self—and stay there.

Let it be noted here that this touching on the lives and teachings of Jesus and Hillel does not in any way involve us in theological conflict. It is really an excursion into the broad—and deep—field of social science. In this field the Jew must strive to learn from the experiences of *dominant* groups.

Dr. Braunstein puts too much into one sentence when he says that Judaism has struggled against the proposition that man is "evil, incorrigibly evil." Now I take the stand that man (and I mean natural man) is evil, but not incorrigibly so. I believe that he makes too much of the stand that some Christians take about incorrigible evil. It is interesting to note that those Christians who take such a stand are generally blandly assuming that their own evil natures are being held in subjugation. For subjugation they should substitute direction. The nature within us can be redirected so that it will, with conditioning, follow the right line without the intervention of the fragment of divinity—but not *all* of the nature within. Eternal vigilance is ever necessary.

"No flight from reality is countenanced by Judaism." Most people will agree that the Jews are realistic, in many ways too realistic. Theirs is the realism of a perennial minority group—and that is not all of realism. Their enlightened self-interest under their minority status becomes a means of survival—but not the only means of survival. They can also survive by learning vicariously from the experiences of dominant groups. Pursuing such a policy they would eventually lose their separate identity, a consummation they should devoutly pray for—if they believe in One God, One World.

" 'The Jew is the emblem of eternity. The Jew is as everlasting as eternity itself.' " Here Dr. Braunstein is careful to let a Christian do his talking for him. He apparently assumes that the words will carry more weight if they come from a Christian. I believe that the talk ended in too smug a tone of complacency.

Basically, the Jew is not different from other human beings. The difference is in his heritage—and that heritage should tend to unite with other heritages that *all* point to, not eternity, but Heaven on Earth. Eternity is too vast a concept for us humans to be playing with when we are mapping courses of conduct.

The brevity of my comments on Dr. Braunstein's address may give them an air of contentiousness that I certainly do not feel. My comments are brief because they are about matters that are enlarged on elsewhere in this book.

Let it be noted here that while I am rather critical of the average Jew, I am almost as critical of the average Christian. The "almost" points to the contribution that Christianity has made to the goal of a pure religion.

Let me close these comments by confessing that the Jew is still very much of an enigma to me. I feel that the Jews should set themselves the task of resolving these enigmas. For one instance, I cannot reconcile their undoubted belief in evolution with a certain setness about them of which they apparently are very proud.

I believe that all the answers can be found in the social sciences, if those sciences are permeated by the spirit of pure religion.

The Jew deserves credit for perpetuating the One-God idea. But what Jew? Not the present-day Jew, but the Jew of two thousand and more years ago. The Jew must be very careful not to rest too much on laurels of the past.

The big question is, "What are the Jews—and Christians—doing today about the implications of the One-God idea?" The most obvious today should be the promulgation of the One-World idea. Jews and Christians are exasperatingly slow in embracing it, as shown by their attitude toward the rest of the world. Both of us like to believe that we are—and hope to continue to be—a peculiar people.

Another inevitable corollary is not yet fully accepted. It is that since there is One God, there cannot be two absolute forces in this world. The idea of an absolute good *and* an absolute evil is incompatible with this idea. It belongs to the polytheistic phase of humanity's thinking.

I noticed that Dr. Braunstein was a very eager and intense listener when men came forward to congratulate him. He had the air—which was genuine—of one who is always eager to learn more, and from others. That is the air that I wish on the Jews as a group. It is an air that the Christians perhaps need even more.

Where do we find inner peace? Luther and Cardinal Newman found it outside their original folds. Most of us find it within our respective folds. The inner peace comes from an adjustment between outward conditions and the problems peculiar to the individual.

The life of John Brown poses many problems. He acquired at the end of his days that inner peace that we all crave. Does that justify his life? Was his peace the peace of God? It is a fair question to ask whether John Brown did not become the crusader as a cover for his neglect of his family.

That seems to be answered by the devotion of his sons.

It again brings out the fact that the will of God never comes to our consciences in pure form. It is distorted by the human channels through which it must pass.

It is interesting to note that this peace of mind was denied, apparently, to Margaret Fuller, who always had her followers and was never in danger of being mobbed. The cause in the case of Margaret undoubtedly was that she did not have the genuine love for her neighbor that enabled her to project herself into their lives. She did not even try; Brown did, although perhaps misguidedly, and he reaped his reward.

The spirit is not measured by the material. The material is but the connecting link between the spirit of God and the spirit of man. "Deep calleth unto deep." We see but the connecting links. But we can sense the spirit by observing these links.

Let us not become mystical about this. The thought is presented merely for the practical consideration that it will help us appreciate the transitoriness of material things, and speed us along the ever-widening road of pure religion. The church must be continually alerted against making the material the measure of the spiritual. All it should do is furnish the connecting links between the spirit of God and the spirit of man. The union is more important than the question of the nature of the connecting links.

Someone has said that we need a new integration of religion, art, science, politics, education, commerce, and finance, not in human aspirations, but in a divine purpose. The catch is discovering the divine purpose without considering my neighbor's aspiration which in turn are rationalized by a study of my own heart.

As individuals do we integrate these disciplines? Very seldom; and we need a better meeting of minds if we are to achieve a *common* integration.

7. SOCIAL JUSTICE

Before proceeding to a consideration of democracy, it seems fitting that we should give attention to a subject that suggests itself almost automatically following a consideration of pure religion. It is social justice or, perhaps rather, social injustice.

Holders of special privileges tend to think of social justice as something already achieved. The underprivileged think of it as being too slowly in the process of being achieved. We must recognize that by social justice we mean the correction of all evil conditions, whether they be economic, social, or otherwise. The object of this chapter is to consider some of the outstanding aspects of social justice.

The early church had, compared with our day, a very rudimentary sense of social justice. Even the Pharisees had a sense that was but a little better than no sense at all. In general they gave as in satisfaction of a duty to God. They gave little thought to the welfare of those who received their alms.

The early Christians gave with a sense of compassion for those who received their aid. In most cases they had a common psychology. But there was practically no thought of doing anything to correct social injustices, partly because their economic status made it impossible for them to be heard. But the basic trouble was the general attitude that "whatever is, is right." The vast majority had no loftier motive than the hope that they could somehow be transported from the oppressed to the ranks of the oppressors. Queen Esther of an earlier day is a case in point.

Religion recognizes that basically the exploited are not much better than the exploiters. Most of them are more interested in becoming exploiters themselves than in justice. They would substitute one form of tyranny for another.

Jesus went about doing good. Should we do likewise? Yes, in the same spirit, but not in the same way. We must remember that Jesus' remarks and deeds were geared to the economy and the society in which he lived, without ever forgetting that his main interest was always the religious approach to a problem.

This is our continuing task today. We must recognize that, for us, the highest form of spirituality is attained through an active interest in the material welfare of others. They in turn will find their spirituality in their thoughts of still others, including us.

We must continue the simple charities of the early Christians. But we must do more. We must become increasingly aware of the need for a greater and more general effort to eliminate social injustices at their roots, always remembering that we dare not pull up too many roots at one time.

We no longer believe in trying to *correct* economic evils by handing out occasional doles. Our ideal is a condition that makes doles unnecessary. Our ideal is an equal opportunity for all to utilize their talents to the best.

When our neighbors are no longer able to take care of themselves, we believe in something more permanent than a dole; and we are more and more looking on this as justice, not charity.

We must be continually striving to rise from the wallow in which special privilege tends to place us. In fact, special privilege is a wallow. Special privilege is an evil because it is out of place. Matter out of place is dirt. Evil is evil only so long as it is out of place.

If special privilege is a wallow, what should we do about it? In many cases we should reject it in the attitude that others can make better use of it than we. If we retain it, we are under obligation to transform it by transforming ourselves. When we rise to the obligations that special privilege imposes on us, then special privilege becomes a right; it is no longer a wallow. It has been absorbed, leaving the impurities behind.

Every part of our heritage is a special privilege until we live up to the obligation that it bestows on us.

But if we make no effort, or too little effort, to live up to the obligations that special privilege bestows on us, how far should society go to wipe out the many unfair advantages that special privilege bestows? Because of the practical difficulties involved, it is better to concentrate on the prevention of future injustices. In individual cases it is difficult, if not impossible, to adjust security improperly won. There is so much room for difference of opinion! This much is certain. Perhaps we are all agreed that the persons who hold the most responsible and prominent positions in our community are seldom the ones that are innately best qualified.

The problem of social justice will never be solved if we use up all our energies to wrest special privileges from the rich few. The first step must be a keen awareness that we are all holders of special privileges. We all hold privileges that are not within the reach of all. Are we willing to change the conditions to make our special privileges the rights of all? In most cases we are not. We do not yet feel strongly enough for our neighbors.

In many cases our special privileges do us more harm than good. But we refuse to recognize it. The idle rich are being embalmed by their material wealth; and they seek release by clinging to it all the more tenaciously.

When this special privilege does more harm than good, the fault is not with the privilege itself, but with the use to which it is put.

I said that the religious approach recognizes our right to strive to excel our neighbors under rules that are fair to our neighbors. Holders of special privilege subscribe to this. But they insist that they are being fair to their neighbors. Therefore a mere statement of a principle is seldom enough. It is an unending task to study cases and over-all effects to determine whether the principle is being violated. It is not easy to point to a special privilege and show convincingly how it violates the rights of others; and still more difficult is it to agree on a remedy if the injustice is recognized as existing.

Let us consider some of these special privileges. It may be the special privilege that allows one to go to college while another must start earning a living for himself and, in many cases, for others. It may be special privilege that came from a lucky break. It may be special privilege resulting from being born white, not black; or Christian, not Jewish; from being born in the right neighborhood or part of the country.

A man who had toured Europe made the observation that it did not seem right that he should leave all that misery behind and return to the land of plenty. Holders of special privileges also have that feeling, but they try hard to smother it by sinking themselves more deeply into their wallow. When holders of much of this world's goods are worried about what the masses are thinking about, they are portraying a lack of faith in the justness of their lot.

One of the most difficult things for a scholar who is also a child of special privilege to see is that if we help a person to help himself, we are not robbing him of his initiative. He simply does not have the religious approach.

Professors of religion are too much concerned about the danger of spoiling people by helping them. They think too much in terms of what the people owe to the church, and too little about the church's obligation to the people. Their attitudes indicate strongly that they believe that the people are made for the church, not the church for the people. Compare Jesus' comment on man and the Sabbath.

They often carry this theory over into the field of economics with disastrous results. They too often conceive of the holders of special privilege in the economic field as being the unselfish benefactors of the underprivileged. Theirs is the viewpoint of special privilege.

There are many people, even among the poor, who think that we need the rich to give work to the poor. They overlook the fact that shares in big corporations can be bought by the poor. If wealth were spread more in accordance with the people's deserts, then we might reach that condition that Walter Lippmann thinks is already here: corporations with managers who are more interested in the workers and the customers than in the stockholders. This is not denying that there are such managers. But how many are allowed by their stockholders to put their interest into practice? Comparatively few.

"Sweet are the uses of adversity." "The blessings of poverty." Those who employ these catch phrases should try them on themselves, not on a temporary, but on a permanent basis. Too often their attitude is, "Let's you and him fight."

"If a man smite thee on the cheek, turn to him the other also. If a man ask thee to go with him a mile, go with him twain. If a man ask a coat of thee, give him thy cloak also." Do we Christians believe in this? It depends on who is doing the asking and doing. Jesus undoubtedly was assuming that it was the underprivileged who were doing the asking and doing.

Canvassers of public opinion polls have discovered that the underprivileged generally ask for less than their just deserts. Chlidren of social privilege generally ask for more. Elaborate this thought to your own satisfaction.

Reform, like charity, should begin at home. We should strive to transform our own special privileges into rights for all. If everyone did this, there would be no problem left. But so long as we are the kind of human beings that we now are, it will be necessary for the underprivileged majority to gradually force the privileged few to give up their unearned privileges.

Some say that this should be accomplished by education and moral suasion alone. The fallacy in this is that too few of us can see the problem through the eyes of our underprivileged neighbors. We lack the religious approach.

It has been demonstrated that people can be truly converted by force. Today it is hard to find an industrialist who does not believe in the right of labor to organize and bargain collectively. Fifty years ago it was just as hard to find one who believed in it. Labor has *forced* the changed attitude on the industrialist.

The industrialist accepts the principal of collective bargaining today partly because he must—it is an inescapable fact. The main reason is, however, that after he has seen it work, he believes in it.

It is also interesting to note that force was first used by the industrialist; labor merely followed his example. As is usually the case, the one whom events have proven wrong was the first to use force.

There would be no need for reform if conditions were perfect. Every invention results in some maladjustment. We justify these maladjustments because of the greater good to society as a whole. But it does not excuse us from doing all we can to eliminate or at least ease these maladjustments.

If one method does not work, it is important to look for a method that will work. If one injustice cannot be corrected, it is no excuse to overlook injustices that can be corrected. Many a person has excused himself from doing anything because the whole field could not be covered. So far as possible, compensatory adjustments should be made to take care of injustices that cannot be eliminated.

It would clear the atomsphere, too, if we said that we fight *for* rights, and duties, and not *against* special privileges. It often makes a great deal of difference where the emphasis is placed.

Many an economic problem that was once considered a necessary evil is now being mastered or has been mastered. We must also consider social changes that have been for the better. And we must not forget how concepts of government have changed and are changing. Jesus said, "I have yet many things to say unto you, but you can not bear them now." We have learned, and are learning, many of those things. In fact, many of *those* things have become *these* things.

Every social change causes some maladjustment. A change in the economic order causes inconvenience to someone. It is even true that every reform probably merely substitutes a minor wrong for a major wrong. It is a common saying that every solution of a problem brings out new problems. Sometimes the problems are created by the reform; at other times they are long-standing problems that are just being exposed to the light of day. But the latter state is generally better than the first.

We still have much to learn on the subject of production and consumption. The big problem is not whether industry will be able to produce. We know it can. The question is whether the potential consumer will be allowed to consume. The production specialist too often has no social conscience. Therefore, he is getting special treatment here. We have many of them posing as educators. Too often they dismiss the problems of social science with a wave of the hand, as being beneath them. Actually the problems are above them. The problems of social science are vastly more complex than their own.

They are often assigned a prominent place in our leading magazines to tell the public about the great things that science has in store for them. They too often take the attitude that as soon as these things are put into production, they will become available to all. They too often are blind to the problem of how the average man will purchase these things with money he does not have. It is a case of the specialist wandering outside his province without proper preparation. He gives too little thought to the problems outside his province. He does not have the religious approach.

Here is a point on which there is a crying need for agreement. It is that there never has been a lag in production because of lack of capital. This is at least true of our country in the past hundred years. Yet it is often used as an argument for easing up on the taxes extracted from the high income brackets. All depressions have come because of low income in the lower brackets. No depression has ever come in this country from lack of production.

Jesus realized that in some cases the only cure is a major operation, as when he told the rich ruler to sell all he had and give to the poor. We still need major operations today because too many of us are still chasing the will-o-the-wisp of enlightened self-interest.

Glenn Frank seems to have grown tired when he reached the last two chapters of his book, *Thunder and Dawn*. He seems to have read too much of Walter Lippmann. In 1929, before the crash, Lippmann said that business had solved its major problems; in 1931 Frank said that business had learned its lesson and confessed its sins. He still had great hopes of business curing its own illness without the bungling aid of government. He believed that the enlightened self-interest of the mighty minority would solve the problems of the whole. But their self-interest simply would not become enlightened.

A speaker said, "We have much to learn in the art of making democracy work." He mentioned the miners, railroaders, and public utility workers as having no conscience about public welfare. He was, of course, partly right. He erred in not mentioning those who cover their lack of interest in the public welfare with a veneer of respectability—those who make extortionate profits; those who create the conditions that cause people to strike.

Still, industrialists are more and more sharing their extraordinary profits, if any, with their employees. This is an excellent step in the right direction. One hesitates to point out avenues for further progress for fear of creating the impression that these works of generosity are not appreciated. However, history and astronomy teach us that the achievement of a goal points to a new goal. For this reason, I am making the observation that profit-sharing with employees merely enlarges the circle of exclusiveness. The next step is giving the customer more consideration; that is, widening our conception of the word "neighbor." Yes, widen it to the point where we will call children neighbors.

The ideal economic condition is that which does not make it necessary for any man to make the acquisition of this world's goods the main goal in life. But we must not blame this lack of economic ideal condition for our own low aim.

We should not be able to say that a man is in business *primarily* for the money he can make out of it. His first concern should be service to others. In the case of the manufacturer, it means consideration for his employee and for his customer. The fact that he must be able to make a living does not alter the fact that making a living should be a by-product, not the main objective.

A worker's first duty is to give of his best to his employer. He should give first consideration to his employer's problems. His own rights will naturally come to the surface in the consideration of his employer's rights. Having determined his own rights in the light of a study of his employer's rights, he should then make a frank stand, without apology, for his own rights.

One child asks another child a question. The latter counters with a question of his own. The first child replies, "I asked you first," and generally wins his point. "First come, first served" prevails.

Let us take a contrasting example. Jesus' opponents ask him a question. He counters with one of his own. They do not say, "We asked you first." They seem to take the more reasonable attitude that they should be willing to do as much as they ask him to do. Regardless of their reasoning, the fact remains that the childish attitude is the selfish, grasping attitude. We should substitute, "First come, first to serve." Not *primarily*, "What can I get out of it?"; but rather, "What can I put into it?"

Employers are coming to the point of accepting the principle that the employee is more important than the thing that he produces. The general public is the employer of the teacher and should do no less than it expects of a commercial employer. This is not to be interpreted as meaning that the teacher is more important than the pupil, but rather that the teacher is as important as any other employee.

"The laborer is worthy of his hire" is something that applies to teachers as well as preachers. A teacher should be free to do some reading, reflecting, and occasionally take a course in something that pertains to his work or his inner growth. A teacher will not do his best work if he is constantly harried by the need to do something besides teach to keep body and soul together.

The public recognizes that teachers are paid too little but does too little about it. How can the public expect the manufacturer to have the proper respect for the rights of others when the public errs still more? House-cleaning begins at home.

There is great danger that the general public, when it gets the upper hand, will be less guided by conscience and the Holy Spirit than the covetous rich. Conscience will be ineffective because they—the majority—are the arbiters of conscience. They are slow to recognize that the surest way of helping themselves, in the long run, is to be very jealous of the rights of the minority. Self-help tends to be self-destructive; other-help tends to build up all, including self.

We must train ourselves to realize that there are many ways in which the law of supply and demand does not operate effectively, particularly where the question of quality, as in teaching, is such an elusive problem. All efforts to pay each teacher what he is worth with respect to the worth of the other teachers within the district have resulted in more injustice than justice. But this much is recognized! Teachers are very much like other human beings. They will respond to the impulses of a generous public and board of education.

Why is the collective judgment of the people sounder than that of special, better educated, groups? It is because the education of the special groups is too much in the direction of how to hang onto the special privileges that they enjoy. The diverse special interests of the general public tend to cancel each other; and the public's mania for impartiality does the rest. There is the other factor that the general public has fewer privileges to harbor.

If the votes of the members of service clubs were segregated and stacked up against the vote of the public and viewed in the light of history, it would undoubtedly be recorded of them that the public exercised better judgment than they.

Service clubs have many pitfalls which they do not see; and do not recognize when they land in them. One is the danger of becoming more conservative than their neighbors who are outside the fold. In the first place, collectively they are the possessors of much special privilege which they naturally want to hoard. Secondly, most of the speakers to whom they listen are like them, or more so.

This is not an argument against service clubs. After all, most of the members think as they would think if they did not belong. The vision of service that it imparts to most of its members more than counteracts its evil influences.

Many public speakers are worried lest the common people misuse their newly-won powers. This has been a perennial worry throughout all recorded history. And yet all the economic and social changes of history that we acclaim today represent the victory of the masses over the possessors of special privilege, whom the educated supported.

Our worry today should not be about the wild-eyed radicals that we always have with us. Rather we should worry about the conditions that make them wild-eyed radicals. Most of them started life as average workingmen. The conditions are created by the smug, sweet, pleasant, complacant holders of special privilege. They lack the humility that is essential to the religious approach.

We should be more concerned about the tendency of the holders of special privilege to reach out for more special privilege. Their initial special privilege is an excellent springboard for the attainment of more special privilege.

Special privilege and nature tend to increase by geometric proportion. We see the need for controlling the nature without us, but we are loathe to control the nature within us that urges us to reach out for more special privilege.

We ex-service men of the first World War were often told by industrialists who grew fat during the war that we were unpatriotic in asking for a bonus and I was inclined to agree with them.

Nobody seemed to think of anything that approximated the G.I. Bill of Rights of World War II. This is not to attack this bill but to discuss conservative attitudes that play into the hands of special privilege groups.

I also remember distinctly selling my war bonds at eighty-three percent of par. I remember defending the system that caused me to sell my bonds at a loss. I thought it was the law of supply and demand meting out justice. It did not occur to me that selfish interests were tampering with this law.

After a rule is made, little or no consideration is given to extenuating circumstances. Many adults, including educational administrators, never get beyond this idea. They believe that rules should always be abided by regardless of circumstances. A rule implies a promise. Therefore most of those people would say that a poor promise is better kept than broken.

I still venerate rules; but I now visualize them as something dynamic that change with conditions; rules that are conditioned by a current estimate of the situation.

It is easy to deduce from the foregoing that there is a phase of conservatism that is not selfish. The mania for doing things according to rules has such a hold on some people that they often stand up for accepted rules that they consider inimical to their own personal interests.

It is this quirk of human nature that the special privilege groups exploit to their own gluttonous appetites. Their conservatism is generally strongest in support of those rules that tend to strengthen their hold on special privilege. They are generally very liberal toward the changing of rules that tend to give themselves more privileges.

Those of us who are in the "have-not" group must realize that if and when we get into the other group, we shall probably turn conservative. Eternal vigilance is necessary if we want to make sure that we will not take the dog-in-the-manger attitude.

We tend to think of our own rights first, and then of our duties. We tend to think of our neighbors' duties first and then, if at all, of his rights. Society, which is all of us, has erred the same way in approaching the problems of the family in a changing economy.

Society has done too much of its thinking in terms of the duties of families and too little of their rights. Society has practically decreed that a child shall not become a wage earner until he is eighteen or more. Society insists that its own welfare is tied up in this. But it is not willing to shoulder its share of the cost of bringing this about. Society has said, in effect, to the providers of the families, "*You* must do this at *your* expense because it is for *our* good."

Failure to recognize this obligation of society gives too many children an unfair start in life. If a rich child and a poor child were running a race and the rich child were assigned a starting position in advance of the poor child, all of us would say, "That isn't fair. No one is entitled to special rights just because he is rich." Unfortunately, it is not so easy to *demonstrate* the many other unfair advantages that a rich child possesses.

Of course, many of these "advantages" are really disadvantages, but the big problem is getting the holders of these "advantages" to recognize them for what they really are. These "advantages" would be real advantages to the underprivileged.

I heard a rich girl say, "I wish I were poor so that I could have a good time like my playmates." Some will undoubtedly say at this point, "Why give to others that which only makes you miserable?" The answer is, "The misery lies in the lack of proportion."

How would I correct it? Not primarily by having the rich toss their abundance to the poor after the manner of one who tosses feed to chickens. The biggest help the rich can give consists in not fighting efforts to eliminate special privilege; to recognize that they are not as superior as they try to imagine.

Are we making progress? We certainly are! As just one instance, we do not have to go back very far to find the rich not even dreaming of sending their children to the public schools to be contaminated by the common rabble.

Religion points to absolute justice. Its pragmatic attitude constrains it to accept anything that moves in the direction of absolute justice, provided it is not moving too slowly. This atomic age is a terrible reminder that perhaps our *rate* of progress is too slow.

Religion recognizes the need for uneven progress rather than no progress, giving help to some when it is impossible to give the same help to all who are in need of it. There is the story of a man who saw two men

97

drowning. Since he could save only one, he let them both drown because, you see, it would not be fair to save one and let the other drown. This is an exaggeration of the mind of muddy reasoning that we too often engage in.

We are prone to be too belittling of the social progress that has been made from Adam to atom. We are fooled by the rapid progress that an individual savage makes when he is introduced to society. Such an individual has one task: to conform. Conforming is almost infinitely easier than setting the pattern. Civilization has set many more patterns—good patterns—than we are prone to realize. All these patterns must be regarded as being subject to change if the need arises; or else there will be no progress henceforth.

What is a liberal? Robert Taft considers himself a liberal. Henry Wallace also considers himself a liberal. Most people consider themselves liberals.

It is possible, by staying away from concrete examples, to give a definition of liberalism that will satisfy all self-styled liberals. They probably all agree that a liberal believes in the right of each individual, in free competition with others, to build his own life.

But to some this "free competition with others" means the law of the jungle. To others it means "enlightened" self-interest. To still others it means the invoking of the religion of love for neighbor.

Nearly all of them consider Jefferson a liberal. The conservatives point to his statement that the best government is that which governs least. The liberals point to his whole life which was a continuous effort to adjust laws, rules, and regulations—and principles—to local conditions, which within themselves have their own laws, rules, regulations, and principles.

When we come to the practical applications for today, we fall apart completely. The conservatives say that governmental activity still tends to be repressive. The liberals counter that government today can be, and does tend to be, liberating—liberating individuals for more creative initiative than has ever been their lot in the past.

In referring to liberals and conservatives of today I am classifying them as they are classified in the mind of the general public. It happens that I myself use that classification.

There is probably no phase of governmental activity that is not considered liberating by some and repressive by others. Almost invariably it is both. At its best it is repressive only on those who possess an unfair advantage. It can also be repressive on some who do not have an unfair advantage. This can sometimes be justified on the ground of a greater good to a greater number. But it definitely calls for more study and more corrective action.

The best judge of whether a governmental activity is repressive is the general public. Its judgment is better than that of any minority group. But the public must also acquire a conscience and a sense of divine mission.

It is possible to have action that is for the benefit of the many, at the expense of a few who already are the underdog. This is a sample of majority rule that is not democracy. There can be no democracy without at least a touch of conscience. The test of democracy is what the majority does when it is in the saddle.

We must be careful that we do not become mystical about this sense of divine mission. I call it that simply because it is not natural. We must rise above our natural instinct for self-preservation at the expense of the other fellow. We must feel that there is enough security for all.

The best way of summing up is to state that the conservatives and reactionaries who call themselves liberal take the attitude that a liberal government does *not*. The liberals and radicals say that a liberal government *does*. To them, the government is a crusader in the interest of setting the stage for making it easier for more people to find their mission in life.

Most liberals were once conservatives. Very few conservatives have ever been liberal, except those who struck it rich and are now concerned primarily about safeguarding their special privileges. Those in general were not liberal to the core. We must recognize that in the liberal ranks are many selfish persons. They will be liberal only so long as liberalism serves their personal ends. All of us would call ourselves conservatives if we were allowed to define the term to suit ourselves. Liberals insist rightly that they are the true conservatives; that those that go by that name should be called preservatists or embalmers.

The basic meaning of conservative is "to put to the best use." The person who gives of that for which he has little need, to those who need it more, is truly conservative. If he does not believe in that, he is a covetous man.

To the casual observer it can easily appear that when I listen to a speaker I am more intent on finding fault with him than on finding the good in his message. As a matter of fact I try hard to follow him, but in most cases I find him taking a wrong turn or starting off in the wrong direction—according to my lights. The reason seems to be that speakers are a good cross-section of the people as a whole on the subject of conservatism and liberalism. That makes more than ninety percent of them conservative. Their general line is, "Let us go back." The liberal line is, "Let us go forward."

This is by way of calling attention to the fact that a short time ago I heard a speaker who started off in the right direction and continued in the right direction. He gave a realistic account of the trials and tribulation of the framers of our Constitution. His attitude was not, "Let us go back to the Constitution of the Founding Fathers and stay there." He pointed out some salutary lessons for those of us who like to take a cynical attitude toward all efforts to make the United Nations a clicking organization.

No, it is very difficult for a liberal to subscribe to the pattern that the conservative presents. I think it is a fair statement to say that the liberal finds fault with the fault that the conservative finds. The conservative is continually blaming people, and things, and conditions that the liberal is convinced should not be blamed.

The problem of special privilege is especially difficult for us because we all, as Americans, are the holders of so many special privileges, and there are too few among us to remind us of the fact. And we too often try to get around them by identifying those who show us up with some "ism" that is repugnant to us Americans.

The rich among us think that we poor don't understand them because of our ignorance. We comparatively rich Americans think that the rest of the world does not understand us because of their ignorance.

Our first remedial step is a confession of ignorance on our part—a confession that we have not appreciated the many special privileges that have been thrust upon us; a confession that we have not sufficiently projected ourselves into the problems of the rest of the world; a confession that we, like Jesus' Rich Fool, are the most covetous nation.

Many of the rich among us think of themselves as the benevolent protectors of the poor. We poor resent that attitude. Yet that is our attitude toward the small nations of the world.

We all crave security or a sense of security. Children crave deliverance from the many insecurities that are the lot of childhood. The desire for security is perhaps the main cause of intolerance. Basically, intolerance rests on the desire to keep something from someone else in order that we may have greater security. Too few of us have faith that there is potentially enough security for all.

We are all entitled to security or a sense of security. We believe that when a man fills a position satisfactorily he should feel secure in that position. He should not be fired as soon as someone comes along who appears to be better qualified. Can this be justified from the religious point of view? It can.

In the first place, it is not easy to determine whether another would

100

be of greater service in that position. Secondly, in this world of insecurity we are entitled to as much security as we can get, provided fair consideration is given to our neighbors' rights.

We should be definitely committed to the stand that everyone is entitled to a decent living so long as he does what is reasonably within his power to provide it himself. Helping others get on their feet is more catching than spoiling. The helpees tend to become helpers.

A sense of security is more conducive to good work than is insecurity. A sense of security is a goal attained. It helps us set our sights on higher goals. It is a stabilizer.

The school directors who took the attitude that teachers would do better work if they were constantly kept on the "hot seat" were all wrong. The fear of dismissal did not make better teachers of them.

The sense of security is gradually lost if the goal is made an abiding place rather than a bridgehead for further conquests. There is no permanent sense of security in standing still.

We must guard against the danger of confusing the sense of security with complacency. Complacency, if nurtured too long, ends up in despair and a sense of futility and frustration. This sense results from the feeling that we are not earning our right to the security that we possess.

8. DEMOCRACY

What is democracy? The three most common answers are:
1. Majority rule
2. Right to ——
3. Freedom to ——

Little or no effort is made to reconcile the first with the next two. But using these three as starting points is much better than never getting started. Enough thinking on the subject brings us around to the concept of democracy as imposing *duties*.

But the word "duty" has unpleasant connotations. These unpleasant ideas can be eliminated by gradually coming over to the idea of democracy as conferring a vision—a vision for service.

This service must be rooted in the pure religion of love for neighbor. And now we are at the starting point and in a strategic position to retrace

101

our steps until we come to what we had previously mistaken for the starting point.

Democracy seeks to embrace all of religion and furnish the forms, tools, and techniques that will speed thought into action. Let us not overlook the interaction here: Action also induces more thought.

Let none be dismayed by the thought that religion and democracy are beginning to look like one. There are still many phases in which—in our thinking, at least—one is different from the other. Religion is still the essence. Democracy furnishes the channels through which this essence can flow; also the fields in which it can come to full fruition. The channels are also funished with accelerators.

The foregoing binder between religion and democracy should make it possible to get more out of—and put more into—what follows.

Too many of us think of democracy as being the framework of our government. We tend to feel that he who operates within this framework is automatically being democratic. This is a grave error. This framework is what *at the time* is considered the best channel through which religion can operate. This framework *plus religion* spells democracy.

This framework contains many curbs on those who do not have the spirit of democracy in their hearts, or on whom the spirit has not taken full hold.

In a very real sense the spirit of democracy *is* pure religion. However, for convenience' sake, I am going to keep on using the term, spirit of democracy, as it is thought of in connection with the forms of democracy.

If any of us still insist on right, let it be the right to build ourselves up for greater usefulness to others.

If any of us still insist on freedom, let it be the freedom to expand into our neighbors' interest.

There is room within the forms for democratic and undemocratic action. It must be so as long as we have individual freedom. Thus, the measure of our democracy is the sum total of our individual practices—and the teamwork between these individual practices.

Individual initiative can result in much undemocratic action. Individuals or groups of individuals often set up strongholds within the channels and call them first-aid stations. Sometimes they really are first-aid stations; but the toll exacted may be too high.

The unprincipled among us are constantly discovering and devising undemocratic ways within this framework. Most reform has as its object the setting up of new forms to put an end to these evil tendencies, or at least to subject them to some control. But they are generally several steps

102

behind these people.

Many of us who shout the loudest for democracy are thinking only of its forms—forms that are sheltering us in our undemocratic practices. The selfish forces at work *in our midst*—under the veneer of democratic respectability—are our greatest danger. Selfishness is undemocratic regardless of the form in which it operates.

These channels must be provided with many branches in all directions to give democratically-minded people a chance to explore without losing caste. This exploring is into the No-Man's Land of new ideas. It sometimes results in branches that become the main channel.

All the present forms of democracy originally began as ideas of individuals and minority groups. Gradually, as the groups grew, they became the majority or a powerful minority. In time their views were *forced* on the governing groups. This force sometimes was revolution. The forms of democracy are a guard against the bloodshed that used to accompany such a change.

Democracy fosters these individuals and minority groups. It is eager to learn from them. They are the source of progress. There are also individuals and minority groups that have unsound ideas. Democracy does not embrace a new idea simply because it is new. Minority groups must look for a slow, often painful, growth.

In a local school, the conventional method of electing class officers is followed. Three persons, generally, get up and nominate candidates. Then all the pupils indicate their choice *from the list of three.* The results are often deplorable. Democracy is flouted. The pupils as a group do not really decide.

For years I have used a different method in my classroom. For a long time I was apologetic about it, although I felt that my method was superior to the conventional method. I was apologetic because I felt that my method did not teach democracy. I was a victim of the human fallacy that democracy is a form ready-cut for us to ape.

People who deplore any deviation from standard forms often bewail the loss that we sustained when we got away from the New England town meeting; but they are against any change in form that would bring us closer to the spirit of those meetings.

My method is to let each pupil make his choice from all the pupils in the class. The two or three or four, depending on the closeness of the vote, who get the most votes, are then placed in nomination. The list is narrowed down until one gets a majority of the votes cast.

The method is very popular with the pupils. They sense very keenly when real democracy is at work, and they relish it. Each pupil sensed that his opinion really counted. Democracy is better *felt* than defined.

Democracy is for any form or technique which serves its ends without doing undue violence to other legitimate ends. Until recently in our country, in the absence of controls, prices kept on rising. In an England with many controls, conditions are worse. It is not either much control or no control. It is a problem of studying each problem on its own merits. We dare not say that either method is undemocratic. The democratic method is the method that works best with due consideration to both short-range and long-range effects.

If taxation to correct inequalities best serves that purpose, then democracy should be for it. Agitators against certain forms of taxation take the attitude that taxation is a form of punishment. Taxation is not punishment. It is asking help of those who can best afford to give. And those who can best afford to give have in general received, gratuitously, the most.

Democracy eliminates old forms that have outlived their usefulness. Or it may extend their boundaries, or restrict them, as the need arises.

We can learn a salutary lesson from our football sales committees. Each year they adjust the rules of the game to conditions that have gotten out of hand. Fears expressed by many, perhaps most, of us that these changes would hurt the popularity of the game have proven groundless.

What a wonderful thing it would be if all of us could take this view of society and law! Why don't we? The panorama is much vaster. Few of us mortals harbor even a dim outline of it.

There is another big difference. The rule-makers of football generally have no personal stake in immediate ends to be achieved by the changes. Their big interest is the improvement of football as a whole. Most of our legislators are too much concerned about how a particular bill would affect them personally or their most influential constituents, and too little about the overall effect. They lack the religious approach.

We build up our individual concepts of democracy by considering the interplay of many attitudes and acts that represent democracy at work, or in action. But practical illustrations of democracy at work often are not sufficiently soul-searching. Too often they are a recital of what *others* should do.

A group of pupils went to the county seat to "see democracy at work." We must try to see democracy at work in our work, in our play, in school, at home, in church—yes, even in politics and business. We must help make it work by getting a clear conception of what it means to us.

An early New England clergyman said, "If the common people are

104

to govern, whom shall they govern?" To most of the people of his day, that disposed of the matter. The idea of self-government was alien to him even though those who governed others were also supposed to be able to govern themselves.

Later Jefferson said, "If people are not fit to govern themselves, how can they be fit to govern others?" His opponents, of course, had an answer that satisfied themselves. It was this: "People of wealth, position, and education are capable of governing themselves *and others.*"

Democracy has great faith in the common man. This is a *relative* faith. For instance, it recognizes that the common man has a very selfish heart. It also recognizes that he has no monopoly on selfishness.

Democracy has less faith in the *uncommon* man at or near the economic top or bottom. At either end, the uncommon man tends to become cynical from a lack of balance between the spiritual and the material.

The common man is the majority. Democracy hails this majority. The dictators dread it because they recognize it as their court of final appeal.

But let us consider some of the pitfalls of majority rule. By majority rule big nations have swallowed up little nations; the Jews have been persecuted through the ages; the South had slaves; the North imposed its will on the South; Russia is swallowing her neighbors; the majority can be blind to the rights of the minority; we can have the dictatorship of the majority. We can have a majority that thinks only of grabbing what it can for itself and leaving the remains for the minority.

A civics teacher said to me, "The majority has more rights than the minority in a democracy."

This might be put down as an academic poser, depending on the meaning we give to "rights"; but he made it plain he meant that those who belong to the majority *deserve* more than those who belong to the minority. This individual seems to do all his thinking in terms of the *rights* of majorities.

Teacher salary scheduling offers a peculiar anomaly. Here we find experts in salary scheduling—on the state and national level—encouraging teachers to probe the problem of teachers' salaries locally from the grass roots up. The result generally is that novices try to do what has already been done by experts.

What makes it particularly bad is that many teachers have a perverted conception of the meaning of democracy. To them, democracy is majority rule and nothing more. They think that majority rule automatically assures justice; or, worse yet, that justice must bow to majority rule. This is something that can easily be verified by anyone who engages a group of teachers in conversation on the subject of democracy in action.

Majority rule without a conscience eventually loses out as a result of its own cupidity. Its less fortunate members—and its enlightened membership—are gradually pushed into the camp of the minority—until the minority becomes the majority. It is now the persecuted majority. In time it suddenly awakes to the realization that it is more powerful than the ruling minority. Revolution! Then the cycle is repeated.

Democracy is trying to eliminate this cycle by giving a conscience to the majority. But conscience alone is too negative. Democracy also calls on the activating divine spirit that causes us to project ourselves into the lives of our neighbors—lose ourselves in their interests. It recognizes only the whole world as being the limit of neighborliness.

This neighborliness must not be for the sake of democracy, but rather for the sake of our neighbors. In fact, nobody should exist for any "ism"; the "ism" must justify its worth to the individual. The curse of official communism is that the individual is made to exist for it.

The spirit of democracy within me bids me to be very jealous of the rights of my neighbor, whether he be of the majority or the minority. We must work overtime to eradicate the too-common conception of democracy as being majority rule primarily for the benefit of the majority.

Even in countries that are not rated as democratic, laws are constantly being passed protecting the rights of the minority groups. The majority need no protection by law except when it is weaker in some respects than a minority group.

Perhaps the simplest way to put it is to say that on the question of rights, democracy, like our courts, knows no majority or minority.

Democracy in action resembles a court of justice more than a lawmaking body. It is more interested in *serving* the ends of justice than in *ruling* over others.

If democracy must choose between justice for the many and justice for the few, it will mete out justice to the many, but it is ever on the alert to make all benefits available to all. It gives help where help is needed to the extent of its resources. It ever strives to point in the direction of absolute justice, but it accepts spotty advance in preference to no advance.

Is majority *rule* always possible? In the 1860 election Lincoln received forty percent of the votes cast. Our system of apportioning senators and presidential electors was aimed at evils of majority rule.

Democracy is not any one thing. It operates under many guises. It stresses the importance of the individual. It also recognizes that the majority comprises more such important individuals than does any minority group.

106

Democracy strives to make a social creed out of the pure religion of love for neighbor. This is impossible if we do not personally possess at least a measure of this pure religion. Democracy moves, not through fear of personal catastrophe, but rather through love for neighbor.

As a nation we, at present, appear to be more interested in averting national disaster than we are in dealing justly with all nations. "He who saves his life shall lose it."

The true democrats among us are often accused of rocking the boat. What they are often actually doing is to remind us that the boat *is* rocking, and that we are rocking with it. Those of us who see only the boat are lulled into a false sense of security. The ocean is still bigger than the boat.

We must guard against taking the attitude that free speech merely means the right of each individual to "say his piece." We must feel a compulsion to listen to him. Our attitude must not be like the attitude of the hangman who allows his victim to say his piece before he is hanged. Democracy does not merely say, "You also have a right to be heard." It says besides, "I am very anxious to know what your hopes, fears, and aspirations are." Democracy is fair to those who hold contrary views.

Democracy is very tolerant of new and alien ideas because it is still growing itself; and because it has faith that it can overcome all new spirits that prove to be antagonistic to it.

It is unfortunately true that many of us who have learned imperfectly the lesson of democracy are less democratic than those who merely try to live up to the old-fashioned virtues. On the other hand, those of us who are imbued with the *spirit* of democracy will find a deeper meaning in these old-fashioned virtues.

A living democracy is a practical democracy. Its watchwords are approach and accommodation.

The approach is a consideration of what would be done in the solution of a problem under ideal conditions. The first requirement to the proper approach is a careful consideration of what is good for my neighbor. Accommodation consists principally in adjusting routine technique to cope with undemocratic forces, and unusual conditions. Democracy can accommodate itself to cope effectively with undemocratic forces without losing sight of its ideals. It likes to work with tools, but it also has weapons.

The democrat who disregards the undemocratic forces at work is not efficient. He must recognize them for what they are, work with them and against them without ever failing to recognize their true nature.

At the same time, we must look for the democratic elements in the philosophies of those who are stigmatized with an undemocratic label.

The democratic spirit is contagious. If we are possessed by it, others will sense it in our deeds and attitudes. They will tend to be possessed by this same spirit. Perhaps they already have it in greater degree than we. None of us live democracy completely. So the first step in making democracy live is to let it get fuller possession of our own hearts.

We put life into democracy when we place service, interest, and justice above rule. When we say that democracy is for majority rule, we must place the emphasis on majority, not on rule.

Democracy is for majority rule because it—majority rule—comes closest to the ideal of giving each individual the freedom to order his own life with, of course, the well-understood limitations. Democracy always embraces majority rule; majority rule does not always embrace democracy. This happens when majority rule is devoid of conscience.

But the individual democrat dare not let the majority make up his mind for him. The strength of democracy is measured by the extent to which its individual members make up their own minds in the spirit of altruism. We are running around in a circle when we say that the individual member of a democracy must let the majority do his thinking for him.

"Since wars begin in the minds of men, it is in the minds of men that the defenses of peace must be constructed." — Unesco.

The minds of men must be conditioned to a recognition of the right of every individual to be different—to be himself. They must be guided by more than the natural heart. They must be lighted up by the flame of divinity. Thus will they impart guidance and meaning to the natural endowments.

This right to be himself is limited to the right to develop his *talents* to the full. The individual's obligation is to use his talents in the interest of mankind. Society's obligation is to make available to the individual all the tools that will further his mission. But when the forces of altruistic democracy set an individual, or a group of individuals, into a favorable position, they have a right to expect an accounting from those individuals.

Most of us detest the religious fanatic. At present we have even more fanatics of democracy. They make a mold of democracy to which all must conform, or else. . . .

Some people say that new ideas are out while we are fighting communism. This is exactly the time when new—creative—ideas must be welcomed. Those of us who are fighting the consideration of new ideas are helping the cause of communism.

Democracy grants the minority the right to keep on agitating even after an issue has been settled. On the discussion level, an issue is never resolved so long as one member chooses to keep it open.

108

In a democracy everything is always on trial, including the rightists. There is no room for smugness. We are all, in turn, judge, jury, prosecutor, defendent, witness, and interested onlooker. We need regulations for those of us who dwell overmuch on one, or only a few, phases of our role. Countries and peoples that are just emerging need more regulations than we that restrict individual initiative—until such a time when there will be less clashing and more coalescing between initiatives. It takes real artistic talent, abetted by scientific insight, to become a true democrat.

The spirit of democracy is the spirit of inquiry, of faith in new revelation. Its mind is not closed as is that of official communism. Let us remember that the doctrines of communism began as individual, minority views. They are now becoming fixed. Let us not fight fixed ideas with fixed ideas. Let our ideas be fluid to change with the needs and aspirations of that important individual whom democracy idealizes—my neighbor. Democracy is humble.

Let us see if we can throw a span across the vast gulf that seems to exist between the concept of democracy as majority rule and democracy as granting laissez faire to the mighty economic minority. It is the problem of preserving both groups for the greater welfare of both.

I believe that a study of local government as it is found in the average community furnishes a clue to the answer. Most local government is minority government with the consent of the majority. The average voter will vote for the representative of the minority who shows evidence of ability and of having a social conscience.

Democracy is not for majority leadership. It is for enlightened majority followership. Even in a democracy the leadership must come from the less than ten percent true liberals. Pity the democracy whose leadership has no clearer vision and loftier motives than its followership! This leadership must be an articulate leadership: It must be able to impart to the majority at least a measure of its vision and sense of mission. Democracy makes it easy to have much interaction between the two groups. In fact, there is no sharp dividing line between them. The sense of stewardship is imparted by the minority. Example is the great convincer to the majority.

As leadership swings from one majority group to another, the new group tends to have a keener sense of stewardship than the group that is displaced. In fact, the displacement is generally the result of the liberals being pushed from the former group into the latter.

But we must recognize that the court of final appeal must be found where the greatest brute force can be concentrated; and then we must set ourselves the task of giving a conscience and direction to this brute force.

That court of final appeal must be the numerical majority. It can be *sheer* brute force. So can the mighty economic minority; but they get their might by harnessing the brutes from the opposing camp. And, fortunately for the minority group, they do not object to being harnessed so long as a semblance of reason is employed.

If we were to substitute the minority as the court of final appeal, the question would at once arise, "Which minority? Who is to decide which minority shall rule?" The answer must necessarily be, "The majority, the court of final appeal." There is no getting away from majority rule.

Democracy must always be careful not to overlook the rights of the minorities that are not dominant. The teachers of Pennsylvania have just been treated to a report on a comparison between their retirement system and the federal Social Security System. It rejects the idea of special consideration for teachers who retire with dependents because such teachers are a minority. We teachers should learn, with other Americans, that if democracy is to survive, we must be at least as careful of the rights of the minority as of the majority. The minority cannot win through the ballot. They must depend on the democratic sense that at least some of the majority possess.

Nothing in the foregoing rules out the obligation of democracy to make this majority stronger than any minority group or combination of minority groups; strong enough to enforce the rights of the weak minority groups, and of itself.

One of the objectives of the forms is to provide channels for those who are at or near the middle. This middle group must reach out far enough in both directions to embrace a majority. This majority must be given a chance to speed its ideas into action.

Democracy's special task is to reach the hearts of the individuals in this majority group. Their needs are more pressing because of their power.

Democracy strives to impress on the conscience of the majority the need for tempering its rule with service and a keen sense of responsibility to those that are ruled. The majority is its brother's sharer, not keeper.

But it must be recognized that there are innumerable groups. All of us belong to majority and to minority groups. So all of us must acquire the democratic spirit that causes us to temper our rule with a keen sense of responsibility toward those in the minority groups. We must strive to make it easy for others to find their mission in life.

What about the filibuster that is sometimes resorted to in the Senate? At its best it is an inarticulate protest against the idea that democracy is primarily majority *rule*. It is a protest against the tyranny of the majority. At its worst it is an illustration of how tyrannical a minority can become.

It, at least, has put us on the alert against the natural tendency for one section of the country, if it is numerically mighty, to try to legislate another section into goodness.

The present national controversy about oleomargarine is one of those rare cases where the line between right and wrong can be drawn very sharply. No national figure can claim that he places the welfare of the people above special privilege if he is opposed to the repeal of the percent tax on oleomargarine. He has not learned the lesson that our pre-Civil War history should have taught him; that one section of the country shall not dictate, through what they call the democratic majority, how another section shall live.

When Branch Rickey opened the door of organized baseball to the Negro, he was substituting example for legislation. And it is beginning to appear that this is something that the South can appreciate.

This thinking about groups must not let us forget that after all it is still the individuals within the group who are important; and the individuals that comprise the minority are just as important as those of the majority. We learn the needs of the groups by considering the needs of the individuals.

Those of us who still think of democracy as being something that confers *rights* have copied our founding fathers too literally. They had to stress rights because they addressed an oppressor king. We still think as though our major concern were to guard against tyranny from somewhere outside our orbit. Instead it should be to guard against being tyrants ourselves. Our main fight should be against our own selfish natures. Have you ever noticed how anxious the underprivileged are to cooperate with a person who is actuated by such a spirit? We need many more such persons if our democracy is to really click.

There is a school of thought that insists that the free operation of selfish enterprise will solve our problems. They point out that the under-privileged are in the majority; that through the equal ballot justice will be achieved. It is becoming increasingly evident that this will not be enough, because too many of us have not learned to think of our neighbors first.

What is the background of Jefferson's statement that the best govern-ment is that which governs least? In his day it was almost impossible to think of a government that did not grant special privileges to the *governing* class; to those who needed the special privileges the least.

Jefferson knew that many an unholy monopoly had been built up through governmental favoritism. He felt, in common with most people of his day, that if this favoritism were removed, then the resulting "free" com-petition would correct all ills. He was a babe-in-the-woods on the subject of extra-legal government. Monopolies as we know them were non-existent in his day.

111

The liberals' immediate goal of that day was a government that would no longer grant these special privileges. They had not yet come to the point of thinking of a government that would try to counteract this unbalance by doing something for the governed—the underprivileged—primarily because they felt that there would be no need for it.

They did not foresee the time when the forces of special privilege would, for all practical purposes, create a government within a government that would stifle competition; that this government would try to run the federal government.

They suffered from an ailment that still has us in its grip; oversimplifying the problem and the solution. We ourselves are oversimplifying when we take the attitude that they thought they had the final answer. The most progressive among them recognized that they were but taking another halting step in what they hoped was the right direction.

It has happened repeatedly that when we as a nation have tried to help a backward people get on its feet, our greatest task was to keep their governing class from administering our aid for its own benefit.

What is the most practical thing to do to set the stage for granting aid to such a government? If the government were deposed, the new government might be composed of men who individually rank higher than those whom they replaced; but as a functioning body they would probably be less efficient than the body that was replaced. Tradition, reputation, acceptance, authority, and general adjustment to the standard forms are aids that are often discarded too lightly. It is different when the machinery is well oiled for the transition. Even here we must guard against imposing our will on an unwilling majority.

The best plan seems to be to accept the government in power and impose such conditions as will be considered essential to the proper functioning of the aid program.

This is a fair contemporary illustration of what kind of government Jefferson had in mind when he said that the best government was that which governed least.

It also helps to explain why Jefferson took a "strict constructionist" attitude toward the Constitution. He was against the stretching of the Constitution only so long as the stretching was in the wrong direction, and he reasoned that the governing class would stretch in the wrong direction. Let us never forget that he lived in an age when the main thought was to *limit* governments. Practically all accumulated ills from the past were laid on the shoulders of corrupt government.

The idea of *limiting* governments was not a bad one—for those days. Government had not yet acquired a conscience.

The Russians are right when they take the attitude that most proponents of democracy take a selfish attitude. But if they are consistent, they will also admit that most proponents of communism also take a selfish attitude. We believe that democracy *points the way* to the fuller life. The fuller life is not in the democracy; it is in the individual.

The Russian attitude certainly calls for emphasis, on our part, on our duties toward our fellowmen as individuals and a playing down of our own rights as individuals. This must not be mere window dressing.

In its beginnings democracy got its impetus from the cupidity of its enemies. The oppressors became too exclusive and the oppressed became too many for the oppressors. It started to put into effect the principle that the majority should rule in preference to *a* minority. Did this solve the problems of democracy? Those who say that democracy is majority rule will answer yes.

All of us, unless we are guided by the divine spirit, will become oppressors if given the power. Franz Alexander apparently places upon the few in society who are dominated by nihilistic tendencies too much responsibility for the threat to democracy. We all must share the blame in varying degrees.

Some will raise their hands here and suggest that "enlightened self-interest" will solve the problem. In practice this enlightened self-interest consists merely in giving the oppressed just enough to keep them from revolting. In time, the line between revolt and submission wears so thin that there is a break—revolt.

Enlightened self-interest does not say, "What is good for the other fellow?" Instead it asks, "What can I do for the other fellow that is good for me?"

No, enlightened self-interest cannot stand up against the onslaughts of human depravity. Enlightened self-interest is to altruism as conscience is to the divine spirit.

Democracy is a spirit more than a form or a technique. England lacks some of the accepted forms of democracy but she has the techniques. Does she have the spirit? She has the spirit, but it is feeble and the flesh is weak.

England is trying too hard to incorporate many of the special privileges of the past into the present without realizing what she is doing. She is conservative.

I am picking on England because we Americans can view her more objectively than we can view ourselves; and because she is perhaps really more conservative than we simply because she has more past to draw on. She also lacks the open spaces to expand that we have.

Democracy as we conceive it today had, and still has, a slow, painful growth. It has been evolutionary. The stages through which it has had to pass are somewhat analogous to travails of a child in its arduous journey to a liberal manhood. This, in turn, can best be understood by considering the evolution of the gang that grows up with him.

The veneration for rules within the gang extends very little beyond the gang limits. A boy who would not violate a gang rule often would not hesitate to steal apples from an orchard. To him a rule is primarily a compact, and he has no compact, so far as he is aware, with the owner of the orchard.

The gang rules were in many cases imposed by the dominant member of the gang. In most cases this dominance was physical. At least it has taught the boy to bow to a higher authority, that is, higher according to *his* lights.

Gradually the circle is widened within which the boy will recognize rules as binding on him. The circle seldom includes the teacher. The teacher is generally a necessary evil.

As children grow in age and experience, new rights and obligations are added. The new spheres are recognized on the basis of recognized common needs and interests.

As the child goes through the adolescent stage, the compacts with childhood gradually are abrogated, but compacts with adults are gradually added.

In the adult stage, many of the compacts with the adolescents are gradually severed. The compacts with childhood are nearly all severed. What are substituted are rules and regulations from above toward which they are headed.

This would seem to be the stage at which the present Russian government has arrived. The next step is to re-open many of the compacts that have been closed. Rules and regulations from above will survive only as they get sustenance from below.

No nation can skip any of the steps in evolutionary progress. We must not expect it of Russia. Russia will have its period of unreasonableness. The announced policy of moving along without Russia, at the same time leaving the door open, is undoubtedly the best.

Certainly by this time it has become apparent that, in their widest implications, religion and democracy are one. But that is merely saying that they have one end. It is practically important to delimit them. Religion is especially concerned with the spirit or motive. So was Jesus. Religion has no definite program. Neither had Jesus. Democracy, if it would endure, must be filled with the religious spirit and then work out a program that will take care of current needs. Two of democracy's handmaids are past experience and prospects for the future.

Democracy is not natural. Animals are not democratic. Living within a circle that refuses to widen is not democratic. Neither are primitive people democratic. Democracy does not regard outsiders an enemies. They are at least potential friends.

Democracy listens, and has always listened, to the voice of the spirit. But the voice is very indistinct, because there are so many other voices competing with it. Democracy is still hearing indistinctly. We must have faith, however, that it is making progress in eliminating false voices without forgetting that new voices, some false, are constantly clamoring for attention.

Joshua listened to the voice of the spirit and imagined that he heard it say, "Go and kill all that stand in your way." Jesus listened to the same voice and heard it say, "Go and save."

This is not an argument against listening for the voice of the spirit. It still is the only way of salvation. But a great deal of patience, and therefore faith, is needed. The voice of the spirit bids us consider our neighbor. Joshua was handicapped by a narrow conception of the word neighbor. With all his shortcomings—viewed from our vantage point—he undoubtedly took a step upward.

Essential democracy is a spirit—growing, expanding, changing. A democracy is not worthy of the name if its citizens are not gradually practicing democracy more and more in their dealings with their neighbors—and "neighbors" should be defined as all with whom they have effective and sympathetic contact.

It looks for the good in all the "isms." It gratefully accepts the good they have to offer, and alters her spirit, form, and techniques to appropriate it.

Our newspapers could help greatly in fostering this idea by publishing more fully the views of the smaller nations concerning our motives. We Americans are too ignorant of the thought processes of other nationals. I do not have reference to other nationals in our midst, but to nationals in their native habitats.

Democracy does not say, "Perhaps some day you will think as I do; then we can get together."

It does not say, "Why doesn't somebody do something?" It does it.

All the aims of democracy are also religious aims. Democracy is religion—plus. We can also say that religion is democracy—plus. Religion looks into the heart of man to determine what must be our attitude if we are to achieve the ends of democracy. Religion studies the conflict between nature and the divine spark within us. It recognizes that nature pulls to ourselves. Therefore, the spirit must pull toward our neighbors to strike the proper balance.

After all, religion is not an end primarily; it is a means. Pragmatically speaking, the end of religion is the welfare of mankind, with a thought to each individual.

Democracy places the emphasis on man's material welfare without, by any means, overlooking the spiritual element. Religion makes the spirit all-important with the material phase as a means and by-product. Both are really ends and means.

While I am seeking to transform my selfish heart, it continues to pull in my direction. My effort must be to effect a proper balance with this pull. Some of us must break the balance in favor of selflessness to counteract the pull of many who do not try to curb their selfish impulses.

Democracy has faith that the altruistic pull of the minority can more than counteract the selfish pull of the majority. The forces are seldom diametrically opposed.

Inertia is another factor that makes it possible to have democratic *action* when only a comparatively few have the spirit of real democracy in their hearts. We have always had enough such individuals to insure slow progress. The atomic bomb serves as a terrible reminder that this progress must be greatly speeded up. This altruistic minority is always looking for new recruits. Come on in; the water's fine!

"We know that *all things* work together for good to them that love God." Fortunately, even selfish people blunder upward. It is the selfless minority who give them direction and speed the progress. In them is the flame of democracy burning most brightly. We must have more such selfless people to give proper control to all the forces at our disposal.

"The oppressed sleep better than the oppressors." Decocracy never uses this as an excuse for being complacent about evils that can be corrected. The best way to help the oppressors—in the long run—is to eliminate oppression.

"If I rise, you too shall rise." Too many of us still believe that we rise only at the expense of others. To that extent we do not have the spirit of democracy in our hearts.

"The voice of the people is the voice of God." It at least is our most reasonable facsimile. We are in this world for service and to speed the ends of justice. Service is recognized, not as charity, but as righting of wrongs; as a balancing of things that are out of balance. The people are not we, but our neighbors. We advance the kingdom of the *spirit* by being actively concerned about the *material* welfare of others.

This is not a one-way street. My neighbor probably numbers me among his neighbors. Perhaps he beats me to it in neighborliness. But I must not depend on it. It is something that easily gives way when I lean on it.

116

As a nation we must take this attitude toward other nations. Not what can we get out of it, but what can we put into it, should be uppermost in our minds. The spirit of helpfulness is very contagious; but we must be careful not to make this contagion our main objective, and it must not be our country's main objective. It is a by-product that is not inevitable.

We can best serve God by serving his creation, chief of which is man, my neighbor. We must learn to lose ourselves in the lives of others in the same way that parents often lost themselves in the lives of their children. This is selfless devotion—and democracy.

Democracy does not take the attitude, "I must help my neighbor because one never knows when one may need help himself." Instead it helps because it feels that the one helped is entitled to it; and that help is its own reward. We rise together, particularly by helping the one who has been less favored than we. Our special obligation is to make available, or help to create the conditions that will help to make available, the tools that are now denied him in the building of a fuller life.

Finally, we are all workers together to speed the ends of justice— Democrats, Republicans, Independents, churchmen, schoolmen, philosophers, all.

Democracy is vitally concerned about two basic emotions: love and hate.

The chief feeder of hate is selfishness. About the only thing we can safely hate is hate itself. We can do little more than hate evil in the abstract. Democracy strives hard to get us to recognize that an evil deed or thought is often largely a matter of opinion.

Even in the case of a person perpetrating a deed that is universally recognized as being evil, democracy probes for underlying causes.

Democracy is tolerant, not because it does not care, but because it cares. It cares for the things it believes in. It also cares for those who believe differently. It cares because it is ever striving for new revelations and new techniques; and because it seeks to win those who hold the wrong beliefs. The first requirement in winning over a doubter is sympathetic interest in his thought patterns. That must be the starting point.

In our international dealings we must strive to learn from other nations. In this striving we shall be teaching them as a by-product of our learning.

Democracy fights intrigue, but its weapon is not intrigue. It recognizes intrigue for the boomerang that it is.

This does not mean that intrigue is never used in a democracy. Other forces besides the spirit of democracy are at work in it. A democracy can be described as a country that has the forms and employs the techniques that, at the time, give the spirit of democracy the best chance to possess the hearts

117

of its citizens.

I just listened to a man with a "Big Name" discoursing on democracy. Most of the audience were awed by his "Big Name" and by the sweep of his subject. But when he got through he had done nothing to clarify our thinking about democracy. One got the general line that democracy is what we Americans have but are in danger of losing and what the Russians do not have.

He assumed that democracy was something all could recognize if they saw it. He did not seem to realize that there are Americans who consider monopolistic practices democratic and labor unions undemocratic; that one group considers a governmental act democratic while another group considers that same act undemocratic. In short, he did not seem to recognize that we have our work cut out for us when we try to get together on the meaning of democracy.

"Democracy has failed; defend it!" This is the burden of many an orator's message. If democracy has failed, why defend it? Why not substitute something that will not fail? It reminds one of the family that is continuously feuding within its own circle, but ganging up unanimously on any outsider who tries to straighten things out for them.

We have reached the stage where thoughts on communism are filling the air. The best way to dispose of them is to read about communism by Communists. It is an indirect but effective way of studying democracy. It is getting away from the natural instinct to defend what is ours at all costs. Real democracy is its own defense.

Democracy is not jealous of the other "isms." Democracy looks for the good in other "isms" for the purpose of self-improvement, and in the interest of tolerance. It looks for what it has in common with these other "isms."

Two persons were arguing about Henry Wallace. One called him a Communist; the other called him a true democrat. And yet many of us say that the two "isms" are so far apart that there is no meeting. We had better spend our energies toward some semblance of agreement as to what democracy looks like in *practice*.

On the other hand, two persons may be pursuing tasks that apparently are opposed to each other, while both are truly led by the spirit of democracy. They are operating in circles, or spheres, that overlap.

We do not make democracy live by building it up at the expense of other "isms." If a democrat and a Communist were to sit down together to discuss their social creeds, they would find many points of agreement.

People are seldom as far apart as their creeds; and they tend to fit their

118

creeds to their personal predilections.

Our concept of democracy is continually changing in the light of new revelation. This thought alone should prevent us from saying that it must be democracy or nothing.

The concept of communism is also changing. At present we seem to be flying apart. Historians will undoubtedly record that our flights were co-ordinated by the human equation and assumed a parabolic pattern.

I suggest that we give the Communists in our midst an honored place in our society. We should listen to them carefully and sympathetically. Then we should look at ourselves to see how much in their charges is true. We should also listen to their hopes and aspirations and compare them with ours. Such a procedure would open the eyes of many of us for the first time to the revelation that democracy is essentially a spirit.

I am, of course, referring to those Communists who are not for over-throwing our government by force. The honored place, of course, is not for the anarchistic Communists. But even here we should strive to learn what made him anarchistic. Anarchists have one glaring shortcoming. They are committed to the theory that there are two opposite forces in the world and that one will inevitably be overcome by the other.

We seem to be agreed now that we should teach *about* communism in our schools and colleges. Will this teaching bring us to an understanding of communism? Not inevitably. We have industrialists who have studied the laboring man for a generation and now understand him less than they did when they started; and vice versa. Many Southerners insist that they are the best judges on the question of how the Negro should be treated because they have given him the closest study.

A study about communism can be worse than useless if it is not con-cerned with what is good about communism. I said "can be" because some of the students will follow their own line of reasoning despite the efforts of a bigoted instructor. They generally succeed in giving the course as a whole a plus value.

Will parallel studies of the aims of democracy and of communism assure understanding? Again not inevitably. It may make Communists out of democrats. The student has practical experience about the shortcomings of democracy. He lacks such experience about communism.

Yes, there is danger in trying to come to an understanding of the aims of communism; but there is a much greater danger in the aloof attitude. Eternal, active vigilance is the price of all the virtues.

What are platitudes? Platitudes are things that are uttered by people who do not sense the keen struggle of ideas that is continually going on.

119

Platitudes may be implied as well as uttered. The speaker on democracy leaned on many implied platitudes. Platitudes are crutches for lazy thinkers—or weak thinkers.

But let us consider the more subtle platitudes. We are being platitudinous when we say that democracy and communism will never mix because they have nothing in common. They have much in common. Our democracy is gradually becoming more collective as collective action becomes more feasible than individual action. Collectivism can be a reservoir of power for individual sallies into unexplored areas.

Life can be pictured as consisting of innumerable strands that are gradually being drawn together in a cable at the same time that new branches are forming and shooting out. The strands *and cable* are pulsing with life.

Collectivism is bad when it seeks to confine before the time is ripe, or when it seeks to encompass all of life. Collectivism should be like the trunk of a tree—most activity is outside the trunk, but the trunk is indispensable.

We must recognize that the official communism of Russia is not the communism of the theorists. It just happens to be a convenient term to designate a phase in the evolution of Russian government and society. It is a phase through which all governments and societies have passed, are passing, or will pass.

It is the phase of unreasonableness largely in remembrance of past injustices—and on unsureness of self. Those who are most unsure of themselves are the ones who try hardest to create the opposite impression.

We like to say that the big struggle today is between communism and democracy. And we are right—from our viewpoint.

But if we want to make progress, we must try to at least understand the Russian viewpoint. To them their fight is not a struggle against democracy. They pay lip service to democracy; and insist that they have more of it than we. They say that the struggle is between communism and capitalism.

So the bone of contention is capitalism—and we will do well not to sidestep the issue. We should begin by agreeing with the Russians that capitalism still has much to learn. It must be permeated by the spirit of democracy; and in the meantime democracy must set up forms for capitalism as it does for every force that is not self-contained.

After all, there is more hope for a democratic capitalism than for a capitalistic democracy.

The Russians insist that the highest form of democracy consists in fighting for the rights of all taken as a group; and then those rights are generally projected into the future.

We must persist—by our lives—along the line that the quickest way to achieve these ends is to be jealous of the rights of *individuals now*. We must also recognize that there is perhaps a stage in civilization in which no ruling class can have respect for the rights of individuals and survive. They would be replaced by a group that is guided by a conscience that operates on a lower level.

They are what they are, not primarily because of what they call themselves, but because of their level of civilization. They should pass through the stage at a faster pace than did *our* forebears because they have an example that was denied those that went before. They need do less groping.

In the meantime, the more advanced people must demonstrate their versatility by showing that while they prefer to work with tools, they also have weapons.

To the average conservative, the liberal attitude is selfish. The conservative looks on every effort to change the rules to jibe with the facts as being materialistic. He refuses to see that practically all rules had such a materialistic beginning. Even if a liberal apparently has no personal stake in the things for which he is fighting, the conservative puts his wishful thinking to work, and creates one. The conservative embraces the collectivism that was handed up from the past, but he is against adding to it—on the part of the government.

In the meantime, the giant corporations are becoming more and more collectivist. And they certainly do regiment those who come under their power. It is the higher-ups in the corporations who have their minds regimented most. These minds are then used to regiment other minds. The conservative generally favors this kind of collectivism and regimentation; the liberal is against it.

The only kind of government regulation, regimentation, and collectivism that the liberals favor is that which will liberate those affected for more intensified activity in new fields. This is a part of the liberal brain that the conservative does not comprehend.

Those of us who conceive of democracy as being just a form are idol worshipers. The idol must return, or move up to, the idealism that created it.

We should work and strive *for* democracy, and not *against* the various "isms." We should be more critical of democracy than of the "isms," because salvation lies in critical self-analysis.

Critical self-analysis by the holders of all the "isms"—and democracy is one of the "isms"—will serve to make us One World ideologically. The oneness in ultimate goals will gradually lead to oneness in immediate goals.

In what fields should democracy be active? In all fields where there is, or should be, activity. We should take the democratic way of life with

121

us wherever we go. The field of social justice is a seemingly never-ending field for democratic activity.

Two thousand years ago, the problem of poverty was partly solved by the occasional handing out of doles. Today we feel that it is a function of the government to try to eliminate the conditions that produce poverty, without reneging on poverty cases that are still with us. And if collectivism and regimentation are necessary to attain these ends, then the government should use these means.

Too few of us appreciate how much we owe to the government, and that we got these benefits through government regulation. The government protects the man of wealth more than the poor man. When we say that the government does more for the poor man, we should mean that the government is striving to more nearly equalize this protection.

Here is one case to illustrate my point. Captain Sutter became a poor man when gold was discovered on his property, because the government was not strong enough to protect him in his rights. It is, of course, fair to ask whether he had a right to all that gold. It is also fair to ask whether it is right for whole family dynasties to live today on ill-gotten—or legitimate—gains of a century ago.

There appears to be no end to the functions that the government has taken over and will continue to take over as a result of *growing common interests*. Many people are afraid of this. Regardless of the age in which they live, or lived, or will live, their line is the same, namely—that what the government has taken over to date is all right, but it is now time to call a halt.

No, it is never time to call a halt. We should take the attitude that as the great majority agree on a program, then the government should take over. To enable us to fold our arms in complacency? No, to enable us to roll up our sleeves and start on new projects.

Practically all that the government is doing today started out as projects of minority groups. As the snowballs became unwieldy, larger groups—and finally the government—took over while new groups started other snowballs. Don't carry the analogy too far. Snowballs become unwieldy in time, you know, even for governments. The snowball analogy, like all analogies, is used to illustrate, not prove, something.

Nowhere in the foreseeable future will there be a time when there will be a lack of projects for groups, and individuals, to work on. It must be remembered that all great movements had their beginnings in small ways.

In our country we believe that the two-party system is superior to the multi-party system; but we draw faulty conclusions from it. Too many think that it calls for an attitude of "my party, right or wrong." Too many of us attach a stigma to a bolt against one's party. There are some who think that there should be an opposition party to every national endeavor. How about substituting an apposition party?

Democracy does not study the doctrines of the opposing "isms" for the purpose of rooting out sinister motives. Its prime purpose is to learn from others. If it does call names, it also furnishes pertinent substantiating evidence.

Would it not be a wonderful thing if the opposition party would think first in terms of what is right in what is offered and take care of wrongs as they become manifest! Can we delude ourselves into believing that we are dealing fairly with other nations when we behold the spectacle of how the two major political parties deal unfairly with each other? If we love not those whom we see, how can we love those whom we have not seen?

Is there any other group of people that is so eager to present to the public what they *hope* is bad about their opponents. And the public thinks of them first when they think of democracy! Is it any wonder that, according to public opinion polls, the public thinks that politicians should be paid less than laborers because they are worth less? This news should first appall them, and then goad them into constructive action.

Do our legislators need religion? They certainly do, and especially by virtue of the prominent position they occupy. The examples they set are followed by many.

They need to be educated in the art of concentrating on issues, not personalities. They need to be educated in the art of not impugning base motives to their political opponents. They need education in the art of considering big issues and not small fragments of them. Many of them still seem to live in the Adam Smith era.

Let politicians realize that when they look harder for the bad than for the good in the policies of the opposing party, then the flame of democracy is very low in their own hearts. Such politicians have not yet reached the "live and let live" stage. Rather their slogan appears to be, "Live, and hope you die." Our politicians must *not* believe that the *selfish* strivings of all the lawmakers add up to the best interests of the nation as a whole.

This consideration of big issues must not result in contempt for the many little issues that are at hand and need attention. Some self-styled thinkers on big issues always disdain to touch the things that are within reach because they consider contact with them degrading.

At the same time they need more courage to attack real evils; to contentrate on real malefactors, and not to speak in general terms.

I consider Drew Pearson one of our country's greatest benefactors. When he attacks he names names, contrary to the methods of most legislators. There is a big difference between naming names and name-calling. But I have often wished that our country had one voice with the following of Drew Pearson, who would concentrate on the doers of good. Such a person could perform wonders. Teamed up with each other, both of them should become more effective.

It is high time for politicians to revise their estimate of the caliber of the general public's intelligence. The politicians of one party impugn all the base motives to the members of the other party. The politicians of the other party return the compliment. The general public believes both, not in ignorance, but on the assumption that those who see all the base motives in others must themselves have a vested interest in those low motives.

It is ironic that the general public creates its heroes of the past from the group that they so much despise in real life.

After every national election there are speakers who rise to remark, "Isn't it remarkable that in the heat of an election campaign we can call each other all sorts of names and then settle the issue on election day without bloodshed?" Then they call attention to countries in which such a thing is impossible.

Faith in the progress we have made to date should not make us complacent about the present state of affairs. A most important question is, "Have we progressed as much as we should?"

This deliberate misrepresentation in a political campaign is irreligious, vicious, unnecessary, and poor politics. In no other field do people call each other names in public as in politics, and in no other field does the general public have so low an estimate of the members.

Here at least the politicians can learn from Hitler. It is that if you repeat a given line often enough, the people will tend to believe it, whether it be true or false.

Every once in a while we are treated to an account of how friendly politicians from opposing parties often are toward one another after they have shot their bolts for public consumption. They think they are fooling the public when actually they are fooling only themselves.

Democracy does not thrive on theatrics. Many politicians are very theatrical. Many of them are undemocratic—in fact, anti-democratic. The politicians' line is the childish line, and it is about time for them to grow up.

The small politician who hands out small favors in the hope that these small favors will loom larger in the recipients' thinking than the less apparent, but more sinister, larger ills, does not have the spirit of democracy in his heart.

A very unfortunate outcome is that the real statesmen in our public life often become infected and, often unconsciously, stoop to the low tactics of the politicians. After all, there are statesmen among the politicians, more than the general public realizes.

In presidential campaigns, the candidates have an especial responsibility to concentrate on real issues, not on "made" issues, or on personalities. They will not impugn base motives to the other side. They will not try to hide behind name-calling.

Whatever faith we have in democracy was *not* given us by the example set by our average lawmaker. And from this group many of our heroes of the future will be picked!

This is important because when we start dealing with other nations, we are prone to carry our national practices into the international field; and we are very much judged by our national practices.

We Americans are often very much shocked when we hear a Russian delegate to the UN "shoot off" about our imperialistic aims. Often he makes statements, apparently for home consumption, that are patently not true. But why should we be shocked? To me it is a reasonable facsimile of a politician in our midst lambasting the opposing party.

Their reasoning is in line with the reasoning of those economists, now rare, who contend that the sum total of the selfish efforts of the separate business men makes for the best interests of business as a whole.

How can we expect to have the proper regard for the United Nations as a unit if our national representatives generally have not learned to place their country above the selfish interests in their districts? More religion, please!

Steffens sounds a word of warning that we must take very seriously. He says that too many of us look on corruption in politics (which he would call corruption in business) as merely a sign of growing pains and that it will disappear in time. Left to itself it will grow instead. It will transform a democracy into a plutocracy. If that is not the trend today it is because of the reforming forces that are always at work.

But we must not despair and think that the situation is hopeless. 'Twas ever thus, only more so.

Are we progressing socially? We do not have to be very old to recall when our neighbors fenced in their front and back yards against us savages. And we did the same thing to them. It turns our thoughts back to the days of walled-in towns and cities.

125

I believe most old-timers will agree that there is much less fighting among neighbors today than there was two generations ago. Any old-time baseball fan can testify to the greater tolerance of the crowd and the greater respect for authority.

But it must be emphasized over and over again that the big question is not primaily whether we are progressing socially and in our economic know how. The question is whether our progress is fast enough to keep pace with our technological progress.

Let us define a good man in the relative sense. A good man is a man who leaves his community a little better than it would have been without him. What is his community? It depends on the man. It may be anything from a very small sphere to the whole world.

This definition definitely has its drawbacks. By it a man can be an asset in one community and a liability in another. It does not fully consider a man's contribution in the light of his talents. It passes judgment on the man in the light of what he means to his community. God undoubtedly has other bases for judging man. Nevertheless it must be democracy's way.

There is many a man whose influence in the community is not appreciated by the community. Perhaps he is administering medicine that the community does not appreciate. Undoubtedly *his* community is larger than the community here mentioned.

Many a good man has not been appreciated by his community even if it comprised the whole world. There are many things about every community that are not good for it to which the majority in the community are blind.

In our South there are many members in the community who are considered traitors to their class because they dare to speak up for the rights of a suppressed group. Yet it is to such as these that we are primarily indebted for the upward march of civilization.

Many good men are needed in every community to consolidate gains and to further new projects to which the community is committed. But if these are the only good men in the community, it and they tend to become pharisaic. Such a community gradually becomes a restricted community.

We have a right to expect that as civilization advances, fewer martyrs will be necessary. No true martyr wants to be a martyr. We all want, and should want, the approbation of our fellowmen. But there are things that are more important than this. Those who choose these more important things are, in various degrees, martyrs.

"He who is not with me is against me" certainly implies that we are

126

to take a stand according to the lights we possess. There is no room for pussy-footing here. If our lights are dim, let us acknowledge it and frankly make use of other lights. If they shine brightly, let us be careful that we are not blinded by the light. If we look intently at one light we become oblivious of other lights.

A few weeks ago I was asked to cast a ballot when I knew nothing about the candidates. I signed it and handed it to a man who was in a better position to judge the candidates. He voted for me and for himself. Was that undemocratic? It was representative government. And, like all representative government, it has many pitfalls.

"It's for the Church; so it's all right." Genuinely religious people will steer clear of this slogan. The church should conduct its business at least on a level with what is considered ethical practice in the business world.

When we buy a railroad ticket and then discover that we cannot go, the management will refund the price of the ticket. Many schools will not refund the money when someone buys a ticket to an event and then discovers that he cannot go.

The school should practice the things that it wants its pupils to practice when they step into the competitive, and cooperative, business world. The school and church make weaklings out of themselves if they fall short here.

Is our church democratic? I think not. Too often it is run by the holders of special privilege. And their views too often are shared by the preacher. Too much thought is given to the church and what the members owe to it. They do not think of the church, and the Sabbath, as being made for the people. They do not share Jesus' view that religious leaders should take an active interest in the material well-being of their constituents.

Professors of religion are not immune to the danger of becoming tyrants through lack of sympathetic contact with the masses. Many of them *are* tyrants.

The church would become more democratic if the low income members were given better representation on the church councils. The *vocal* part of the church is not democratic.

The church is very undemocratic when it says that as soon as a person has been confirmed he shall become a financial supporter of the church. The connection between money and the means of grace is too close. After all, the idea that the new non-wage-earning member is himself contributing is generally a delusion. It merely means but an added burden to the wage earner in the family. Why not wait until the member has become a wage earner before expecting him to contribute? Surely the church cannot afford

127

to be less altruistic than the government. The government does not expect that its young citizens shall give of that which they have not. The government never says to the wage earner, "Your load shall be heavier because of what we are doing for your children." Instead it lightens the load. And it is the church that pays the most lip service to paying according to need.

To say that the church does not *require* parents to pay more as a result of the children they are bringing up is missing the point of my argument. My argument is that the church should take a definite stand on the issue.

Some will say, "Think of the added burden on those who have no children to support." The answer is, "Think of the much greater task of bringing up the children."

It is ironic that the church, which is supposed to foster the pure religion that should motivate democracy, should be so undemocratic.

All this is in line with the religious attitude that we should equalize inequalities wherever possible.

Compared with the church, the sporting world is very democratic. It is more responsive to public opinion. This is probably because the public has so much more chance to evaluate it and make itself felt. The sporting world does not have that wiser-than-thou attitude. Certainly the church should try harder to discover what is going on in the minds of the masses. Similarly we should spend more time to find out what is in the minds of children.

The concept of the universal brotherhood of *men* does not necessarily mean the mingling of those whose ideas and ideals are far apart. We should get each other's viewpoints and then more or less go our own ways. Diverse interests and gifts call for diverse fields in which to employ them.

There are many who raise the bugaboo that the granting of equal rights to a people of another color necessarily means the mingling of the two races. We need only to look at our problem of the foreigner to answer that question. Many Americans are prejudiced against foreigners. In such a case foreigners do not try, with a few isolated exceptions, to impose themselves an those who want to have nothing to do with them. There will be as much mingling as the more exclusive class will choose to tolerate.

I feel that some proponents of racial equality are doing more harm than good in publishing pictures of the white and colored races mingling indiscriminately. The unfortunate thing is that it places the emphasis in the wrong place. It misses the point that tolerance means granting others the right to live their own lives as we demand the right to live ours. Mingling is incidental. The amount of mingling that will result will depend on the desires of both parties. I have had the personal experience of discovering that when I find people with whom I would not care to mingle, they generally have the same feeling toward me.

I must hasten to add that the right to live their own lives means the rights of others to the privileges that we enjoy. If there is to be any restrictive zoning, it must be self-imposed.

Let us enlarge on the statement that love believes in meting justice to my neighbor even if it means a minor injustice to me. On the question of tolerance toward Negroes, there is the selfish besetting fear that tolerance will mean that the Negroes will tend to gravitate toward the most tolerant. Boiled down this fear amounts to this: We are afraid that we shall be forced to do what we expect others to do.

One argument is that the Negroes should be kept down South and tolerated there because it was Southerners who caused them to be brought to America. This is equivalent to saying that children should pay for the sins of their grandparents.

More of us need that keen sense of the untapped potentials within ourselves that will cause us to be willing, and anxious, to mete justice to others even if it means a *greater* injustice to ourselves. There is always virgin territory beckoning for settlers. To such people the "greater injustice" proves to be a mirage.

The *spirit* of democracy along with the spirit of pure religion is found in the hearts of men throughout the world. Some Russians have it, and some Americans do not have it.

It can exist without the forms of democracy; and it can also be absent within the forms. But, generally speaking, the forms are a great aid to its spread. The spirit of democracy cannot live in the heart that is not expanding and reinforcing itself. Democracy tries to teach us to rule well our own hearts, not other people's hearts. On the positive side it is for "live and help live."

9. "BOTH-AND" vs. "EITHER-OR"

"We must choose." This sentence has come to stand for intolerance. If the virtues and vices were clearly delineated, then we could choose without much thinking. Then there is the further fact that we are not agreed on what, in practice, are the virtues and vices.

The great truth calling for acceptance today is that we do not live in

129

a world of opposites. What is *every* man's goal in life? The satisfying life. When we get down to cases, we find differences, but not opposites.

Communis*m* and capitalis*m* may theoretically be opposites. But very definitely Communis*t*s and Capitalis*t*s are not. Human beings—God's creatures—are not opposites.

Nature and spirit are not opposite. Nature was moving in a generally upward direction before spirit-guided man appeared on the scene.

So let us bring apparent opposites together. They will soon find that they are related. Two profound(?) thinkers arrive at hypotheses that are diametrically opposed. But when they become practical, they generally come close together. On the other hand, two persons may subscribe to identical creeds, but they will be different.

True tolerance does not consist *mainly* in finding areas of agreement between two groups; rather it is recognizing areas of disagreement, *and putting up with them.* In the putting up with, many points of agreement will emerge. And the points enlarge into areas.

Marxian and official communism are based on the theory that communism and capitalism are irreconcilable. It recognizes the power for selfish ends of the despots of capitalism. It is up to us proponents of democracy to *demonstrate* the power of the divine spirit to redirect our natural talents.

Fortunately, Communists pride themselves on their pragmatism. Their masses can be convinced by a workable democracy and capitalism.

From our end let us not make the mistake of calling the two irreconcilable. A thorough understanding of the *problems* of democracy leads to an interest in the problems of communism, and vice versa.

We must put an end to attaching a stigma to straddling as such. Straddling is possible only where a barrier exists between two camps. It is not always a problem of choosing camps; it may be one of removing the barrier, or of being big enough to straddle it. It is substituting both-and for either-or.

We visit cruelty on others because of the subconscious feeling that we are thus driving it from our own doorsteps. Good and evil are both boomerangs that to most people lose their identity in passage because they change their form.

The one who says, "We (you) must choose," all too often assumes that in the consideration of a given issue the lines are clearly drawn between good and evil, between right and wrong, and that the choice is simply whether we want to be on the right or on the wrong side. The human race could really make progress if it were as simple as this. In the New Testament is found this passage: "We know that all things work together for good to them that love God." This suggests, at least, that there is more harmony in apparent opposites than we are prone to realize.

A recognition of these facts dares not result in our taking no stand. But the stand should nearly always be somewhere between the two extremes.

Such a stand nearly always results in the charge from both extreme wings that we are in the camp of the opposition. Actually it means that we have achieved that rare combination of projection and introspection that is the one hope of the world.

It is distressing to have a speaker crash the headlines in a tirade against those of us who are concerned about parental delinquency. He took the usual line that it is one or the other. He talked about social delinquency— that is, the delinquency of society in not making proper collective provision for the youth of the land. I could have added individual adult delinquency alongside parental and social delinquency. I am thinking now of those adults who are not parents and those parents who no longer have children of the impressionable age. I am thinking of their delinquency in the individual examples they set for the rising generation. I am also thinking of their delinquency in refusing to admit that they have a responsibility in the bringing up of the rising generation. Somebody will undoubtedly say here that everybody's business is nobody's business. The shirker in particular uses this line.

There is more adult than parental delinquency in the drinking problem. It is the adults who have more money to squander than the parents who are setting the worst examples. Children seldom want to emulate their drinking parents; but they often try to emulate the bad habits of other adults. The evil effects of bad habits in the home are much more apparent than are the effects of the same bad habits outside the home. It is not at all unusual to find a child forming a habit that is the exact opposite of the bad habit of the parent.

Why could the speaker not speak about social delinquency without finding fault with those who are mainly concerned with another phase of the problem? It undoubtedly is an effort, consciously or unconsciously, to flaunt his own superior insight.

Professors of religion are too prone to take the attitude that the world's salvation lies in the literal acceptance of their personal theology. How wonderful it would be if all the world could be of one mind; that is, my mind! They should give more thought to James's definition and Jesus' practice of pure religion. Jesus emphasized that there were others, outside his fold, doing good.

It will help our reasoning in the chapters to follow if we here care-

131

fully consider the fallacies of the "either-or" attitude of mind. Jesus' uncompromising stand on clear-cut issues between good and evil has had rather unfortunate results. In trying to apply this stand of his, we overlook the fact that in actual practice there are few, if any, such clear-cut issues. There are almost invariably good and evil forces at work on both sides. And the possible and needful remedies are many and varied.

The world's theologians have not done their part toward making this world One World spiritually. The big stumbling block is their either-or attitude—either my way or none.

Too many of us go to church regularly to hear ourselves lined up with God, and the rest of the world with the devil. We Christians are so prone to think that our way is the only way. We can continue to believe this if we recognize that if we go deep enough we find that there is but one pure religion, regardless of how many names we give it. Christians and Jews are agreed on pure religion. We differ on the approach. The big task for us Christians is to come closer to the grand objective of pure religion by attending to our own knitting. We must remember that Christian theology is but *one* of the handmaids of pure religion. Instead, it spends too much time probing the No-Man's land between itself and the other theologies, mostly for the purpose of discovering reasons for maintaining its separate and aloof existence.

This is basically a book on attitudes. But if techniques were left out it would be a book on airy nothings. But we must be clear in our minds as to their respective legitimate functions. Attitudes are fundamental. Techniques are means of attaining desirable goals. We must continually build up techniques that help to give our attitudes proper outcomes. Attitude-technique are both-ands that must move forward together. On the other hand, it must be recognized that in a book such as this it is often advisable to do no more than suggest the *direction* that the techniques should take.

Why is it that so many, perhaps all, reforms fall short of their goal? It is primarily because people who are involved have not sufficiently adjusted their attitudes and techniques to the new conditions.

And it should be recognized that even where there was much adjustment of attitudes and techniques to projected new conditions, there must still be much readjustment when the new conditions arise; because actual new conditions generally turn out to be different from the projected new conditions.

Conservatists have the habit of borrowing techniques from history without considering the attitudes that originally give impetus to the techniques. These truths have been presented in other settings and in other

132

terminology. But we must approach the great problems of civilization from many different angles in the hope that if one view does not register, then another view may accomplish the purpose.

Educators often debate whether the school or the home should perform a certain function. In most cases the answer is that it is a responsibility of both. Renewed activity by the school in a particular field does not in general cause the parents to complacently fold their arms in the attitude that their work has been taken up by another agency. When the school assumed a responsibility for the child's health, the parents also assumed a greater and more cooperative responsibility. It is both-and.

The both-and philosophy needs qualification. Too often teachers are given new tasks without regard to what shall be eliminated to make room for them. It is really the wrong application of the both-and philosophy. The essence of this philosophy is that there are many approaches to the solution of a problem and that many can work at it at the same time. It does not mean saddling more work on a person who already has enough.

The "experts" seem to be as much addicted as any to the false notion that proving the unsoundness of another's position automatically proves the soundness of their own. Naturally they do not say so and would deny the indictment; but their general attitude betrays them.

Right now there is much talk about forming, with the United Nations' sanction, a United States of Europe. We must be careful that we do not draw conclusions via the either-or philosophy. In thinking of the work of the United Nations as a whole, we must remember that there is much that must be done by subsidiary units. We, a United America, a United States of Europe, a United Russia, a United Asia, and a United Nations, all must work toward the same end.

We run into the same either-or philosophy when we consider the problem of student government. The same principles govern.

We are told that if we all contributed one tenth of our income to our religious organizations, they would have close to twenty billion dollars instead of the less than two billion that we do contribute. The implication is very plain. What a tremendous amount of good would have been done, and could be done, with those twenty billions! Anyone who makes such a statement should be ready to present a program for the proper use of that money. It assumes that if the church had enough money, it could do almost anything. It places an unhealthy emphasis on the power of money. It overlooks the teachings of history that worldly wealth has often been the ruination of many a church group. Money can be abused by churches as it is abused by people, primarily because the church is administered by people.

The church dare not assume that it has the consecration and that all it needs is the money.

In politics, our big lay task is the prevention of the conditions that call for legislative action. The politician—the term is used in a good sense—has the task of making the best of a bad situation. "There ought to be a law," should never be used by the laity as an excuse for their laxity.

Lippmann exhibits a distressing tendency to think in terms of "either this, or that." He believes every man must choose between a theology that is authoritarian and his own "high religion." Plainly he feels that the two are incompatible. I, of course, would call his "high religion" high theology. Still more distressing is his inability to see any middle ground. Certainly Jesus spoke against authoritarian theology and his "high religion." Lippmann talks of them as being opposites. Jesus speaks of them as having one origin. Neither is centered on my neighbor's good.

After we are committed to both-and, we must not make the mistake of expecting miracles from it. Even both-and can bite off more than it can chew. As an instance, I heard a preacher say that if we had contributed the money that is needed to build one battleship toward the Christian missionary movement in Japan, and had implemented it with consecrated missionaries, we might not have become involved in World War II. He, at least, recognized that money alone is not enough. He also recognized that the missionaries must be really, not just formally, consecrated. He overlooked the immense obstacle of lack of agreement on the part of us Christians as to what Christian living is.

Is it true that material advance often means spiritual retrogression? Is it true that we lay less stress on spiritual values than did our forefathers a hundred years ago? If the answer is yes, then we should go back to the ways of our forefathers. But I am convinced that the answer is no. The material feeds the spiritual and the spiritual feeds the material. Materialism goes hand in hand with spiritualism if a reasonable effort is made to make progress available to all. Too often it is you, *or* I, they *or* we, material *or* spiritual. We reason that since the past enjoyed fewer material comforts, therefore it excelled in spiritual things. It should be both-and.

If we look about us we shall see that, in general, people in the lowest economic levels are poor churchgoers. We are dodging our responsibility to them if we take the attitude that their economic plight is the result of the kind of people that they are; and that that also explains their religious attitude. No, they are merely demonstrating that the spirit does not spread well from a poor material point of reference.

There should be little room in the economic world for the "either-or"

134

philosophy. But economics is still too little possessed of a social conscience. We too often don't like to see our neighbors get anything because we feel that it will tend to take something away from us. We must feel strongly that we rise with our neighbors, not against them, or at their expense.

But our faith must go deeper than that. We must believe in justice to our neighbors even if it means a lesser—sometimes greater—injustice to us. If we must pinch, let us pinch where it will hurt the least. In a family, where we live one another's lives, this policy is carried out effectively. The extent to which we as a nation are one big family is the extent to which this policy is carried out. The implications for the family of nations are obvious.

Too often we take the attitude that we must choose between competition and cooperation. We must have both at one and the same time. Competition and cooperation are a great team. We adults should not try to hide the competitive spirit that we display so openly in sports. I like the picture of the boxer who helped his opponent to his feet so that he could knock him down again. How drab life would be if we had no one to emulate or excel! Let us quit thinking of competition and cooperation as being opposites. Yes, even conservatism and liberalism can be a great team. Both are necessary. Conservatism prevents chaos; liberalism assures progress.

A decade or two ago it was stylish for "progressive" teachers to make fun of teaching by the bell. Consciously or unconsciously their attitude was that others should conform to them. They seemed to be unconscious of the self-discipline that there is in meeting a deadline. Conforming is doing things "by the bell." And even among the most progressive, life activities consist mostly of conforming. Civilization advances by learning to do more and more things by the bell to release our creative energies for activity elsewhere.

Free enterprise should connote the ideas of competition *and* cooperation. Does the religious attitude favor competition, the desire to excel? Whether we are thinking in terms of excelling our own previous efforts or excelling our neighbors, religion is for it.

If this were not so, how could we find a religious sanction for competitive sports as we know them? The schools foster competitive sports. Is it religious? The big question is whether competitive sports tend to instil the religious attitude. I am firmly convinced that they do.

That person is considered a traitor to the spirit of play who does not try to win. We should just as frankly try to excel our neighbors; but in contests that give our neighbors a chance; in contests in which we do not have a running start or superior equipment. This, of course, means superior equipment that is not natively endowed or acquired by fair means.

This rivalry must always be held in bounds by the law of love. Is it not true that love knows no law? Yes; but that does not rule out law. The law must know love. This law of love, under another name perhaps, is the base of pure religion. The theologies of the world must rest on this foundation. And they must strive harder than ever to get together on details.

We all operate in circles; or, better still, spheres. There are no opposite spheres. But they may be overlapping. We have, or should have, competition and cooperation where they overlap. Let us be sure that it is a cooperative competition; and a competitive cooperation.

Of course, strictly speaking, spheres do not overlap. They merge or amalgamate. The sphere is really the ideal toward which we should aim. Our existence lies somewhere between a circle and a sphere. But let us not leave this without reminding ourselves that even circles are never opposites. They may be separate, overlapping, or one may be completely inside the other.

The choice is not always between "both-and" and "either-or." It may be between either one and "neither-nor."

Some people take the attitude that it is all right to do harmful things in a moderate degree. There is no moderate degree to harmful things. At the same time, we must recognize that there are many things that are beneficial in a moderate degree and harmful in a higher degree.

In a full consideration of this complex problem, we must look for the many concomitants of even the simplest acts.

10. NATURE

Nature is the ~~bogus.~~ *bogey man* To some poets nature is serene and peaceful; to others it is violent and vicious. To some, nature is satisfied with its share; to others it is always grasping for more.

The nature within us is very elusive, even to those of us who are comparative experts in self-scrutiny. It becomes a blur to us if we do not try to analyze the forces within. Nature has a logical place earlier in the book, but it seemed fitting to build up our strength and assurance before analyzing it; and then mostly in its manifestations.

Before man appeared on the scene all of life was nature. And this nature

136

was slowly but surely improving. This improving was definitely the result of the survival of the fittest.

This nature was ruthless in the acquisition of that which was needed to satisfy an immediate want. It was ever pushing upward. It was always *reaching for the light*. Nature was very ambitious—for itself. Its evil lay in its potential ability to increase in geometric proportion. It was too crowding. This very potentiality, under the proper guidance, can be the source of great good. It needs a stabilizer. We can furnish it.

The distressing thing is that we find this selfish nature within ourselves. And yet we should not be distressed. Nature is essential to our mortal existence. But it tries, often successfully, to take possession of us. We Christians call it the Old Adam. We call the spirit of God within us the New Adam. Nature is often evil relatively. Sin is in the *spirit* within us that does not curb the promptings of nature or give it the proper direction.

What is *human* nature? It is nature plus reason—imperfect reason. The Tree of the Knowledge of Good and of Evil marks the crossing of the hump. But it did not take imperfectly reasoning man long to detect more humps ahead—and uninviting landscape; drudgery. The gap between his reasoning and his work was seldom closed. Work tended to be considered a hindrance to enjoyment. Work was considered a curse. In general, work was that which did not *immediately* satisfy a want. Even in his earliest beginnings man was probably wishing for the life of animals, as some intelligent(?) people are doing today.

Some of the first things that reason learned *imperfectly* were that we can build ourselves up by pulling others down; that we can take things that others need now and store them for our future use; that we can drive suffering away by inflicting it on others; that to be supremely happy we must make others do our work for us; that the satisfaction of the carnal appetites is the supreme bliss.

I just read about a penniless foreign nobleman who came to this country and expected the same deference that his rank would have given him in the old country. Practically all of us Americans are agreed that the idea is silly. But fawning on parasites is not peculiar to the peoples of other countries. We Americans are also good at it.

All of us have speculated on what we would do if a certain opportunity for evil should present itself. In most cases when the opportunity presents itself, the still, small voice within saves us. That is why the still, small voice should be nurtured.

A generation ago it was customary for traffic officers to hide for the purpose of giving people more rope with which to hang themselves. They followed a natural instinct. Like all natural instincts, this is not all bad. It is an instinct that we, and traffic officers, cannot afford to discard entirely. But it should be the exception, not the rule. Prevention, not punishment, should be the dominant thought. The still, small voice is interested in the *prevention* of evil deeds.

Character insurance companies assert that there is absolutely no external way of telling who will, and who will not, remain honest in his trusts. Those of us who honestly examine our own hearts know why this is so. We do not know when we shall wrench ourselves loose from the promptings of the still, small voice.

Human nature has not changed in kind; it is changing in degree. Even today we are still engaged in learning how to channel nature to work for us. This takes the evil out of nature. Reason is *approaching* perfection.

There was no Devil when life was all nature. Reason introduced him. When our reason leads us to inhuman acts, then the Devil appears on the scene. A scapegoat always comes in handy.

Reason is constantly setting up, and enlarging on, codes of proper conduct. This is morality. It is guiding our conduct on the basis of what *others* think is right. This implies faith in *others*. The Holy Spirit is aborning. The Old Adam, still strong, is being driven into a corner.

Nature cannot subscribe to these codes of conduct. It is amoral. The Devil is found only in immorality. But amoral nature can be made to help set the stage for spriritual growth.

Children should be taught the difference between their evil, or sinful, natures and evil, or sinful, acts. They should be taught the need for substituting for their naturally evil desires, good deeds. Good deeds lead to good thoughts and the two gradually succeed in mastering evil thoughts. Evil thoughts can probably best be mastered if they are thought of as weeds. We should be keenly aware of the lack of abiding satisfaction there is in translating these thoughts into action. We must guard against sayng, "You might as well say it (or do it) since you are thinking it."

I am sometimes very bitter about the fate that gave others a better break in life, in certain respects, than me. I am not nearly so bitter about the fate that gave me a much better break than the average person. My attitude is not the religious attitude. I cannot completely control it. But I can guard against putting these selfish thoughts into practice. This selfish instinct is the key to our desire to perpetuate our special privileges. It furnishes the key to the question as to why the common people can better govern themselves than be governed by those of greater erudition.

I mentioned selfish persons. In a very real sense we are all selfish; but by selfish I mean persons who make no appreciable effort to curb their selfish natures. An unselfish person gives the sprit a chance to work on him.

The spirit is different from nature in that there are no limits of area and volume to its expansion. For nature, the earth is the limit. For the spirit, the universe is the limit. Too many of us allow nature to chain us to its limits.

This is not theory without practical application. We all know how flat is the satisfaction of merely our carnal appetites. Our spirit needs to expand and soar. It needs a vision. It is a vision.

Inhuman, natural (amoral), moral, religious: Human beings can be put into these four classes. When reason makes an improper application of what is recognized as good theory, it may lead to an inhuman act or attitude. This lowers us below the level of animals.

Have you ever heard of an animal as being sinful, covetous, or as destructive as man sometimes is? In the case of vicious animals it can be laid to the dawn of very imperfect reason.

The Tree of the Knowledge of good and of evil enables us to rise above the animal level, or to sink below it. We sink below it when we do not know when enough becomes too much; *or in our desire to hear and say something bad about others.*

When our reason leads us to an acceptance of standards of conduct that are considered correct, we are being morally correct. This *generally* is above the animal level.

Religion is making an entrance when we try to improve the standards, provided that the improvement is not primarily for our personal benefit. We have an example of humanity stumbling upward when striving for our selfish ends also happens to be what our neighbors need. Civilization's climb is slow because much of our progress is of this kind.

Let us note particularly that we are born natural. In the process of maturing we are inhuman, amoral (natural), moral, and religious. We acquire our personal label on the basis of which of the four traits holds the upper hand in the ordering of our lives. Only religion uses the upper hand wisely.

Despite the fact that I have drawn a sharp line between nature and human nature, I am going to use the terms indiscriminately, as is generally done. The division was merely to place the blame where it belongs—on imperfect reason. This enables us to apply the remedy in the proper spot.

Nature working on us mortals produces many an enigma. The enigmas are probably the result of the conflict between nature and the spirit within us.

In the earlier stages of civilization, people tend to regard all those outside their orbit as enemies. They do this despite repeated demonstrations right in their midst that as we get to know others the reasons for enmity gradually vanish.

The enigma lies in an exactly opposite human trait. At least it appears to be exactly opposite. It is the common attitude that those who were brought up and got their training and education outside our community are better than those who developed here at home.

As Jesus went about doing good, the big shots in each community, with rare exceptions, were opposed to him. The common people, with some exceptions, were for him.

The exceptions among the big shots were those who could view their own special privileges in something approaching a true light. The exceptions among the common people illustrate the enigma. The opposition was based on geography.

The common people of Judah and Samaria sometimes turned against him. The opposition was based on the fact that he was a Galilean, a kind of foreigner. The people, including the common people, of his home town of Nazareth, also turned against him. Why?

Perhaps a partial explanation is that we do not like to admit that those who got the same training that we got turned out better than we. We tend to assume the "What does he think he is?" attitude. And then we point to something in his past that we *hope* will place him in a bad light. Few of us have risen above the urge to build ourselves up in the estimation of our fellowmen by pulling others down.

"May the best man win!" is a slogan to which we subscribe almost one hundred percent when we apply it to two contestants in whom we have no personal stake. What a whale of a difference the personal stake makes in a controversy! Our suspicious attitude toward others is a reflection of our own selfish nature that too few of us take the trouble to analyze. When we come to a peculiarity of our natures that cannot be rationalized, it is up to us to give it proper consideration in determining courses of action.

To many of us wallow in the slough of selfishness under the pretext that "they all do it." We try to achieve security by trying to keep all we get. We do not have the faith to believe that we get by giving.

Anti-ism is a relic of the dark ages. In those days it was difficult to think of life as being anything but a struggle *against*. We must condition ourselves to thinking of life as being a struggle *with*. Let us be only against the *anti* in communism. Let us persist in giving credit to communism where credit is due.

As one step in that direction, let us remind ourselves that it is not communism, but human nature, that makes the ruling powers in Russia so ruthless. It is after all the basic feeling that there is not security enough for all; that we build ourselves up by pulling others down.

I do not like animal stories; stories that are designed to show how animals are superior to us humans. Such stories deny the power of the spirit over nature. Animals have no spirit as the term is here employed. They are all nature.

The enlightened self-interest group is the be-kind-to-animals type. They like animal stories. They are glad to help others provided they will be allowed to continue to look *down* on those that are helped. The helpees must learn to stay in their place.

It would be unfair to say that Plato did not recognize nature as a force to be subdued or directed. It *is* fair to say that he did not properly gauge its strength, persistence, and devious ways of operating. He thought that intelligent people could be educated to rise above their selfish natures; that they would be in a better position to say what was good for the less intelligent than the less intelligent themselves. The evidence is that it is not so.

We all, regardless of degree of intelligence, tend to point our logic in the direction of our interests, which in turn are generally directed toward our special privileges. In other words, we cannot think straight when our own special privileges are involved. We tend to believe what we want to believe.

When I was fourteen years old I read a weekly series called "The Liberty Boys of '76." I thought they were true despite the fact that the Liberty Boys fought in every battle of the Revolution. My main reason for believing them true was that I wanted to believe them true.

"You cannot change human nature." The persons who say this may be technically correct, from a short-range viewpoint. But it is nearly always used to justify a do-nothing policy. There is almost no end of illustrations that we can use to show that much that we do, or do not do, is the result of custom, not the promptings of nature. Reason, custom, and love can be great allies in giving proper dircetion to our natural impulses.

Nature is a great regimenter. It regiments the conservative. This is just another way of saying that it regiments all of us in varying degrees. The nature that is unguided by the spirit tries to put a stop to all spiritual growth. Nature must not be allowed to guide us. Here is a case of the blind leading those who are capable of seeing.

Nature, like the spirit, craves a sense of security. It thinks it finds it in grasping for everything within reach, and sitting on top of that which it cannot use. It is human nature to take the attitude that for a thing to have value it must have substance.

Children also crave this sense of security. Few children want to move from one community to another. Their desire for a sense of security is stronger than the quest for new adventure.

A child is naturally generous until he discovers that his generosity costs him something. The next stage is as far as many of *us* go. This stage harbors the feeling that we cannot give without losing as much as we give. It is the attitude that we must choose between ourselves and the other fellow. It is the "either-or" philosophy. It is the attitude that parents often assume in trying to impart to their children a philosophy of life.

Old folks like to talk about how they brought up their children better than today's parents do. Their talk is almost invariably in terms of how they repressed them and piled on tasks. It is fair in a case like this to take a look at the children that they brought up. Would we want our children to be like their children?

We must learn to look on nature more in terms of how it is to be guided and put to use for good rather than repressed. We must recognize how important to the children is the sense of having some choice. Let us note in the natural world about us that when we pull out a weed, a product of nature, we make room for a useful product of nature to grow. Nature cannot be ignored in our hearts either.

What is the religious attitude toward the play instinct in children, and adults? When Jesus set up children as examples, he was undoubtedly thinking of them in terms of their natural play instincts and not in terms of what their parents generally tried to make of them. Does anyone believe that he favored robbing children of the good times they have at play? Can we reconcile the doctrine of the natural depravity of the human heart with the promotion of the play instinct in children? It is easy if by depravity we mean selfishness.

The Puritans believed in thwarting the selfish natural instincts. We believe in directing them. What is play but the doing of things that bring immediate satisfactions?

Let us turn to those who should be the least susceptible to the promptings of nature—the philosophers. When the philosopher says, "All I know is that I know nothing," he is generally trying to show off his superiority. Pride in humility is false pride. What we need is people who are humble in their humility. Philosophers take great delight in tearing down what other philosophers have built up. They are following an instinct of nature. Will Durant amply illustrates this in his *Story of Philosophy*.

I hope I shall never be guilty of tearing down for its own sake. I try to tear down where is seems imperative that another structure be erected.

Those of us who have tried have discovered how difficult it is to overcome the feeling of natural superiority to less advanced races. Our superiority is not a natural one. It is an inherited one—or a phantom.

The Pharisees of old were a superior people. They also lacked the important quality of real humility. We all know where Jesus placed them. We should not lose sight, however, of the fact that behind this natural feeling of superiority is wishful thinking, which is also natural. It helps to explain our fear that other people's wrongs may prevail over our rights.

There is great need for a study of the pre-war German people and nation. Many observers have remarked that as individuals they were excellent people to get along with. They perhaps come closer than any other European nation to exemplifying the virtues that we teach—except one. That is the virtue of real humility. They felt themselves superior to other *peoples*.

Leaders in German thought had fed this feeling of superiority. The result naturally became a feeling on the part of the German people that they were collectively the "World Shepherd" predestined to lead us sheep into greener pastures.

In our pride we Americans sometimes say that we are the most philanthropic nation on the face of the earth. We point to the *fact* that we give more than any other nation. We should ask ourselves whether we are giving more *of ourselves* than other nations. We should give more consideration to Jesus' evaluation of the widow's mite. We have a right to question the philanthropy of the man who often talks about his philanthropy—and that goes for nations, too.

It is high time for us as a nation to start thinking about our fellow nations on the subject of balance of trade and other nations' monetary debts to us. We often call the people of debtor nations indolent at the same time that we do not let them do for us as much as we are doing for them. When they try to sell as much to us as we are selling to them, we object that it would be bad for our economy. *Their* economy all too often does not concern us. We are *wielding* the upper hand unwisely; in fact, maliciously. And cartoons that portray the indolence of other nationals certainly do not contribute to world amity.

Jesus found the employer class most in need of humbling. His parable of the generous employer who paid all alike shows that he recognized a generous impulse in that group when he saw it.

Lincoln Steffens studied corruption in local and state politics. His conclusion was the same as Jesus': that the greatest malefactors were the "honest,

143

upright" leaders of the community. These "honest, upright" men were always the bitterest opponents of reform. Few people can view their special privileges in the proper perspective. Fewer still even recognize their special privileges as such. Such people, for practical purposes, deny the brotherhood of man. Saying that we are brothers under the skin is no help if we keep it under the skin. Keeping it under the skin is rank hypocrisy.

Perhaps it is not too much to say that all superiority complexes have a core of inferiority complex. Some people's main objective in life seems to be the application of the veneer of superiority. And the veneer can often be fittingly called special privilege.

What is the religious approach to the evil that is within our own hearts and our pupils'? It should consist of a frank appraisal of our own inmost thoughts and desires. This should not be for the purpose of pouring them into the ears of others, but to convince *ourselves* that we have need for continuing humility. Children should recognize that these evil thoughts and desires are not peculiar to themselves; and that, if recognized, they can be controlled.

My experience is that when teachers go back to college classes, they generally proceed to cheat at a faster clip and with more finesse than their pupils. It can also be easily observed that those who cheat the most are generally those who simply cannot understand what is wrong with children nowadays.

Shall we let the theologians and pseudo-religionists escape? I have particular reference to those professors of religion who get up in their pulpits and cast aspersions on the motives of those who disagree with them, or who do not live as they do. They are too proud of their humility. Theologians, succumbing to their natural bents, often take greater delight in flaunting their superior knowledge than in trying to understand God and to interpret Him to His followers.

Begging the question seems to fit in well here, because professors of religion are so expert at it. It is a first cousin to casting aspersions. It is basically the attitude of "Of course I am right, and of course you are wrong. Can you not see that I am led by the spirit?" Many people stay away from church on account of such preachers.

The idle rich *sense* the essential dignity of the man who toils. That is why they are so panicky about all efforts to give him something resembling an even break. They feel, and rightly, that if the common man is given an even break, they can no longer be parasites. Certainly their approach is not religious. They are children of nature. They are not doing enough of a constructive nature to the heritage that has been bequeathed to them. They are like pampered children. They are not conditioned to seeing in its true light the "something-for-nothing" that is theirs. Perhaps this helps to explain why we are prouder of our background than of what we have achieved through toil. Perhaps it adds up to just another effort to assert a natural right to our heritage. What we do get is another example of the self-destructiveness of selfishness.

It is surprising how many speakers and writers today venture the statement that higher wages mean higher prices, and that the net gain to labor is nothing. They do not come forward with the equally true statement that higher prices *should* mean higher wages. They carefully refrain from making the observation that in the last few years prices have risen more than wages. They are children of nature.

When Jesus spoke about taking the lowest seat, he was undoubtedly thinking of the common human failing of improperly evaluating our own qualifications and rights. He did not hesitate to speak about his own qualifications and rights—and duties.

What about this very human failing, that perhaps all of us have, of being much prouder of our abilities than of our accomplishments? Perhaps all of us would rather have it said of us that we could have done a thing if we had tried, than that we tried very hard, but it was too much for us. We must recognize this peculiarity of our natures. Perhaps the explanation is that we are proud beyond measure of those gifts that seem to distinguish us from the animals.

Are adults more conservative than children? Are civilized people more conservative than primitives? Robinson in *The Mind in the Making* goes into this very deeply. And he comes out with the observation that the less civilized people are, the more conservative they are. If savages do not seem conservative to us, it is because their conservative ways seem radical to us. Why is man naturally conservative? Because nature recognizes no guiding spirit. It fails to recognize that much of this spirit dwells in *man* and is to be used by man to solve new problems as they arise.

Young people tend to be more conservative than old people because they have learned imperfectly the principle of living within the rules of the game. They do not recognize that laws were made for man, not man for the laws. They are more *conservative* in their interpretation of laws *that they accept* than are grown-ups.

I am not satisfied with the result of my investigation of the question of whether youth is conservative, liberal, or radical. I am thinking particularly of people between 21 and 30. I am picking 21 because it is the beginning of the voting age. It is well known that from this group came

Franklin D. Roosevelt's strongest support. A goodly part of his program was security for old age. Is not perhaps their adventurous spirit but the quest for a security they do not yet feel? Their seeming lack of conservatism is in the field where they have not yet accepted the rules of the game. They have not learned to temper justice with mercy—to use a popular expression. I would prefer to say that they have not given the word justice sufficient flexibility.

I take the attitude that we mortals start life almost one hundred percent conservative. After our education is completed, or rather, after it has reached its limit, more than ninety percent of us are still conservative. I see no evidence that education has made us teachers less conservative than others.

Analyzing prejudices is the first step in eliminating them. We shall do well to analyze our personal prejudices of the past that we have overcome. Such analysis should help us dispel prejudices that we still hold. Here are some of my past prejudices. When I was ten years old, I had never seen a foreigner, a Republican, a Catholic, a Jew, a Negro, or a Chinaman. To me they were all a bunch of crooks except the Negro. My literary heritage explained my attitude toward the Negro. My feelings were shared by the adult population with which I lived. In fact, I merely reflected their feelings.

Here are feelings I carried into my young manhood. I thought foreigners were incapable of harboring the finer instincts that I fondly imagined were commonplace with us. I thought that it would be forever impossible for Americans and Chinese to meet on the same intellectual level.

Children have prejudices, but they were not born with them. Prejudice is pre-judging on the basis of irrelevant evidence. They cannot be blamed for having prejudices when we consider how guilty we grown-ups are. It is not unusual for parents to vent their spleen through their children as stooges.

What is the difference between prejudice and intolerance? The prejudiced person is often addicted to "proving" by analogy. He often gives the things of the spirit a material measure that does not apply. He forgets, or never knew, that analogy never proves; it merely illustrates. He places too much weight on surface evidence. He does not dig sufficiently for cause and effect. He deliberately avoids evidence that would tend to disprove his point. One is tempted to say that there is a close correlation between prejudice and ignorance until we recall the blind prejudice of the "educated" holders of great special privileges.

An intolerant person takes the attitude that, since he is right, no one else can possibly be right. He gives too little consideration to the possibility that he may be wrong, or that perhaps both are right, or partly right. He gives little or no consideration to the fact that the opposition probably is just as certain that they are right as he is. The Pharisees "knew" that they were right and that this young upstart by the name of Jesus was all wrong. So they did not see why such a heretic should be allowed to continue. A compendium of what the "best" people of Europe thought of Washington, Jefferson, and their ilk would be very sobering for those of us who view the current scene with that superior air. The intolerant person gives little heed to the principle that everyone who stands up for what he thinks is right is entitled to consideration.

There is no particular merit in being tolerant about things that to our minds matter little. Tolerance is worthy of the name only if it is on issues on which we feel very deeply. If teachers and parents were to set an example of tolerance and lack of prejudice, the pupils would acquire it almost automatically. This is true of all the virtues. Example is the best teacher. Prejudiced and intolerant persons err too much on the side of trusting others too little. Love for our neighbors errs on the side of trusting a little too much. This is going more than half-way. This is the margin on which the world moves forward and upward.

We all have a streak of stubbornness that can best be corrected if we try to analyze it. We are sure that we have chosen an unwise course or method, but we are too stubborn to change. We bump into a door and we kick the door. Feeding our stubborn nature becames more important to us than our own welfare. What is the basic cause of this stubbornness? It is an indirect protest against the many inevitabilities of life. It says in effect, "How long must I bear this injustice?" Gradually we should learn not to rail against the inevitable.

Parents here have an enormous obligation which they too often fumble. They refuse to recognize their children's limitations. The child would rather create the impression that he is not learning because he does not apply himself, than that he is too "dumb" to learn it. Parents are the same way.

Teachers often hear parents say, "Johnny is bright enough, but he will not study." They are right about the not studying, but they miss the point that, in most cases, the main trouble is that Johnny is not bright enough.

Let us not make too much of the story of how Thomas A. Edison's teacher told the mother to take him out of school because he could not learn. Certainly there is danger in this direction, and all possibilities should be explored.

But still more certainly one of the main causes of juvenile delinquency

147

is the insistence of parents that their children perform the impossible. This persistence gradually builds up an inferiority complex which gradually acquires a veneer of superiority complex.

Parents must steel themselves to the need for taking the word of an expert third party on the question of their children's abilities. They should give more consideration to the principle that positions should be prepared for, and filled, by those who can best qualify for them. It is a hard pill to swallow; but swallowing it will turn out to be the lesser of two evils. The limitations of our native endowments are stone walls that simply must be recognized.

Why do parents and teachers often take such an unfair attitude toward children? Not because they are parents and teachers, but in spite of it. The big reason is that they are human beings not yet sufficiently touched by the divine spark. If we parents and teachers had enough real religion, the problems of maladjustment would practically disappear in a generation.

Let us take a look at the history of education. What stands out? Certainly one thing is the tyrannical teacher. What will stand out when the teachers in the year 2000 study the teachers of 1950? The same, in less degree. The verdict will be, in effect, that we gradually assumed the religious attitude, regarding our pupils as people and neighbors entitled to as much consideration as adults.

It is not at all unusual to find a group of adults getting together and agreeing to do certain things individually by a given deadline. The deadline arrives, and in many cases the work is still undone. Those who did not meet the deadline are generally those who say, "Why doesn't someone do something?"

Our problem is to guide our natural urgings into the proper channels. Children portray these urgings much better than do we adults. What we need to do is find these forces in our own lives. Perhaps it is not wrong to say that all the drive is in nature. The direction is in the spirit.

Follow through; be as good at the end as you were at the beginning. I notice a distinct tendency on the part of the writers of our best books to ease up in the last chapter or two. One reason is a natural tendency to ease up toward the end; a desire to get finished; tiredness. Another important reason is a desire to sermonize in terms that are too sweeping. They often are peculiarly inept in making applications to the current scene. They spread out too much, like nature.

More thought and study should be given to the theory that nature tends to improve itself; that desirable traits are more likely to be transmitted than undesirable; that children tend to have higher I.Q's than the average of their parents. I do not believe that the present generation has a lower I.Q. than the preceding generation, because the higher birth rate in the low group is counteracted by the tendency of nature to improve.

We need to remind ourselves repeatedly that nature was moving in a generally upward direction before man appeared on the scene—but ever so slowly! We do not have the patience to depend on eons to effect the change, as did nature. Man's native ingenuity speeds the process. The divine spark speeds it even more. It is no exaggeration to say that the divine spark accelerates nature's progress ten-thousand-fold.

This again points to the conviction that "all things work together for good to them that love God," including nature.

We definitely are all children of nature. But we are constantly striving or should be, for adoption into the kingdom of the spirit. This is religion, viewed from another angle. We are sons of men and sons of God.

We must have faith that the world is generally surging upward. Otherwise we should have to conclude that God created a failure. A study of history can give us that faith. I said "can," because we have many history teachers who have not caught that vision.

Ludwig bemoans the life of pure contentment that the natives left behind after they were discovered by the white men. Then he proceeds to describe the life that they left behind them. I shall use only one illustration. The men did nothing but build houses and fight. There were three women to every man because in every war, every man of the conquered enemy was killed. This tells a tale of greater devastation and woe than the worst that World War II could produce.

The trend of all existence, as we know it, is from chaos to order—and we are part of that trend. Are we doing our part to help it along? Or are we fighting it?

11. CHILDREN—THE JUNIOR PARTNERS

This chapter is introduced because of the importance of children as junior partners. Everything written here could easily have fitted into one of the other chapters. It also serves as a refreshing interlude to the surrounding chapters. This explains why this chapter is short. Children will be flitting in and out throughout the chapters.

Perhaps every teacher insists that he teaches pupils, not subjects. The remark has become so commonplace that we are prone to take the attitude that we are all living up to it. Those of us who really live up to it are often viewed with suspicion by the other members of the teaching corps.

There are still many teachers who approach their teaching subjects as so much to be forced into the children in a given length of time. Children's likes and and dislikes, gifts and shortcomings, are almost entirely disregarded. Many teachers still take the attitude that if children detest a certain thing, that is sufficient reason for them to do it.

This does not rule out the performance of unpleasant tasks in the classroom. It does rule out the hard way until the possibilities of other ways have been fully probed. It should be recalled here that material progress in the upward march of civilization is dependent on finding easier ways of doing things for the purpose of finding time for other and new things. This thought should be ever with us as we plan our work for the classroom, and outside.

We adults should occasionally ask ourselves this question, "How would I treat this child if he were as big and strong as I, and retained his present faculties?" An easy answer would be that the world would soon go to rack and ruin. Admittedly this might be an intolerable condition. This projection will serve its purpose if it will teach us to use the words, "You must!" very sparingly.

In the aggregate, teachers are more unreasonable in their attitude toward pupils than pupils are toward their teachers. The teachers have the upper hand. The upper hand is generally the most unreasonable.

This should be a good place to consider why children almost universally do things behind the teacher's back that they would not do in the open. We like to tell them that we teachers are brave; we do our things in the open. We do not admit that we have lined up behind us authority, the parents, the adult world, the police, heritage, the law, the courts, tradition, physical might (except in the upper grades and high school), and mental maturity.

By what are pupils backed? By other kids.

When we speak about the inhumanity of children toward children, it is a serious question whether we should blame it on their natural bent or on their imitation of us adults. Perhaps the greatest difference between the inhumanity of children and that of adults is that the children have not yet applied the veneer of respectability.

Children are just as sensitive to unjust and unpleasantly true criticism as we are. We are often fooled by the thin shell of callousness that they are using to hide their fluid emotions. We all know how easily these emotions can break through this shell.

Our shell is thicker and more pliant. That is why we tend to boil within instead of exploding like children. We are not more sensitive than children. The fact is that we force children to swallow what we are not willing to swallow.

Are children people? They are; and they are entitled to at least as much consideration as we adults. This does not mean that they should receive the same treatment. Neither does it mean that we should act like children when dealing with them. They want to imitate adults, not children.

Once upon a time I walked up to a teacher's desk. "Well, what do you want?" he snapped, without looking up. The expression on his face when he discovered that he had snapped at a teacher and not at a pupil is something that I shall never forget. He immediately did an about-face and proceeded to exude mush from his whole being.

The attitude of the adult world toward the juvenile world is perhaps the best single index to the kind of progress civilization has made. The adult world is in the majority and the majority is increasing. It has the upper hand. Is it using it wisely?

It is; at least more nearly so than has ever been the case in the past. It is really beginning to regard this emerging world as including the junior end of the partnership.

Of the worlds to which we are more or less strangers, the child world is closest to us. If we cannot form a competent liaison with this world, how can we expect to penetrate other worlds?

A man's attitude toward the child world—an oppressed world—is perhaps the best index of the kind of man he is.

There is a great deal of dwelling nowadays on the fact that a generation or two ago children did things for their parents; now parents are doing things for their children. Of the two, which is better—or worse?

First of all, World Wars I and II were *not* brought on by the children of this generation. Their job is to undo our damage.

Civilization took a real step upward when parents—who always have the upper hand—started to think more about their duties to their children and less about their children's duties to them—just as it was a great step upward when employers started to think of their duties to their employees.

I make bold to say that he who has the upper hand and refuses to think of the welfare of those under him is a parasite. Parasites can well be defined as people who are very much exercised about the danger of spoiling people

151

by helping them. What we need is a crusade to put an end to the worship of parasites.

Children are not little rebels. They are more conservative than we are. Children are very strong for observing the letter of the law. They are more interested in being technically correct than in being fair. Their idea of fairness is abiding by the rules. They seldom question the rules, except occasionally when they are personally involved. Their rebellion comes from their failure to recognize a course of action as being according to the rules of the game.

It is very difficult to teach social justice to children. To them injustice consists in not observing the rules. It is very difficult for them to see that the rules may be unjust. They feel that a rule that all must abide by under a given set of circumstances must be fair. They fail to see that differing circumstances may make it impossible to mete out justice by the application of the rule.

Give a group of children a hypothetical case in which the application of the rules of the game would result in plain miscarriage of justice. They will almost invariably stand up for rules, not justice. I have tried this many times, always with the same result. We must teach them to think of rules as being primarily boundaries within which we can operate freely, rather than think of rules as being straitjackets. Naturally there will be rules within rules.

My conviction here is bolstered by my recollection of the type of thinking I engaged in even in my early manhood. I recall that when I was a victim of injustice through the application of the rules, it never occurred to me to question the fairness of the rules.

There are many people who carry that kind of thinking with them to their graves. They, like children, are always trying desperately hard to fit into a pattern. They are not creative.

Is this to imply that children are not creative? Not at all. It does imply that they need special guidance in being made to see new fields in which they can put their creative talents to work.

Young people are not addicted to old ways of doing things simply because to them there are no old ways. All ways are new. In that respect they can view new ideas more judiciously than older people.

We must try to make children see that the rules of men are not necessarily the law of God; that rules are made for men and children, not men and children for the rules. Shall we add here that since rules are for men, they should be applied only when they can be of service? The answer is yes if we consider all the individuals that are affected by the rule.

I have seen professional instructors teach volleyball to small children by the same rules that adults go by. The result has been a game that consists largely of serving. I have changed the rules to make them fit the maturity of the pupils and the result has been a game that is interesting for all pupils. Teachers must feel free to adjust and adapt.

Children should feel that we do not like to hand out punishment; that it is at best a necessary evil. If punishment is in the form of an assigned task, it should by all means have value in its performance that the child will recognize. Punishment should be educational by continuing the task of education.

I realize that from a purely logical point of view, a strong case can be made out against requiring work of an educational nature as punishment. We can dispose of it by adhering to logic, if we apply logic to conditioning factors. One of these is the attitude children, and all of us, assume when we are asked to perform a useless task.

Deprivation of privileges should be reserved for those who refuse to perform an assigned task; or who plainly are not improving their attitudes through the half-hearted performance of an assigned task.

Here again we should look into our own hearts to try to ascertain how we would react if someone did to us what we are doing to the pupils. Perhaps still better is a recalling of our school days for the purpose of determining what teacher attitudes we appreciated and what we did not.

Children must not feel that they are performing other people's tasks. That is drudgery. That is the fault with many tasks assigned to children in the home. Children must not feel that parents are deliberately trying to make things difficult for them. That is exactly what parents are often trying to do: build up other people's characters by assigning tasks to these people.

Big and little, large and small, important and unimportant, all are relative terms. There are such things as big mice and little elephants. Many a thing that is little from our viewpoint looms very large from the child's viewpoint. We can never understand a child's problems if we make no attempt to apprehend his perspective. Many a task that to us seems small is not small in the child's thinking.

Children subscribe to many conventions within their own circles that seem very foolish to us. Those of us who are least tolerant about the matter are generally those who are very slavish in our adherence to conventions within our own circles. If we are not willing to overstep our bounds because children consider the restrictions foolish, then we should not expect them to overstep their bounds because we consider their restrictions foolish. If we fall short here, we have not yet accepted children as neighbors.

Parents help children build up their characters when they are setting examples of genuine self-discipline; and when they are helping their children find the work that is peculiar to their abilities and interests. This is the opposite of repression. There is too much thinking in terms of repressing children and too little opening up of new avenues for them .The parents' big perennial problem should not be the bringing up of their children, but bringing up themselves.

It is very difficult for us to become adjusted to the fact that children have needs that are just as real for them as ours are for us. We feel that since many of their needs are transitory we need not be much concerned about filling them. Are not many of our adult needs also transitory? To us our needs are more transitory than a child's needs are to him.

When we consider how we pamper our own desires, we also should consider the child's desires more than we do. In other words, we adults should think more in terms of our duties and the child's rights. This, if started early enough, will generally preclude a delinquency problem.

An unskilled adult can easily turn the foregoing into pampering. Naturally, care must be taken that the child does not form the habits that the adult is trying to avoid.

Should children be taught to speak up frankly for their own rights? Perhaps the best answer is that that is something they can do without being taught. They need instruction and example in the attitude they are to assume in presenting their cases.

Can we learn from children? Children live in a world of wonders. Do we? Or have we lost faith? If we lack faith, we have lost it along the way. We were born with it.

Youth envisions a great adventure around every corner. Are we too old to dream? We should gradually begin to realize as we grow up that the most permanently satisfying adventures are adventures in the spirit.

It is dismaying to hear people repeatedly tell children and adolescents that they should not wish to grow into manhood and womanhood, because that is the period of worry and suffering and onerous responsibilities and frustration and futility and despair. What a picture to present to the children! Just as though creative activity ended with childhood!

But the children persist in wishing that they were grown-ups. But they cannot help being influenced by what they hear the adult population say.

Adults often overlook the fact that children do not want the Wonder World handed to them on a platter. They want to explore and find it for themselves. They do not always follow the right leads, and they do need direction, but the exploring must be done by them.

154

The "child-centered" school very often tries to hand out predigested food. There is a principle in child psychology that is often overlooked in these "child-centered" schools. I shall illustrate it with the picture of the dog who looks up at his master as if to plead, "Give me something to do." Children delight in performing tasks assigned outside themselves. It is needless to go into details here as to the many pitfalls to be avoided. They can be found through a study of the methods of the teacher who does nothing but assign tasks.

Most to be pitied are those who live, move, and have their being without a blueprint, frame of reference, anchoring point, aim, or sense of direction. Poor aim is generally better than no aim.

Children expect us to do more than let them do as they please. They also enjoy doing, within reason, what other people please. They expect mature adults to set up major blueprints; but they ask for the liberty to operate with a great deal of freedom within these major blueprints.

Freedom within limits is more liberating than freedom without limits. Freedom must be freedom from something. Freedom must be able to view with satisfaction the thing from which it is freed.

Freedom must also be freedom *for* something. The "for" leads to new anchoring points.

Let us be on our guard against exalting parental love unless we are definitely agreed on what we are talking about. Parental love, if it is to deserve the name of love, must be centered in the child's welfare based on the child's interests, abilities, and capacities. Such love is not primarily concerned with the vocation the child will choose, but rather with what kind of man, or woman, the child will be; and they get to be real men and women by learning to be real boys and girls.

We are always setting an example for the child. He is always watching us and trying to imitate us. Sometimes he imitates too well. He tends, however, as he grows older, to discriminate between things that are worthy and things that are not worthy of imitation. In most cases he grows up to outshine his parent. If we do not believe this, then we do not believe that we live in a world that is progressing.

12. PLAY

This chapter continues in the spirit of the one on children. Play and children are both very important. It is to make us keenly conscious of the important role that play has in the child's life, and should have in our lives, that this chapter is presented as a separate topic.

Play is spontaneous imitation. It is make-believe. It is doing the task at hand out of pure enjoyment—doing it for its immediate satisfactions. It is this last definition that I have in mind when I speak about making play out of work.

Making play of work promotes efficiency. Promoting efficiency has the sanction of religion.

Play is natural. It is another example of what we can do with nature if we use it right.

The right to play is in the child's Bill of Rights. Adults should exercise it, too. The play instinct should not be lost sight of as the child gradually shifts to work. Work can be made play.

This must never be used as an excuse for shirking work that is onerous. No one will ever succeed in making play out of all work.

Life is a quest—a never-ending quest. But it is not a fruitless quest. We achieve goals that point to new goals. Their hue gradually becomes more spiritual and less material. We gradually get in tune with the infinite in the spirit of play.

Every summer most people attend at least one reunion. They engage in sports. Almost invariably they say, "We should engage in more sports."

They would come closer to the core of the truth if they said, "We should do more of our things *in the spirit of play,* as do children."

Children like to emulate us adults. But on the question of play they will not give in. They will have their play. There is only one plausible conclusion: They need it badly. They need it to feed their spirit. Children suit the action to the thought much more than do we adults.

And, let me repeat, children naturally shift from play to work as they grow older. Or they may do even better. They may learn to make play of work.

As children grow older, they must more and more school themselves to the need for plunging into a task even though the immediate satisfactions are lacking. The wise person will seek to build up these immediate interests.

The true play spirit does away with the habit of doing the hard things first. It does the most interesting things first and builds up interest in the tasks that are to follow. When we think of doing the hard things first, we are thinking of tasks, not play. We should so adjust our tasks, or adjust our attitude toward them, that we find immediate satisfactions in the performing of them. People who at a distance appear to be hard-working men are generally people who have learned to make play out of work. They project

156

themselves into their work instead of keeping it at a distance.

We must all have goals; but there is such a thing as concentrating on a goal so intensely that the immediate task becomes very tiresome and boring.

We can have goals that are only a short distance ahead or just around the corner, or we can have goals that are years away. Calling attention to the need for having long-range goals should not imply that they should *consume* our interest. There should be many intermediate and immediate goals. Goals that are nearby enable us to take an interest in tasks that otherwise would be boring.

Why are nearly all boys aspiring to be great athletes? Is it because they feel that after a hard grind they will be in the public eye? No, it is primarily because the road itself to the top looks very inviting to them.

We adults can learn much from this. How much drudgery we give to our work because we refuse to see any adventure in the task at hand!

We need more philosophers who, while having a clear picture of the long-range goals, concentrate on the more immediate goals; philosophers who teach us to play. Whenever I read of philosophers in ivory towers, I picture a philosopher in a dungeon. He is not free.

It is the people with the play instinct who rise to the task at hand, clear away debris that is within reach, and so make the task of those who follow easier. They are the ones who can afford to take an occasional look back, with justifiable pride, on what they have left behind.

Have we teachers learned this lesson? We consume too much nervous energy wishing that the period, or session, or day, or week, or month, or semester, or term were over. Perhaps I should have added "or life." What an example! The teacher's attitude too often all too plainly is, "Let's get this distasteful task out of the way, and some day perhaps we shall be able to enjoy ourselves."

Once again we are faced with the question of whether we are giving our children enough of a fruitful nature to imitate. Are we willing to make the drastic adjustments in our own lives that we expect of our children? Too often not. Too often children imitate us to the extent of dreading work as much as we do. Children can be led to move from play to work without the unpleasant coercion that too many of us consider inevitable.

This is all a very beautiful picture of the beautiful present, but what happens to the beautiful present when competition rears its ugly head? The right kind of competition will help to make the beautiful present more beautiful; and competition need not have an ugly head.

Life is a constant striving to excel. So is play. We adults should frankly strive to excel in the spirit of play. Children delight in knocking one another down and picking each other up. They compete and help at the same time.

In an effort to give this idea a practical twist in the classroom, I often try to impress on my pupils that they should cooperate in their lessons about nine-tenths of the time and compete the other tenth.

Some educators believe that we should not stress the competitive spirit in the classroom; in fact that it should be eliminated entirely. They are the "all-or-nothing" type. They are not very adjustable.

Yes, they will go so far as to say that children should be taught to lay the stress on beating their best previous effort, but there they should stop.

Let us turn to bowling to clarify the issue. It is very easy, physically, to bowl alone. We can concentrate on beating our best previous record. But do we? Very seldom, and then generally only because no opponent is available. Is the desire to select an opponent to vanquish irreligious? Not at all. It is in the very spirit of religion.

Is the bowler generally glad to help his opponent improve his game? Yes. Does the bowler delight in bowling against an opponent who always loses? No. He would rather bowl against an opponent who always wins. There is too much looking back in continued static success.

This is the kind of competition that we should strive to build up in the classroom. Mediocre bowlers are seldom jealous of the success of the top performer. They select as goals, performers who are just a little ahead of them. Children in the classroom should be taught that this is a desirable attitude.

Children voluntarily or involuntarily condition themselves to this line of adjustment. I have seen children in the height of ecstasy because they achieved a bare, passing seventy. I have also seen children in the doldrums because they dropped to ninety-two. This is as it should be. The joys of life are not restricted to those of us who are highly endowed.

Let us turn to competitive sports. Superficial thinkers on the subject are very prone to think that sports do more harm than good. They think that competitive sports create poor sportsmanship. But do they? It is more probable that they merely expose to the public gaze that which has always been there. Watching children at play makes it all the more apparent that contests merely bring to the fore selfish traits that children already possess.

Shall we consider here competition with my neighbor? Can this be best considered under the heading of play? It can be if we think of the competition that is engaged in in the spirit of play. Vying with my neighbor in the spirit of play enables me to see and sympathize with his problems and aspirations in a way that would otherwise be impossible. Nevertheless, I shall leave my neighbor with this brief mention in the assurance that he will continue to occupy the stage in the pages to follow.

Jesus says that the Kingdom of Heaven is for those of us who become like little children. Of what childish traits was he thinking? We can best answer this by studying children and the play instinct.

In the spirit of play, children strive to emulate those who are definitely above them. They are not jealous of the superiority of those whom they try to emulate. They strive to excel where that possibility exists. They make play of work by choosing objectives that are close at hand. They live in a world of wonders. Has that world vanished for us? They do not hide their enthusiasms. They are frank.

This last sentence in particular suggests that there is great need for refining all these play instincts. This is a job for us adults. But we must be very careful that we do not confuse refining with smothering.

I do not know whether there is etymological kinship between play and pleasure, but I do know that they are inseparable. Or are they? Is all play accompanied by pleasure? Yes. Is all pleasure accompanied by play? Apparently pleasure is basic. Play is *an* agent.

What about pleasures that cloy? It would be better to call them pleasures that cease. We are here making pleasure objective, when it is intrinsically subjective. Pleasure is not in the thing that is supposed to produce it. It is in the subject that acts upon the thing.

It is this confusion that makes it so difficult for youth to appreciate that old age also has its pleasures. They think too much of the outward acts and objects that produce their own pleasures. They do not appreciate that it is these outward things that cloy. They do not appreciate that these external accessories become less and less necessary as the years go by; that they, in fact, tend to become a hindrance to pleasure.

Is it any wonder that youth cannot understand these things when we consider how many middle-aged and old people do not understand them either? Too many persist in concentrating their attention on the externals that are gradually slipping out of their grasp. They think too little about the things that are left and about the new things that are taking, or should be taking, their place.

Many of us allow our lives to be marred, sometimes ruined, by our attitude toward forbidden pleasures. We tend to feel that we shall never be satisfied until these pleasures are ours. This is particularly true of young people. They waste too much time brooding over pleasures they cannot enjoy.

159

There should come a time in our lives when we shall be able to bask in the pleasure of beholding young people enjoy the physical pleasures without regretting that those pleasures are no longer ours. It is because so many of us oldsters are maladjusted that children cannot look for much guidance from us.

Children should be frequently reminded that the withholding of one pleasure can open new vistas that might otherwise be forever closed to them.

A lady wrote to a doctor, "Dear Doctor, what shall I do with my gray hair?" Back came the reply, "Admire it." This is the spirit of play.

Old people too seldom look within for pleasure. This is ossification.

The best preparation for old age is a keen appreciation of the transitoriness of the external agents of pleasure and a firm faith that old age can have bread that youth knows not of.

All this adds up to the conviction that the spirit of play need not be dead in the hearts of the old folks. In fact, with the intensified realization of the transitoriness of life, greater stress can be placed on the ever-present.

What do children learn from play? Many things. They learn to abide by rules that are agreed to by them and by others. They learn to respect recognized authority. They strive to excel, but not by taking advantage of others.

Sports blaze the way for the economic world. A poor boy who excels in sports has an even chance with the rich boy both in school sports and in sports out of school. This is too often not true in the economic world. If a child of a special-privileged parent were given a running start in a contest, it would be no more unfair than the more than running start he gets in the social and economic world. He also has better running equipment. This theme is elaborated elsewhere.

Sports, of course, are not the perfect example. There is racial intolerance in some of them. This will gradually be worn down. Even here the intolerance is not bred by the sport. The sport merely accepts the condition, or does not fight it hard enough.

In games where many players participate, rule-makers are continually on the alert to equalize opportunity between those who are highly endowed by nature and the lesser fry. When weight begins to count too much, the rules are modified to counteract this tendency. The same thing holds true of height.

There appears to be no end to the number of lessons that the social and economic world can learn from sports. Why do children take to sports? Certainly one reason is that they find a democracy there that they do not feel in their points of contact with the adult world.

160

The sporting world recognizes only *tentative* limits. These are not set so high as to take the heart out of even the best athletes. Athletes set higher goals for themselves than for others. This is as it should be. We are not so easily disheartened if we are allowed to set up our own goals. The poorest student will play hard at his school work if he is given goals that interest him and that will make it possible for him to achieve *more* than his teacher expects of him. Then he will gradually relinquish his "what's-the-use" attitude. This idea will be developed more fully in the chapter on education.

What shall we say of the sporting world's too great emphasis on the importance of being the top performer? This is an outcropping of nature that is also present in the economic world. There is plenty of evidence that the sporting world is slowly beginning to realize that continually straining toward something higher is more important than just being a winner.

There is a sense—and this is especially evident in the spiritual realm—in which we are all winners, and one in which we are all losers. We are winners in that we are continually attaining new objectives and losers in that we often do not try hard enough, and new goals are constantly looming up before us.

My neighbor can be regarded as a catalyst. He gives greater interest to my quest after higher and still higher goals. He unconsciously translates for me academic interest into a crusading interest.

13.   CREATIVENESS AND REVELATION

The first book of the Old Testament begins with Creation. The New Testament ends with Revelation. But creation, or creativeness, did not end with Genesis and revelation did not end with the New Testament. They are still our sustaining forces. Creativeness leads to new revelation and revelation leads to more creativeness.

I grew up with the idea that creativeness meant making something out of nothing. For that reason, until recent years, I have been impatient of those educators who talked about exploiting the creative urge in children. Finally I saw the light. It dawned on me that creativeness means what we make it mean. I now subscribe to the generally accepted definition that

161

creativeness is doing things with less expenditure of energy to make room for greater effort in new directions; to make two blades grow where one grew before; to look for the spiritual behind and in the material.

It also means to use wisely every precious minute available. Recently almost half the pupils were out of school on account of closed roads and sickness. Parents, teachers, and pupils were heard to remark that it would have been better to close the school because everything that was taught then would have to be taught over. Does not everything have to be taught over and over again before it becomes a part of the child? Granting that conditions call for a change in the teacher's plans, must a teacher be so lacking in creative ability that the pupils will say, "We didn't do much more than just waste our time?" It is better to teach half the pupils than none of them. "Impartiality" can cover a multitude of sins.

Jesus was adept in applying common sense to every situation that confronted him. What does this mean? It means, in part, that he carefully weighed all factors, chief of which were the spiritual. Common sense is used here as over against a hard and fast application of a rule. The criterion is what is just, not what is the law, or rule.

The law should be a general guide. When it no longer serves this purpose it should be modified.

Unfortunately, many people make common sense mean doing the things that will bring them the greatest material return. Their common sense should rise to the occasion by demonstrating to them that such an attitude makes them poor company for others. This knowledge should start them on the road to altruistic service.

Those who lack this common sense also are poor company for themselves. But they are ignorant of the cause and generally persist in the acts and attitudes that will make them still poorer company for themselves. This explains why many people get grouchier by the year.

Those who possess this common sense are on the road to becoming better and better company for themselves and for others.

How is "the bliss of solitude" achieved? Some get a synthetic version of it by turning away from the world. Others have it thrust upon them because the world has turned away from them. This is the enduring type. It prepares the possessor for living blissfully in this world as well as out of this world.

Blissful solitude comes to those of us who put into practice the conviction that we cannot escape from ourselves. We must do the things that *we* are convinced are our lot to do. We must *face* the issues of life, not turn our backs to them. The life that is outwardly turbulent through its

162

refusal to withdraw from the issues of life is the one that has discovered real peace within.

Peace of mind, or the Peace of God, does not come to us immediately after our first stand for the right. The first reaction often is utter confusion and doubt. It is only as we persevere in spite of this confusion and doubt, and keep on probing the merits and demerits of the points at issue, that peace gradually envelops us.

It is largely because most of us are so afraid of the sneers of the onlooker that few of us have real peace of mind. We succumb too readily to the name-calling tactics of those who are opposed to us.

Mark Graubard in *Science and Emotional Outlets* persuasively presents the case against the century-long waves of history. Let us identify a few of them. They are: (1) the other—worldly early Christian wave; (2) the Crusades; (3) the anti-witchcraft wave; (4) the Age of Reason wave; (5) the technological wave; (6) the psycho-analytical wave. These later waves, of course, are not century-long.

He describes them all as emotional outlets for that mass sense of frustration, futility, etc., that piles up between waves. My personal interest lies in the analysis of the causes of these insecure senses. I shall do no more here than to preface it with the remark that it goes back to the individual sense of futility to which we all are subject at times. The solution goes back to the individual that helps to make up the mass. When we have enough individuals in whom this sense of insecurity is not the dominant theme, then the waves will disappear. Religion must fight these waves.

Is it possible to develop a technique that will tend to nullify our tendency toward those well-known periods of mental ups and downs? I feel that my own experience can be a great help. As an adolescent and a young man, I had my share of those periods. When I noticed how rhythmically those periods came, I set myself the task of reminding myself, when the depressive periods came, that they would not last long. And it worked! For me the waves have become mere ripples.

There are many articles constantly appearing on what to do when those periods come. There should also be many on how to gradually eliminate the waves. Once we learn to live with our depressive periods—to face them— we discover that they are not depressive at all. Basically it is a problem of self-adjustment to a situation. It is the problem of what I can contribute to the situation.

Let me inject a very apt analogy here. All of us know people whose physical appearance is repulsive. I used to try to imagine how repulsive it must be to live with such people. I have since had the experience of

163

having had intimate dealings with such people. And the experience was not repulsive at all! I had faced the situation!

Here is another illustration. When World War I came along, I enlisted in the infantry because I considered that the toughest spot in the army. I figured that if I picked the toughest spot in the beginning it could not get any worse. And I was right!

To this day when I am in a crowd that is scurrying for a favored spot, I generally wait until the forward are all accommodated. Then I take the cream of what is left. And the cream is real! Note that these cases are different from that of the early bird. The early bird pays the price.

Learning to share, and to give more than our share to those that insist on it, is one of the keys to our inner spiritual storehouses. It is one of the keys to living. Learning to live is learning to adjust ourselves to the vicissitudes of life. Those of us who wade into and breast the vicissitudes of life have learned to live.

We must believe that the whole can be greater than the sum of its parts. We must believe that into the union of the parts there will go intangibles of great worth. If we reject this, we must reject the idea that man is a creative being. Man at least activates values that were inert before. Creativeness makes the whole greater than the sum of its parts. It follows the spirit into the workaday world and makes the prosaic poetic. It creates new spirit.

It seems fitting here to again remind ourselves of the opposite of creativeness—nihilism. Nihilism is making the whole equal less than the sum of its parts. It consists in stifling the spirit.

We are being nihilistic when we seek to stifle our neighbor's creative efforts; or when we seek to deprive him of the gifts that would make him more creative.

We must recognize that we all are nihilistic at times. Perhaps everybody is creative at times. Our task is by our creativeness to drive nihilism into a corner and keep it there.

Jesus went about righting wrongs, doing good. Is it too far-fetched to say that he went about doing things the best possible way? The best possible way is the way that produces the best results for the effort expended. How does civilization advance? By learning to accomplish more by the same or less effort.

Particular pains must be taken not to build up the egos of those who are the ringleaders of evil. I believe this is one of the biggest mistakes teachers make. But a special effort must be made to have pupils recognize real merit in their classmates. We must learn to give recognition to the creative efforts of all regardless of talent. We must recognize that the one-talent pupil can also be creative.

Our constant aim should be to make the head and heart one. We should condition nature and intellect by the spirit, so that we shall be able to truthfully say that our natures pull in the right direction. All things should tend to become one. It is creative to make things work in harmony that were at cross purposes before; to direct the forces already in existence in the right direction.

As I am writing this book I am spending less *time* on my class work than ever before; and I am getting a better response and better results than ever before. The pupils seem to be absorbing much of the renewed spirit that is permeating my whole being as I am writing—and thinking. Creativeness is contagious.

What is the difference between skepticism and cynicism? Cynicism can result from skepticism. So also can faith. Faith is built on a foundation. Skepticism can remove the things that don't count, or that are inimical, thus revealing a solid foundation.

If skepticism is only concerned with finding out what is wrong with things, then it leads to cynicism.

Skepticism precedes, accompanies, and follows genuine faith. The faith that is afraid to investigate is not faith, but doubt. The faith that is doubt calls names instead of investigating.

In the physical realm it is easy to distinguish light from darkness. In the spirit world it is not so simple.

Those who are most steeped in superstition—which is darkness—are most eager to shed their darkness—which they think is light—on others.

Those who are possessed of the most light are very eager to absorb more light from others; and, in the absorbing, make it possible for others to absorb light from them.

Light looks for more light; darkness looks for more darkness.

Let us not be too certain that we have more light than our neighbors. Our very certainty should put us on our guard.

A clergyman's talk on "The Superstitions of the Pennsylvania Germans" evoked a long train of thought in me. He brought out that superstition is an erroneous adaptation of pure religion; that many superstitious folks must be accepted with their superstitions, in the hope that a growing sense of the implications of pure religion will slowly turn them from their superstitious ways. He might have added that many of our forbears, whom most of us label as having been very religious, were really very superstitious instead.

165

He also reminded us that the Pennsylvania Germans have no monopoly on superstition; that it is found throughout the world. He might have added that it has existed through the whole age of man. The early and all succeeding Christians have in varying degrees been in its grip. The forms of the theological groups become a superstition to many adherents.

We ourselves will speed the day of pure religion if we recognize that the early Christians who formulated our theology were also superstitious folks. This early theology must be considered in the light of the superstitions of that day. This calls for more frank admissions than most Christians have the faith to make.

How much creativeness and revelation is found within the theological organizations? Very little. Very often they accept new—creative—ideas only when they can no longer escape them. They are grudging evolutionists.

It is difficult to be creative without calling some form—or some phase of the form—in question. Theological leaders are very much afraid of this. Their attitude can perhaps best be expressed as follows: "If you stray far from the forms, then the Devil may get hold of you."

They forget that it is this very exploring that leads to the Tree of the Knowledge of good and evil. It is here that we really begin to live—or die. It is here that we can demonstrate that we are sons of God. We can choose!

True faith never believes that it has apprehended the whole truth. It continually places itself on trial for the purpose of discovering deeper truth. Faith and skepticism, skepticism and faith, can form a wonderful partnership. Faith takes the attitude that the best available is better than nothing.

The young teacher has the special obligation of recognizing the possibility that his ideas are half-baked. His skepticism has not yet led to anything on which he can build with assurance. An almost universal tendency of young teachers is to criticize their predecessors in front of their pupils. This is the result of a false sense of their own importance; and also of an effort to cover their many inferiority complexes. Old teachers are not immune either; only here the sceptic has become the cynic.

I feel that the "pursuit of happiness" is a very unfortunate phrase. We do not catch happiness. It catches up with us when we take time out to give thought to our neighbors. This must be taught to children and to others by example. It is comparatively easy to sense this spirit of genuine neighborliness in others.

It is also easy to see when this neighborliness has selfish ends. It then does not ring true. It is an attempt to buy happiness. Too many of us think

166

that we can discharge our obligations along this line by joining a service club. We don't *fully* discharge our obligations by giving a certain amount of money or material to be dispensed by *others*.

Many adults wish that they were children again so that they could again know real happiness. In view of this, it is refreshing to hear Aristotle say that a child cannot be truly happy; that such a state of bliss is reserved for mature adults. Certainly he comes closer to being right than those adults.

It is too bad that we have any teachers of our youth who believe that the degree of our physical maturity is the best criterion of our stature. So the important thing is for the teacher to firmly believe in the importance of the things of the spirit, and by his example impress this sense of importance on the youth of the land.

Perhaps Aristotle was thinking of the spiritual state of those old people who have the sense of having fought the good fight—and won. But we must broaden our concept of happiness to include the state of those of us who have the sense of doing our part in the great quest.

By happiness, I am thinking of a more or less chronic state of satisfaction that is not complacency. Pleasure is more a thing of the moment. The distinction is analogous to that between climate and weather.

It is easy to make the wrong application from the statement that happiness catches up with us as we are engaged in doing our duty. Such an attitude does not rule out the doing of the many little things that bring us immediate pleasure. It does rule out pleasure seeking as a main goal.

"Is this the best possible use to which I can devote my time?" is a question that we must be continually playing with. The criterion is genuine happiness as a by-product.

"If I were a millionaire, I would give most of my money to the poor." How often have we hear this or similar statements! In most cases it is offered as an excuse for not doing anything until we are millionaires.

We run hither and yon, we wrack our brains, in the quest for release from boredom, sense of futility and frustration, loneliness; and then we say that we are too busy to go about doing good.

It is interesting to note that the practical reformers, who see life at its seamiest, are also the men of faith, for they also see the forces at work that will inevitably better the world.

Many an outwardly turbulent life harbors a serene soul; serene because of the knowledge of a mission faithfully fulfilled, or being fulfilled. The converse is patently true. A sense of progress is a sense of adequacy. An outwardly serene life can be inwardly very turbulent. Its nature depends on whether the surface turbulence is caused by outward or by inward maladjustment. The flat existence is not the happy existence. It denies the transcendental.

I am indebted to Symington's more or less objective study of the attitudes of conservatives and liberals. Some of the findings are: that liberals generally enjoy frequent periods of isolation for inner musings; that they are more optimistic than the conservatives; that they are restless and happy; that they think the world is improving; that in general they exemplify the difference between introspection and introversion.

Is the savage state the happy state? Most people will agree that the more people are steeped in savagery, the more superstitious they are. It is difficult to see how a superstitious person can be a very happy person.

Superstitious persons place their dependence on something outside themselves that must be humored. They lack the inner sense of security. To the extent that they are superstitious, they are not religious.

There probably has never been an age when people did not look back to an age of less material comforts that, they thought, brought the people of that age more happiness and contentment than they themselves were enjoying; and the present age is no exception. But almost invariably they are not willing to try on themselves the things that are supposed to have brought happiness to past generations.

They will reply that they would no longer enjoy these simple pleasures in the knowledge of what is now being enjoyed by most people; that it was different in the past when all the people had to put up with like discomforts.

But there never was an age when people enjoyed equally the good things of life. There was more desire to discriminate in the past than there is now. And people were at least as miserable as they are today.

One writer thinks that we no longer like to work as our parents did. I distinctly recall hearing the same thing nearly fifty years ago. He writes that we no longer have the veneration for the dignity of work that the Founding Fathers did. Has he forgotten that in "Those Days" it was considered a disgrace for a member of the upper crust to be caught working?

Many of us who do not like workmen's unions like to say that the unions are for less work and more pay, *and nothing more.* We say that the unions have made us lose our veneration for work. As a matter of fact, it appears that the unions deserve the most credit for getting the upper crust off its high horse in its attitude toward work.

One thing is certain. Those with the strongest nostalgic urge are the ones who wish the hardest that they had more of the material things that are supposed to bring unhappiness.

Here and there in our country we have religious sects who are actually trying these things out on themselves. Some of us envy them. We tend to take the attitude that they are asserting their democratic right to be themselves. Actually they are not being themselves at all; they are being their ancestors. They are addicted to at least a mild form of ancestor worship. They are not creative.

The right to freedom does not guarantee freedom. Along with the freedom to expand is the freedom to crawl into our own shells; and the freeedom to expand must have bounds if it is not to end in chaos. Freedom without limits is meaningless.

In this connection, it should be remembered that most restrictions on freedom are self-imposed. We are still our own worst enemies.

Freedom results from breaking down barriers between fields, and learning to move back and forth without getting lost. It also results from sallies into chaos, provided the boundaries are well-defined. Philosophy is the integrating force.

"Sing to the Lord a new song," chants the psalmist. A new song has been the need of every generation. It includes that generation's addition to humanity's spiritual storehouse.

Unfortunately, to most of us the material storehouse looms vaster. It is something we can see and feel without any contribution from ourselves.

But the spiritual storehouse can be explored only by those of us who are making our own contribution.

Really loving our neighbors is a spiritual contribution. Living our faith in the power of the spirit is the key to the world's salvation—if enough of us carry through.

So many famous writers take the view that the dissatisfied mind is the unhappy mind. Nothing can be farther from the truth. It is the satisfied mind that leads to unhappiness. There is no happiness in stagnation.

From this they draw the conclusion that most progress comes from unhappy minds. No, the crusaders are the possessors of the happiest minds. It is the traditional, idle rich who are made miserable by fighting progress.

I just came across an article by a psychoanalyst who divides people into three classes. The vast majority he classifies as normal. At the bottom are the neurotics. At the top are the perfect men. They are without fears and prejudices. Their lives are properly balanced. They have peace of mind. But he does not envy them. He thinks they do not have enough drive. He does not realize that true contentment comes with the conviction that they have not taken their duties lightly. It is persons who hold this conviction who are the real drivers. The satisfaction is more in the knewledge of

169

having performed a noble service than in the outward results that have been achieved.

The religious approach would largely eliminate the boredom of those whose main interest is the *pursuit* of happiness. In this connection it should be noted that the happiest people generally do not laugh the loudest. Loud laughter is often an effort to force out something that is not here.

The sense of futility and frustration that in varying degrees is the lot of all of us is undoubtedly a major factor in building up a climate of intolerance. The religious attitude will tend to eliminate this sense. This climate of intolerance can very aptly be called "The Great Obsession."

Natural growth has definite limits, maximum and minimum. Spiritual growth has none. Too many of us limit our spirit by our nature. That is why few middle-aged men would imitate old men. The spirit too often becomes ossified with the end of natural growth.

Physically we are past our peak at thirty. Spiritually the peak should always lie ahead. It is because of the submergence of the spiritual that the average man of thirty does not look forward to the age of sixty with pleasant anticipation. Whose fault is it that the man of thirty does not want to imitate the man of sixty? It is largely that of the man of sixty who sets such a poor example. Few of them realize the importance of the spiritual element, or realize it too late.

Each of us should be concerned with this question, "Am I a success?"

I believe that the best single criterion is found in our answer to the question, "Would I want to live my life over again!"

I believe that the success does not want to live his life over again. He is satisfied to live his life in the present. And he views the future with eager anticipation. "Unless ye become as little children, ye shall not inherit the Kingdom of Heaven."

A child does not want to revert to infancy. His eyes are on the future. An adolescent does not want to revert to childhood. His eyes are on the future. Why can it be said of so few of us adults that we do not want to revert to adolescence? It is primarily that the growth that lies ahead is not natural growth. It cannot be discerned with the natural eye. We do not make good enough use of the power to think that has been bestowed on us. This leads on to the greatest fear and dread of all: fear and dread of—old age.

We should so spend our youth that we can build up to an old age of real satisfactions. What is the creative approach to the problem of old age? Should we talk to children about the problems of old age? We most certainly should, and always in a vein of faith and hope.

170

At all ages children should be taught to think in terms of the differences between them and adults. These discussions, among other things, would tend to make the teacher more tolerant of the child's viewpoint.

Too many adolescents view the period of old age as a period of unmitigated evil. They conceive of the period of their youth as being a race against time. And that attitude all too often leads up to an old age of unmitigated evil.

I recall that as a child I used to stand and gaze at old folks who just sat. I could not understand why they did not run around and have a good time instead of just sitting and being miserable. This is not denying that old folks often sit and are miserable; but it is an argument that it need not be so, and the time to start preparing for our old age is in the days of our youth.

Children should understand that we adults also marvel, and never cease marveling, at their seemingly eternal activity. They should recognize that we sympathize with them in their need for activity. But they should be gradually conditioned to the ideal of satisfactions not connected with physical activity. They should recognize that theirs is not a race against time, but a race *with* time. They should recognize that time is with us, not against us.

Why do so many people face certain death with so much despair? I am thinking of more than the natural trepidation we have about a new step or adventure. I am thinking of the utter despair that seems to envelop so many of us. The main reason is lack of love for neighbor in our spent lives.

The well-spent life does not regard death as something that lies ahead. Instead it centers its anticipation on an old age of keen spiritual enjoyment. Death is regarded as something that hovers overhead, or that follows on behind, to give us a gentle push at the right moment.

How can we expect world peace when there is so much turmoil in the heart of the average adult? The blame is primarily the individual's. But a greater measure of social justice would be a big boost to the individual's quest for a sense of a more clear-cut mission in life.

Spiritual growth, when bodily growth has ceased, presents problems that are poorly handled by most of us. Here the older people should give us a direction that is so sadly lacking.

How few of us agree with Browning when he says,

"Grow old along with me;
The best is yet to be—
The last of life, for which
the first was made!"

171

What is the source of "that tired feeling?" Often it is a symptom of spiritual lethargy. Men in their thirties are apparently most vulnerable. This is the period when physical vigor starts to decline. Before these men look *up* to the fututre; now they begin to look down. And they tend to make this physical decline the measure of spiritual change. This is the age at which many men make or break themselves spiritually. For them life (or death) begins at forty.

Our prime trouble is lack of faith in humanity. Humanity is nature plus spirit. Nature improved slowly before man appeared on the scene. Are we to believe that nature-plus-spirit will do less?

We must have faith in the might of right. Why are we worried about what Russia will do to Asia? If they will help them, they deserve our thanks and applause. If not, there is enough of the flame of democracy in Asia to guard against the return of a darker age.

Our main concern should be our task, not Russia's task. Let us buckle down.

We must conceive of a world, created by God, that is constantly evolving naturally, materially and spiritually. Otherwise we should have to conclude that God created a failure.

The picture of nature moving backward is an optical illusion. The illusion is created by the much greater upward movement of the spirit. The material advance is dependent on spirit and nature.

By spirit I mean that which raises man above the plant and the rest of the animal kingdom.

This is the Age of the Common Man—and of the Uncommon Man. Saying the first, and not the second, savors too much of conforming to a standard. This uncommon man must not be confused with the cynical uncommon man that is described earlier in the book.

It is, or should be, the age in which the common man is accelerating his rate of speed in getting at least a glimpse of the vision that possesses the uncommon man farther front and up.

It is the age in which the uncommon man is beginning to see more clearly that the *starting point* in his philosophy must be the hopes, aspirations, and commonplaces of the common man.

We have a great deal to say about the paths our individual journeys through life shall follow or lay out. I have special reference to the spiritual trail. The scenery along the way can best be made beautiful if we make an effort to see to it that each point is originally picked out for its intrinsic value—not something that just happened.

172

But it will still happen that many of the points just happened. Many of these points can also be made points of interest if we throw enough of ourselves into them. This is just another approach to the point that we should condition and be conditioned.

Art consists in finding the consummatory in the instrumental. It makes ends of means, thus making the means stronger as means. Practically speaking, for us mortals the ultimate end is our neighbors' welfare, always remembering that our neighbors are also members of the "we" family. If this may seem too prosaic, we can expand the horizon and say that interest in our neighbors' welfare points to the ultimate end: order from chaos.

When I become impatient of the means that must be resorted to in order to achieve an end, I deliberately slow *up,* instead of speeding down. This slowing up affords me a chance to look around and up. Almost invariably I discover an end in the means. I am being artistic.

Our basic shortcomings are those of every age. Every age fails to appreciate that preceding ages faced problems similar to its own. The big trouble is thinking in terms of opposites. The material and spiritual are constantly set in opposition. We reason that since the past enjoyed fewer material comforts than we, it necessarily excelled in spiritual things.

It takes effort to hold someone down. This is what exhausts many people. And the greatest exhaustion is spiritual exhaustion.

Why does every age persist in believing that it is slipping spiritually? It is because spiritual progress can be apprehended only by the spiritual eye and mind. It is also a relic of ancestor worship.

We are still too much addicted to ancestor worship. We persist in believing that we are descendants. Actually we are ascendants.

When a lie is repeated often enough, we tend to believe it. We have called ourselves descendants so long that most of us think that's what we are.

In our mind's eye, when we look back to the past, do we look up or down? Most of us look up; and are overwhelmed.

It is difficult to persevere if we feel that we are gradually, inevitably, slipping back. This has always been humanity's predicament. We persist in believing that when God created us, he created a failure.

This present age is preëminent spiritually. So has been perhaps every preceding generation *up to its point.* We are gradually moving up, not down.

When we read about the past, we tend to read the thoughts of their noblest souls. The noblest souls of the present have not yet been canonized in our thinking. But we must also see the past's bad as well as the good, so that we shall not become discouraged by the amount of bad we see so easily in our day because we are part of it.

I am indebted to Rudolf Allers for many excellent leads that I got from his *Ideas, Ideals, and Idols.* One of these leads brought me to a conception of an idol as an ossified ideal.

Many of my leads led to conclusions contrary to his. In fact, I got the very definite impression that many of his ideals never had to become idols; they were idols from the beginning.

He has a "line" that I find very irritating. It is that somehow our fore-fathers apprehended the spiritual values that escape us moderns; that the dread of old age stems from a lack of faith in the past. I think it stems from a lack of faith in the present, and future; from a failure to recognize that as physical activity *decreases* there should be an *increase* in spiritual existence; but that existence must be found within, not in the past.

We should be continually reminded that giving does not always involve taking. In fact, there is more give than take in every creative effort. At the same time, we must recognize that in nearly every reform measure there is give and take. And we should not be weary in giving even if it involves taking.

This condition is present in nearly every new law and every governmental activity. Politicians should learn to candidly study the creative phases of a new governmental activity, even if it was sponsored by the opposing party. Instead we generally have our whole attention directed to repressive phases. In the interest of its contribution to the state of mind that will insure world peace, if for no other reason, politicians of opposing parties must learn to play fairly with one another.

I feel that it is very unfortunate our highest government officials should consider it necessary to state that the selfish interests alone of the nations should be sufficient reason for working for world peace. The unfortunate phase lies in the fact that too few recognize that to achieve those selfish ends, many unselfish deeds are necessary. It is the wrong approach.

Let help to others be expressed in terms of what it will do to others, not what it will do to us. Let us have an end of sugar-coating our altruism with selfishness. The aftertaste is bitter.

The Friendship Trains have shown better than anything else that people do not need the assurance of material returns before they will act. The best way to give democracy a chance to live most fully is for our public officials to exhibit a real faith in the American people.

The selfish approach is the platitudinous approach. It is a true general

174

statement that does not give sufficient consideration to all the factors involved in a fair disposition of the case. There is always a begging of the question in some phase of it.

There are people so wrapped up in themselves that they do not know there are satisfactions to be had in denying themselves for the benefit of others. Denying oneself can be enriching oneself.

Self-denial can call up inner potentialities that we did not know existed. Self-denial can be a substituting of new values for old. It can be a substituting of better values for lesser values.

Children should be schooled to the need of resigning themselves to denied pleasures. They should have faith in the healing power of compensations. At the same time, they should be schooled against the danger of becoming complacent about correctable evils. Professors of religion too often preach faith and patience in enduring hardships that can be eliminated. Jesus would have been more concerned about *eliminating* those hardships.

Should we feel remorse for actions taken that bring disastrous consequences? Not if they were based on the best judgment available. We spend too much time judging isolated acts by their consequences. More attention should be given to the reasons that led to the acts. Nevertheless, disastrous consequences should certainly lead to a retsudy of the problem.

I am sometimes appalled at my callousness toward suffering that cannot be helped. My redeeming quality is that I am not callous to suffering that can be eliminated or eased. There are too many people whose hearts melt over someone suffering from an incurable disease, but who have hearts of flint when they survey conditions that are the result of unfair rules of the game or of unfair administration.

Can the statement that the end justifies the means be disposed of easily? It can, as a general statement. But it becomes very complex when we come to a consideration of case studies. The end justifies the means if the means do not cause a greater injustice elsewhere. We must exercise our sense of value in disposing of the case. Let us beware lest we swallow platitudes whole.

It is creative to use all yardsticks available to encourage, prod, and evaluate my efforts to excel. This effort must be in the direction of helping others who have been denied some of my gifts. It must strive to find for me my niche of greatest usefulness, without forgetting the quality of my versatility. It recognizes the need for continuous self-improvement for greater service.

These yardsticks can be my best previous efforts, my neighbor, and even those opposed to me.

I just gazed on a man who has a keen sense of his own importance. But didn't I say that, pragmatically speaking, man is the center of the universe, and isn't he a man? Yes, but he does not have the same keen sense of his neighbor's importance, who is also a man. He does not have the religious approach. Just as un-religious is the self-deprecating man who does not believe what he says.

There is a great difference between egoism and a sense of mission. There is a vast difference between being impressed by the importance of *me,* and being impressed by the importance of *my mission.* All of our presidents who are generally rated as "great" had a keen sense of the importance of their mission. It is very easy for those who are so inclined, to find in Jesus only a great egoist. The greater the sense of mission, the greater is the charge of egoism that may be laid against a person.

I just came across a news item of a Negro in a southern state who won the right to equal pay with whites having the same qualifications. He was an elementary school principal. He received over five hundred dollars a year while a white principal with the same qualifications received over fourteen hundred dollars.

The southern whites claim that they are superior to the Negro. Why should they then be afraid to give him an equal chance to compete with them? Superiors should be able and willing and anxious to give inferiors at least an even break and still have faith that they themselves will come out on top.

We must get over the idea that inferiority or evil will win for other people, while we must be good to win. This describes our attitude toward Russia. We say that democracy is basically sound, while commnnnism is inherently bad. Yet we fear that communism will encircle the globe, while our good democracy is in danger of fighting a losing fight.

The westerners are afraid of giving the Japanese-American an even break. These people's grasping ways, if any, are largely a defense against the ostracism that has been imposed on them. They will quickly fall into our ways if we accept them as members of the brotherhood of men.

Similarly, the rich are afraid to give the poor an even break.

Most of us will accept all the foregoing statements except the ones that touch us. Then we will try to explain in what way our case is different from the other cases.

I am more indebted to Max Lerner than to any other writer. Particularly evocative has been his *Ideas are Weapons.* I was especially pleased that he shares my views on Walter Lippmann. We all love company.

But the thing that first struck me was the title. It had, and still has, a discordant sound. I am still puzzled by his quotation that men have thoughts, but ideas possess men. Ideas are images and images can become idols. And idols often possess men. I must hasten to add that this is a restricted view and that it is meant to be no more than a scratch on the surface of a complex idea. Let us not let the idea possess us. I realize that I am going round and round. But there can be worth-while accretions in such a process.

Generally speaking, it can be stated that optimists and liberals conceive of life as being an unending *quest*; while pessimists, radicals, and conservatives regard life as being an unending *battle*—offensive for the radical and defensive for the conservative. Both are idol worshipers.

Weapons suggest battle; tools can suggest a quest. I suggest substituting tools for weapons. Let us at least give tools first place and us weapons only as necessary expedients.

This is all in line with my objection to such hymns as "Onward, Christian Soldiers" and "The Son of God Goes Forth to War" and even "A Mighty Fortress is Our God." These hymns all are based on the assumption that life is primarily a battle. Battles are scars—often necessary scars—on the whole picture. As our common conception of the quest becomes clearer, the need for battle begins to wane.

Is the quest really unending? From the viewpoint of us mortals it is; and that is what counts to a practical man. But we can make progress that in *our* eyes is considerable.

I hope I will be excused for making this observation: When we exchange ideas, are we exchanging weapons? Do not opposing forces have the same common, grand objectives?

This should give practical meaning to the statement that all things work together for good to them that love God—that there is one all-pervading Spirit.

Are weapons ever creative? Let us think of them as being used to set the stage for creative work with creative tools. At the worst weapons are nihilistic.

This book is also concerned about the need for a more detailed study of what attitudes must be cultivated if we do not want technological progress to leave social progress hopelessly behind.

What would happen if the whole population of Pennsylvania were transferred to an undeveloped country of comparable size with an abundance of natural resources? Assuming that they leave everything behind except what they have in their heads, I believe we will be agreed that within a generation they would have developed an economic security vastly superior what they found when they got there.

177

What about the former inhabitants of the country who are assumed to have moved to Pennsylvania and started in with all the material equipment that the Pennsylvanians left behind? Their technological progress would be held back by their ignorance concerning economic and social adjustment. Within a generation they would probably be trailing the former Pennsylvanians.

This is just another illustration that environment is not everything. Heritage is more important, except possibly in long range.

The mathematical laws of this machine age are complex. Comparatively few people master them. But once they are mastered, they make the solution of many complex problems comparatively easy.

It is too seldom recognized that society presents problems that are much more complex. Formulas often fail because too many factors are variable and unpredictable. The expert sociologist has mastered much more than the expert mathematician. I am assuming it is understood that account must be taken of sociology's interplay with economics, religion, etc. We have become adjusted to them without sensing their complexity. But to the individual who has not stopped growing, they are complex indeed. That individual is not so quick to jump to conclusions, but he is always ready to probe and take a trial step.

Two ants living together on an apple were getting on each other's nerves. Simultaneously both decided to get as far away from each other as possible. So the two started off in opposite directions. We all know what happened.

Enemies are not as opposite as they fondly imagine. Two persons are at enmity over trifling things. In their own thinking they are far apart. We who view from the sidelines generally place them both in one spot.

These simple illustrations can be of great help in setting the stage toward an understanding of many complex problems—problems with many apparently irreconcilable elements. It should help us better to understand the statement that it is easier to build up than to tear down; because in an absolute sense there is no up and down. Let us remember that absolutes still point the way in many cases.

Einstein's Theory of Relativity is simple compared with the problems that are posed by man's dealing with his neighbor. More ingenuity is required in giving all the factors their proper weight. Robinson probably used an unfair comparison when he stated that our social thinking has progressed much less in two thousand years than our scientific thinking. This can be accepted if it is not meant to give more credit to the scientific thinker than to the social thinker. When the scientist takes a forward step, the

178

materials do not argue about it. They go along in dumb admission. This is not true of the materials, human beings, that the social thinker works with.

Oh, yes, human beings also change, but ever so slowly. Nature changes, but ever so slowly. Do we have the faith that can appreciate this slow change for the better?

When we study history, we see the less than ten percent of the people who had a vision of progress. We seem at home with them because the "radical" things they stood for have now become commonplace to us.

The less than ten percent among us are generally overlooked. If they are thought of at all, it is as rockers of the boat. Yet it is on them that the hope of civilization depends.

The Pharisees often accused Jesus of rocking the boat. They could not understand why he was continually poking around in things that seemed well set. Their attitude was, "Never mind the essence; consider the surface."

What is creative *thinking?* It is what we say it is. I like Robinson's definition. It is that creative thinking is the kind which leads us into new fields of endeavor and which makes new applications. Less than ten percent of us do that kind of thinking but more of us can learn to recognize that kind of thinking when others engage in it. It is the key to progress.

These less than ten percent of thinkers are in the forefront. The mass of us lag on behind, but we slowly move in their general direction because there is no enlightened leadership in our own midst.

Whether we are Christians or Jews, we must guard against the "know-it-all" attitude. We must recognize that none of us know the whole truth; that we should all be humble searchers after the truth. The know-it-alls did not get that way as a result of *thinking.*

Saying that we do not know it all does not imply that we should not try to get as much revelation as possible. The really humble person is the person who has really tried and found himself wanting. He has also discovered the power of the spirit. Without this discovery, he does not possess the gift of humility, but ends up with the curse of despair.

This helps us to explain why ninety percent of us remain conservative in our attitude toward our heritage. We don't examine our inmost thoughts and desires sufficiently. We lay too much stress on inheritance and too little on the part that we should play in the unending—but satisfying—quest. It helps to explain why so many of us Christians feel that revelation ended with the writing of the last book of the New Testament.

An important step toward creative thinking is the habit of committing our thoughts to writing. This should be subject to repeated revision. It should be our inner sanctum to which no one has access until we are ready to reveal it. Ideas do not become compartmentalized if they are all kept in the head.

Jesus said, "I have many more things to say to you, but you cannot bear them now." He never said them. He meant that, guided by God's spirit, all God's people would gradually come to a clearer apprehension of God's will. And all God's people are those who have the religious approach.

Life tends to become a vicious circle if we do not put enough of ourselves into it. And it is full of minor vicious circles. Most so-called vicious circles are really spirals; or they can be transformed into spirals. It is what we generally get when we work along on the assumption that the best available is better than nothing. The more we stretch the spiral, the greater the progress. The big danger is the possiblity of a break in the spiral— too great a break from form.

Spirals are not all progressive. Our imperfect reason often extends the spiral in the wrong direction. Those of us who live without design tend to revert to, or stay within, the vicious circle.

The individiual who lives without design tends to become worse. But in every large group, there is a spiritual leaven that counteracts this tendency.

Jesus said, "Destroy this temple, and in three days I will raise it up." I think we can draw the conclusion that spiritually it is easier to build up than to tear down. All our selfish efforts tend to tear down others so that we may rise. But the sum total of our fewer unselfish acts more than counteracts this drag on progress.

"All things work together for good to them that love God," is more than an idle saying. Many a selfish thought is unknowingly transformed into an upbuilding deed. Even selfish people strive upward.

We teachers must have faith in the children of America. What a refreshing, and rare, thing it is to find a teacher who has faith in children! What a need there is for us teachers to listen in on the spontaneous conversations of children! We would discover, some of us for the first time, that children have ideals—lofty ideals.

Children wear their enthusiasms on the outside. We are attracted to the adult who does the same with his genuine enthusiasms.

Children are quick to forget injuries inflicted by others. We too often allow resentments to ruin our lives. We too often see slights when none are intended.

Children are growing. Are we? Children are constantly acquiring new ideas and ideals. In our search for new ideas and ideals—philosophies, if you wish—we must be careful not to pull out too many old roots at one time.

In economics we learn that goods have place utility. Services may also have place utility. A thing that is worthless to us may have great value for our neighbors. We adults should think of these things when we deal with children. Children are neighbors too.

We must learn to live today, because when tomorrow comes it is still today. We cannot escape today. So we had better face it as a child faces it. He ties his daily activities in with the exciting question of what the morrow will have in store for him.

This is no argument against planning for the future. The child plans more than the adult. But he needs guidance and example from us. Those who plan best for the future are most keenly aware of today.

One of the rocks of the foundation on which civilization rests is our propensity to conform. Visionaries often forget this. Conformity is the taking-off point for all creative work and thinking. Where it is possible to conform, that conformation makes it possible to concentrate more fully on other matters.

Here is something in which we adults are sadly lacking. Think of all the bad habits we adults would eliminate if we were not so sensitive to criticism! Jesus criticized even his friends. It should be a wonderful help if some of us adults would get up the nerve to organize clubs whose main object would be the ferreting out of our personal faults. Many of us would be terribly hurt, but the end results would be very salutary. We should be more self-centered to the extent of being more critical of our own faults.

If we try this, we must be alerted against a great danger; the danger of becoming mere conformers where we were perhaps creative before.

On two sparate occasions, I have suggested to my pupils that the closest friends get together and tell one another's faults with a distinct understanding that they would take the criticism in the right spirit. In both cases some girls took me up with lasting good results.

I once sponsored a boys' club in which the initiation ceremony consisted in having the members of the club bring up all they had against the candidate. The criticism was confined to real faults, not supposed real faults. The results were very salutary.

When we say that we should try to see ourselves as others see us and then endeavor to conform to their sense of propriety, we must be aware of the necessary qualifications. The cynic and chronic fault-finder need this advice. It is poor advice to the creative artist. Outsiders often do not sense the creative urge that actuates him. He must be willing to put up with the sneers of the unseeing onlooker as being the lesser of two evils. In this case conforming would be the greater evil.

We used to have "finishing schools" for women. I believe the name is no longer used, but they certainly lived down to their name. Even the most liberal colleges today manage, in spite of themselves, to finish some of their students. Probably all of them have some of these finished products on their faculty. And I am definitely not excluding the theological seminaries from this picture.

The finished product is easy to picture and detect. The difficulty is in placing those who are in the twilight zone. The thoroughly finished product has been cut down here and padded up there to fit into a predetermined pattern. This pattern may have been set by others or by himself. He is in the way of becoming a solid citizen of the community, or a solid member of the faculty. Every liberal knows how solid these finished products can be.

Most people who are in the wrong generally have drifted into their positions by stages so gradual that they are not aware of any inconsistency. I have read that if a frog in cold water is placed on a hot stove, he will gradually stew to death without experiencing any discomfort. This is just another illustration of why the upward climb of civilization is so exasperatingly slow.

Among the most sinister enemies of democracy are those higher-ups who impose their wills on those over whom they exercise some control. They make their puppets appear as though they were exercising their own initiative when they are merely reflecting the views of their masters. These puppets often sink to the level where they fool nobody but themselves.

It is perhaps at this level that their influence is greatest. These puppets often achieve an outward prosperity that deceives most onlookers. These onlookers begin to feel that if they will also become puppets then they will also improve their material prosperity and enhance their social status. So they turn cynic and become puppets.

And the higher-ups watch their puppets perform and label it "Democracy in Action." And the new puppets proceed to forget that they are puppets and begin to make puppets of still others. The greatest puppet-makers are the greatest puppets. It takes a puppet to make a puppet. The very name of puppet reminds one of the noise made by a motor when it is about to give up the ghost.

Those who have the most regimented minds are the loudest complainers about government regimentation. I just read that the bankers of the state are asking the state to pass a law making the closing of the banks on Saturdays during the summer months mandatory. Many of those bankers often have complained, and are still complaining, about too much government regulation and regimentation.

One of the obligations of the highly endowed is to furnish light and guidance to the less favored. At what point does this degenerate into puppet-making? The answer lies in a consideration of attitudes.

All those who take the attitude that they can learn nothing from those below them are puppet-makers. All those who make others feel that it is dangerous to engage in any unregimented thinking are puppet-makers. Many professors of religion are complacently resting in this pitfall. A pitfall can be so great—compared with the man who is resting in it—that it looks like the whole world to him.

It again boils down to this: The creative leader says, "Show me;" the puppet-maker says, "Let me show you."

These are things about which I have done much thinking: nature, evil, good, democracy, religion, philosophy, education, morality, children, play, work, tolerance, intolerance, impartiality, detachment versus perspective, prejudice, love, humility, pride, tradition, heritage, conservatism, liberalism, radicalism, nihilism, inferiority complex, superiority complex.

Emerson's mousetrap, waste, human rights versus property rights, neighbor, family, community, One World, competition, cooperation, God's seeming indifference, happiness, misery, example, coercion, Divine discontent, complacency, sin, truth, spiritual hunger, satisfactions, rewards, pain, pleasure, God's kingdom, ethics, self-pity, selflessness, Christianity, Judaism, Jesus, Joshua, Moses, evolution, provincialism, accident, human waste, service, ambition, laziness, enthusiasm, cynicism, hope, despair, despondency, delight, revulsion, benefactors, malefactors, saints, sinners, Pharisees, clannishness, keeping up with the Joneses, snobbishness, aloofness, hero worship.

Realism, idealism, pragmatism, ideals, goals, objectives, introversion, extroversion, the laws of learning, economy in learning, transfer of training, liberal education, cultural education, the classics, romanticism, naturalism, Darwin, DeVries, Washington, Jefferson, Houston, Lincoln, Wilson, the Roosevelts, progress, retrogression, security, sense of security, security and special privilege, sin and crime and duty.

Children, play, and sports; old age and contentment; something for nothing, scepticism versus cynicism, jumping at conclusions, enjoyment, rugged individualism, laissez faire, ardent detachment; heredity, heritage, inheritance and environment.

Attitude and technique, individualism, sin and evil, special privileges versus privileges, introspection, politics as practiced in the U.S.A., communism, conviction and conscience, humanity and inhumanity, nature and amorality, Old Adam and New Adam, reason and emotion, logic and psychology, philosophy and superstition, religion and superstition.

14. PHILOSOPHY

We all, regardless of age, have ideals. If ideals are not philosophies, they at least suggest philosophies.

I clearly recall an ideal that I cherished as a small boy. I had definitely made up my mind as to the kind of life I would lead as soon as I could leave school and start earning a living. I would move to a simply-furnished one-room shack, existing on the bare necessities so that I could spend a maximum of my income for candy. That ideal plainly suggested my philosophy of life.

I got my ideal from a bachelor who lived like that. The only difference was that he spent all his extra money for drink. This man was dull. His sensibilities had been blunted by drink. He was unresponsive. Nevertheless, he was my ideal. Children are enthralled by the cynic. It is probably because cynicism is a new field to them.

The cynic can be said to have lost faith in beliefs. To him beliefs are opiates. He no longer dreams. It would be better to say that the cynic in him does not dream. No one is a one hundred percent cynic.

The have-nots whose minds are set on material acquisitions as panaceas are much impressed by the cynics among the haves. To them, the cynics are scorning as from a lofty position the things that the have-nots are looking up to. They are looking forward to the time when they will also be able to look down on the things that now appear so alluring. To them that "lofty" position looks very alluring. If they do achieve it, they discover to their sorrow that it isn't lofty at all.

The cynic does not sense the spirit that underlies the material. He does not realize that this spirit makes itself felt only as we think of the material in terms of our neighbor's welfare.

Unfortunately grown-ups also tend to be enthralled by the cynic in a group of people. Those grown-ups have not emerged spiritually from childhood. The average adult ideal, in its essence, is but an elaboration and an embellishment of the childish ideal. The spirit is not given sufficient weight.

We all have philosophies of life that are constantly changing. We are all philosophers. However, for convenience I am going to use the term to apply to professional philosophers only. The context will make it plain when I mean others.

When we come to a study of philosophers, we find that they have the same basic difficulty we average adults have. They find it difficult to give the spirit proper weight. And they, like us, have trouble in trying to determine what is a proper spirit.

184

I just read a churchman's review of the report of the President's "Commission on Higher Education." The churchman complains that too much stress is placed on the "needs of the times" and too little on "abiding values." He follows the usual line of not defining these "abiding values." Even if he had defined them, he would still have been faced with the necessity of showing how they contributed to the solution to the problems of practical religious living.

No, abiding values are not extracted from the air or from philosophical or theological musings. But we can get at least a hint of them by studying the needs of our neighbors; and by noting what effect such an attitude has on our inner selves. Philosophy must learn to be pragmatic. This pragmatic attitude must lead to the conviction that for a thing to endure it must have merit. Many of us believe that communism has no merit, but will still permeate the world. We must believe that communism will not stand without merit on its side. Communism will not rise above its level. Yes, those things outside our orbit must also have merit if they are to endure. Or are we afraid that they do have merit?

There is a vast difference between folding our arms and waiting for communism to collapse, and buckling down to democracy's task.

The religious attitude recognizes that a multiplicity of factors generally produces a given effect. It does not, however, fold its arms until it is sure all factors have been considered. Such an attitude leads to a do-nothing policy. It is this consideration that enables us to be tolerant of those who are led in another direction by these factors.

Logic exists outside our minds. It is the aggregate of all the factors that operate in a cause-effect condition or movement. Those factors are spiritual and material. Reason is the attempt to weigh these factors. It must depend on psychology (psycho-logic). Psychology is the logic that the mind can grasp.

It is for this reason educators are becoming increasingly aware that in a learning situation all logic must be conditioned by psychology. A logical presentation is meaningless if the mind cannot follow it. If the mind cannot follow the steps in the right order, it means that the steps are too numerous for the mind to retain; or that the steps themselves are more complex than appears on the surface.

Now that logic has been isolated and identified, we shall continue to use the word in the sense in which it is generally used. In this sense it is that part of real logic the mind can apprehend and apply.

Which is more important, reason or emotion? Reason is basic. It is not a question of one or the other. The question is how much reason is to be swayed by emotion. It all depends on whether the emotion rests on spiritual values, and what weight we give to the spiritual values. When we say that a man is swayed by emotion and not by reason, we mean that his reason is swayed by emotion.

Religion *feels* the truth of things that can never be proved by logic. Philosophy must learn to lean on religious experience. Life is so complex—there are so many cross-currents and counter-currents contributing to every life situation—that logic is never able to give consideration to all the factors. Logic cannot be the sole guide. Even if all factors were recognized, logic would have to bow to the limits of the human mind as to the number of things it can consider at one time; especially since not all factors operate with equal or uniform potency. We must help logic by losing ourselves in the lives and interests of our neighbors—a highly contagious business.

Emotion is a safer guide than logic. I refer to the emotion of love for neighbor. Why is it safer? A hundred years ago the industrialists who thought that labor had any rights were few indeed. In their arguments they relied on logic. They were generally right so far as they went; but they did not present all the evidence! Harry C. Link said in 1940 that psychology had *proved* we were more selfish then than we had been ten years earlier. As his only proof he offered the acknowledged fact that more people favored local relief in 1930 than in 1940. He used logic. But he did not present all the evidence! We can sense all the factors better than we can see them. Sensing is emotion.

Love *senses* justice better than logic finds it. As love grows and expands in the light of new revelation, democracy follows in its wake.

There is need for a sense of compact between parent and child, between teacher and parent, between the powerful and the feeble in our land, between nations. It is a role of religion and democracy to foster this sense of compact.

This sense of compact strives to wipe out special privilege and prevent the rising of new ones. It does not depend on physical or mental superiority to achieve unfair ends.

A necessary step in the building up of a *religious* philosophy is a survey of the current philosophical situation for the purpose of determining what makes it creak.

Creaking is not necessarily a sign of old age. A child's cheap new toy often creaks. Philosophers' and others, may draw their own analogies here. I cannot refrain, however, from observing that the creak in many a philosopher's philosophy sounds like heavenly music to his own ears.

I am not blind to what philosophers have done for mankind. I believe that they have helped to teach men tolerance. But they are seldom creative. Instead, they too often merely rationalize the results of other people's creative efforts.

The philosophers of Athens set a good example to those who were less tolerant than they when they merely laughed at Paul, instead of throwing rocks at him.

Considering the start that Plato gave them, it is too bad that the status of philosophers today is such that apparently no one is thinking of asking the leading philosophers of the United States and Russia to get together to try to point the disagreements, if any remain after due deliberation, in the direction that will lead to an eventual solution, and to a present workable compromise.

What would happen if they did get together? Nothing much perhaps. Too few can cross the metaphysical line and come back with only that which has meaning and application in the workaday world.

Franklin D. Roosevelt thanked God that our country was not run by college presidents and philosophers and teachers. So do I. The apostles looked on a sick man and started a dissertation as to what caused his misfortune. Jesus looked on the same man and healed him. He was not blind to the issues that they raised. Neither did he think them unimportant. But he believed in clearing away debris whenever the occasion allowed it. This is where we teachers and philosophers and college presidents are so often lacking.

I once attended a conference on higher education. Those who participated in and engineered the discussion were, with one exception, the type that disdains the considering of matters that occupy the minds of ordinary people.

They imagined that they were living in a rarefied atmosphere. To me it seemed stuffy. The moderator was a young man who oozed book learning.

They were concerned about a problem that interested me very much. I have forgotten what that problem was because they never came to the heart of the matter. They persisted in viewing from a distance and with "philosophical" detachment.

Perhaps the fairest way of summing up is to say that the main trouble with philosophers is that they are human beings. They are guided too little by spirit. Or better, they have trouble telling a good spirit from an evil spirit.

A philosopher, taking a *detached* view of Jesus' ministry in Palestine, would have decided after the crucifixion that here was another effort gone to waste; that the next generation must fight the same battles they would be

187

fighting if Jesus had never been born. The view would have been different if he had *attached* himself to Jesus' ministry.

The longer I live the more I look up to the workers of the world and down on professional philosophers. I look up to the plodder who performs the menial tasks of life for me. I look up to the person who *does* things. I am, of course, now comparing him with the thinker who remains aloof. The worker at least projects himself into the life of his neighbor who is similarly situated. However, his frame of reference is too restricted. Too many philosophers merely say "Come on in; the water's fine!" They do not bridge the gap.

Well, in spite of the fumblings of philosophers we are making progress. But we must speed up the *rate* of progress. Material advance is running ahead of spiritual advance.

I have read *Philosophy in American Education* by a group of philosophers chosen by the philosophers of the nation. The overall effect of their contribution can hardly help being salutary. But I feel that it was too lacking in the religious approach.

"Man is incurably religious." Not by my definition. It probably means that man is incurably under the spell of transcendentalism. "Pure" philosophers have plenty of company. Most of that company seek to rationalize their instincts under the heading of superstition. Superstition recognizes a force that operates independently of the workaday world; but which can make its influence felt in this workaday world. Abstract philosophy has done little more than refine this instinct.

"Pure" philosophers are to the real philosophical world as the superstitious are to the rational folks. Neither is rooted in the workaday world. They are too much concerned about what is beyond the roots and out of their reach and control.

The truest philosophy is not dispensed by philosophical technicians. These technicians are a necessary evil who, in a few cases, liberate themselves by recognizing the limitations of their specialties, and get started on the road to true philosophy and pure religion.

The most important thing in the world is that which we think is most important. This is subjective philosophy. If it were so, we should be placing ourselves into the position of not believing what we believe. We teachers must be very keenly aware of the implications of this bit of philosophy. We must strive hard to see the things that are the most important things in the world to the pupils. This is another step in the direction of understanding pupils, and people in general.

We pure religionists must recognize that there is a deep well of living water on which we must draw continually. Behind it, and pervading it, we must see, not some omnipotent element—that is, impersonal—but God. We must also recognize that superstition is an erroneous adaptation; that it tends to shackle free will.

We need a spiritual pragmatism, a pragmatism which seeks out those things that our common and individual experiences demonstrate to be spiritually uplifting. We discover these best things by trial and error, and vicariously. The trial and error method calls for more exploring than is done by most of us. Too often when we find an experience not satisfying, we try more of the same thing when we should in most cases try a new lead.

A satisfying experience must call for more exploring, but with greater assurance. We must remember that our own spiritual needs constantly change; or at least the physical channels need constant revamping.

The philosophy that I envision uses the law of love as a starting point. My ideal philosopher, instead of viewing with detachment, throws himself into every problem that he considers. He recognizes that the human equation can best be evaluated by his own immersion in the problems he is considering. Jesus is my ideal philosopher.

Pure religion must rediscover for us the pragmatic truth that man is the center of the universe and that such a man is my neighbor; and philosophy must take great pains to absorb the idea. The Theory of Relativity points back to the individual. It makes my neighbor the measure of things.

If we learn from astronomy that man is infinitesimally small, we must *not* draw the conclusion that he is correspondingly unimportant. A who is big physically is not more important than a little man. We *can* learn that man's spirit has no physical limits. We *must* learn that "man" includes children.

The religious philosophy starts with the things that we experience. Its conception of the mind is based on the things that we jointly discover by exploring our minds. It rejects predestination, not as something that is not true in the absolute sense, but as something that does not fit into our practical program. It plunges into the problems of life and living. It takes a stand.

In line with my insistence that a workable philosophy must begin with man, my neighbor, as the center of the universe, is my picture of man's world as a lighted core with darkness all around. The scholars are probing and penetrating the edges of this darkness. In that sense they go in. Education begins when they back out and make the proper integration with the known. The spirit eliminates the flatness.

Life as an unending quest can be defined in terms that will include all

189

individuals. The quest of all is the satisfying life.

Too many of us take the attitude that when this, or that, *end* is achieved, we shall have the enduring satisfying life. The *end* in the aim ruins the satisfaction. It is not an end but a direction that should be our aim. The satisfaction is in becoming, not in being.

The religious philosopher does not promise to bring heaven to earth in the absolute sense, but he promises to bring it closer. He has faith in the efficacy of evolutionary reform, something that Garrison and Brown lacked. This is not meant to place these two outside the fold, but rather as a recognition that none of us have the religious approach in all phases of our thinking.

The religious philosopher is always alert to the moral and religious implications of all phases of the sciences. The economist must consider the moral implications of his economics, etc.

The center of Jesus' interest was the human heart. The curse of philosophy is that it views the human heart with too much detachment. Philosophers may argue that they are viewing man as God views him. God does not view with detachment. He sees through man and lives in him. This should be the aim of philosophy. Jesus often let his imagination soar as do philosophers; but he always came back to the core of his interest. Philosophers too often try to find the virtues in outer space.

The foundation on which the religious philosopher must build is the well-being of man, his neighbor. This foundation is not absolute. It shifts. It changes. But it is always there. This makes the question, "What is good for my neighbor?" the great criterion. And my concept of "neighbor" must continually expand.

In this neighborly expansion, we must be careful not to by-pass too many islands of opposition—groups of people who do not understand us and whom we do not make sufficient effort to understand. Granting others the right to live their own lives and pursue their own interests does not include a shutting of our hearts to their interests. There should be a continuous effort to understand them and to make it easy for them to understand us.

To often children are consigned to islands of isolation. The isolation continues until they grow up into something that has some resemblance to us.

This policy of making my neighbor's welfare the foundation is a guard against biting off more than I can chew. Jesus has been accused of narrowness because he chose a comparatively restricted core of interest. For instance, he has been accused of evading the problems of government that

190

were weighing heavily on the minds and hearts of his followers. He was merely putting first things first.

Some philosophers still say that their main role is the erection of the superstructure, or skeleton, to which the man of the world will add flesh, blood and spirit. To me this seems like an awful confession for a philosopher to make. It is a confession that he lacks the divine spark.

Those who erect only the skeleton are definitely the "Misters" in the philosophical world. The real Masters and Doctors of Philosophy in most cases do not answer to the name of philosopher.

This again brings us down to a peculiar shortcoming of philosophers and teachers; a distressing inability to apply their theories to a hard and cold fact. Too much theory, too little practice. Too much induction, too little deduction. Too much insistence on ideal conditions, too little consideration for actualities.

Religion has a keen sense of values. Philosophers often lack it. They lose it in their quest for impartiality. In practice they often take the attitude that impartiality calls for calling unequals equal. It is especially distressing to note with what a condescending air the name of Jesus is often mentioned by philosophers.

Apart from all theological considerations, how can anyone ignore the profound influence that Jesus has exerted on the world's thinking for nineteen-hundred years? Few philosophers give him this recognition. They would probably deny the charge. I am not thinking in terms of what their answer would be if they were asked the question directly. Rather I am thinking in terms of the total effect of their pronouncements.

Philosophers delight in emphasizing the need for detachment in considering a problem, thinking that this makes for impartiality. From their deliberately chosen lofty position, they delight in looking down on the pageant of the ages and name Confucius, Buddha, Plato, Socrates, Jesus, Luther, Paine, Jefferson and Lincoln in the same breath. This, they think, is true impartiality. It very often happens that he who deliberately sets out to be impartial becomes very partial; while he who thinks primarily of justice generally achieves impartiality. Impartiality, like happiness, cannot be achieved by a frontal attack. They both are by-products more than aims.

What is Walter Lippmann's "high religion"? It is essentially traditional Oriental philosophy. It is pharisaic. It is self-centered, egoistic, despite every effort to portray its altruistic phases, if any. It is the kind of philosophy that Jesus spoke against. I say this despite the fact that Lippmann thinks he and Jesus have the same philosophy. He quotes one statement by Jesus to show that he and Jesus have the same religious approach. He refers to Jesus' remark on casting pearls to swine.

How does the church fare here? Too often it sounds like Walter Lippmann. No, it does not use his words, but the overall effect is about the same. It has too much theology and too little religion. With Jefferson, religion came first. He always refused to engage in a public discussion of his theological beliefs. He believed in putting first things first. To him theological disputation was not a first thing because it almost never results in a meeting of minds.

Too often professors of religion have transformed their religious heritage into something static, which does neither them nor anyone else any good. They, like the rest of us, pay the penalty of being human beings. Is is this fact that makes us accept *their* gospel with a spoonful of salt.

Lippmann has a strong hold on a large segment of the American public. That is why I have devoted this much time to him. He has amply demonstrated that in the fields of sociology, economics, and government he is a poor prophet. Unfortunately, in the field of religion and theology it is not so easy to *demonstrate* the fallacy of his position.

I believe that what is true of Lippmann is true of philosophers in general: a distressing ineptness in appraising the current scene. It is because they lack the religious approach. They give too little thought to their neighbors' good. They fail to realize that the prose of little things can add up to a mighty symphony.

Perhaps it would be fairer to say that the bane in their method of analysis is their mania for rooting out hidden meanings when the dominant meaning is as plain as the nose on your face.

What group of people most nearly resemble philosophers? Teachers. They also are often engaged in rooting out hidden meanings. They fail to realize that the obvious is often very difficult to evaluate

S. L. Frank seems to have come closest to a satisfactory religious philosophy in *God with Us*. In considering the transcendental he never loses sight of the individual. He is not taken up by the paradoxes. He is concerned with going only as far as is necessary to satisfy the intimation of eternity and infinity that is in each one of us. That is the way he begins, but he does not keep it up. He ends up with an apology for his own theological beliefs.

Real philosophy—that is, a workable philosophy—begins and ends in religion. It is a phase of religion. Only the philosophy of the absolutes, whatever that is, outreaches religion.

Penetration, insight, and perspective. Carrel wrote a book *Man, the Unknown*. Will Durant called it very penetrating. He undoubtedly intended that for strong praise. But is it enough for a work to be merely penetrating? Insight presupposes some knowledge of purpose and relationship with the known. Penetration is objective; insight is subjective. The larger perspective is the true philosopher's quest.

I am thinking of philosophy much in terms of what it has been, because what it has been still has a strong hold on many philosophers today. The salvation of philosophy lies in a recognition of the insidiousness of this hold—insidious because many philosophers would deny that it still exists.

"Might makes right." "Right makes might." These are more than academic posers. The former is used by those who insist that what we accept as right today was imposed on the weak by the mighty in the past, and custom has made it appear right in our eyes.

We can accept this as fact without overlooking its baleful aspects. It leads to war. "Right makes might" leads to world peace. It is the spirit of religion and of democracy.

"Might makes right" forces the selfishly expedient to be accepted as being right. "Right makes might" puts might behind the right.

There are many injustices in the international field that are generally regarded as being right; but close analysis will show that the conditions were brought about by the physically mighty nations of the past. And the mighty nations of today are still creating such injustices.

We would not be confronted with a Palestine problem today if other nations had not presumed to determine *for the inhabitants of Palestine,* and the surrounding area, what their immigration policy should be. The people of the surrounding area cannot help being affected by Palestine immigration. In this connection, we should remind ourselves that a Jew's fatherland is the place of his birth, not of his ancestors' birth.

Might, like the majority, cannot be by-passed. Its mood must be imbued with a transforming love, or it must be overpowered by a greater might. Might without a conscience is self-destructive. By its selfish exclusiveness it gradually cuts off its own support. Unfortunately, it is often succeeded by a might that is just as conscienceless.

What is right? Logic does not have the answer. It gets lost in its own labyrinth. This world is a poor place for one who is a logician and nothing more.

Logic cannot be independent; it will be conditioned by nature and by love. Making love dominant insures thinking of right in terms of my neighbors' interests.

Love gradually makes it impossible to choose wrong when the choice lies between being on the side of the "right people" and being on the side of right.

Love does not answer the question, "What is right?" But it certainly points in the right direction. Love without a trace of understanding is unthinkable.

"It had to be." Really? The chances are that many other conditions could have been, and we could rationalize them just as glibly as we presume to rationalize the conditions that came into being.

Here is where historians err, perhaps more than any other group. To illustrate my point. I should like to call attention to an article I once read on the fifteen decisive battle of the world. The author took the attitude that every one of those battles turned out right; that if in any one of them victory had gone to the other side, then humanity would have been set back immeasurably.

They overlook the fact that many apparently opposing forces tend to assume a parabolic pattern; that the losers would eventually have pursued practically the same course that was pursued by the victors; that even in our selfish ways we tend to go in the same direction.

"It had to be" is just as much as saying, "Whatever is, is right." And this definitely means that might makes right. Physical might will not make the world right. Helping and giving will. Conservatives seek to perpetuate the things that "had to be."

There is one phase of this problem that we shall do well to consider very carefully. There also are many things that really had to be. But that need not mean that they have to be today. The progress that civilization is making is tied up in this truth.

Here is a graphic illustration of how things that came to be "had to be."

We read in the Old Testament that when the people got tired of the uncertainty of rule by judges, and asked for a king, they were told by their prophets that this was contrary to God's wish; that they were seeking to substitute king rule for God rule. But they persisted and got their wish. And shortly thereafter they reached their highest eminence—materially, at least—under King David and King Solomon.

So in all the succeeding generations the ideal of perfection was a *kingdom*. And the Messiah for whom they were looking—and are looking— is always envisioned as a king. And when Jesus talked about the spiritual realm it was always the *Kingdom* of Heaven.

What possible bearing can a religious philosophy have on the teaching of such a dry subject as mathematics? A great deal. Mathematics is probably the most poorly taught school subject. That is because it appears so easy.

Have you ever heard of that large segment of the general public who speak of teachers in two breaths? In the first breath they say, "You teachers certainly have it easy!" In the second breath they say, "I would never be a teacher! I couldn't stand it."

Then there are the teachers who say, "You mathematics teachers certainly have it easy." Then in the next breath they say, "I could never be a mathematics teacher." The "driest" subjects call for the greatest ingenuity on the part of the teacher.

Mathematical "experts" apparently have looked everywhere except in the classroom for an incentive to a greater interest in mathematics. They have set up various distant goals that always leave the pupils cold. Their attitude has been, "Take an interest in these immediate computational exercises and the more or less distant future will reward you."

Some day perhaps they will learn that the incentives *and rewards* can be found in the operations themselves.

"Written" problems in arithmetic generally do not generate interest. The reverse is generally the case. And it is a good thing that it is so. Children need practice in the fundamentals much more than they need practice in deciphering written problems. There is hardly a written problem in eighth grade arithmetic, as an instance, that the average adult does not grasp. When the eighth grader grows up, he will also be able to work that problem, regardless of whether or not he could work it in eighth grade.

But in the field of fundamental operations we have a different story. Here facility does not grow with the years; it grows with practice. The satisfactions for the children must be found in the task at hand rather than in some remote goal. The pupils do find their satisfactions here despite all efforts of experts and philosophers to direct their attention elsewhere.

Every student of mathematics, when he studies the history of mathematics, is struck by the slowness with which the human mind grasped mathematical concepts that seem so simple today.

Similarly, a student of the social sciences is struck by the persistence with which those things which we regard as the amenities of life were resisted by man in his upward climb *to* civilization; and in his climb from a low form of civilization to a high form. The picture is not complete if we do not recognize that he is still climbing and resisting. For all practical purposes he is insisting that nature be allowed to regiment him. I hope it is recognized that when we come to the present *he* becomes *we*.

We have allowed our minds to be regimented on the subject of Lincoln and the Civil War period. Many of us today consider it close to sacrilegious to question anything Lincoln said or did. We are still under a hypnotic spell on the subject of what we think the Civil War decided. This is why I am drawing so copiously on this period. Nothing has yet been finally decided by us humans.

What causes intolerance? Selfishness? Yes; and that suggests other causes. A big cause is lack of consideration of all the factors that produced the condition that some deem intolerable. Too many people assume the attitude that if they can find one valid reason to bolster them in their stand, then they hold the one key to the solution of a problem.

Let us use the analogy of a place on the terrain for the problem that calls for solution. The problems of life are generally laid in a social, economic, and religious terrain that is rougher than the terrain that we generally see around us. The road we take to reach the objective is analogous to the solution of a problem.

Sometimes the nature of the terrain enables us to reach the obective in a straighjt line. But even if the terrain is flat, we often find that we have to make many turns (follow custom or habit) to reach the objective. Sometimes the inherent nature of the terrain forces us to take a devious route. Sometimes the terrain is so rough that we move away from the objective. It is not always easy to keep an eye on the objective, or even to keep it in mind.

Let us use another analogy. There are many legitimate forces pulling at many different angles on a problem. Some of these forces are diametrically opposed, although they may not be of equal strength. All these forces must be given consideration. This is where so many of us fall down.

Let me use one illustration here. It is an argument about dependency payments to workers. Some argued that dependency payments ran counter to the principle of equal pay for equal work, and they were right. They erred in thinking that they had to make a choice between the two. Each principle should have been given its proper weight, which, it is recognized, is not easy.

There are people who insist that they will never sacrifice a principle. Actually they are continually sacrificing principles. If they are doing the right thing, they are sacrificing lesser principles for greater.

Principles operate in circles or spheres that overlap or intervade. Perhaps it would present a truer picture to say that lesser principles are assimilated by greater principles. And in the assimilation the lesser principles are making a contribution.

Some say that they will not sacrifice a *basic* principle. Right; but what is a basic principle? It depends on the viewpoint. Allowance must be made for other viewpoints. We must compromise, not with evil, but with other human beings who also have basic principles.

The role of philosophy is the synthesis of the disciplines found by specialists in their special fields and their integration with those found by other specialists in other fields. These fields often overlap. There are also areas not covered by any field; or only partially covered. It is one of the special tasks of philosophy to cover these areas, and prepare them for new specializing. The specialists themselves are philosophers to the extent that they contribute their bit of synthesis and integration. Philosophers must not accuse specialists of narrowness when their restricted field was deliberately chosen with full knowledge of its limitations.

But much that goes by the name of synthesis and integration is rationalization. This was particularly true of pre-Civil War thinking.

There is perhaps no better way of summarizing this pre-Civil War type of thinking than to consider the life, thought patterns, and attitude of Francis Lieber, who had reached *his* maturity in the 1850's.

Here was a man who was definitely a leader in setting the thought patterns of his age. Lincoln acknowledged his indebtedness to him. What was the main burden of his message? It was this: Whatever is—in this country and England—is right. We have developed the traditions, mores, institutions, conventions, habits, etc., that will gradually bring us heaven on earth. We have a Constitution which guarantees that each form will exert just enough influence on society to insure its optimum development.

He gloried in the thought of what a boon to mankind the Civil War would be. *He gloried in war.* He had acquired a veneration for the possibilities of war when he was a youth in Prussia. His attitude was that the strong arm, properly *wielded,* would usher in justice. It was to him that preachers generally turned for material for their sermons, and not to Jefferson.

He even exemplified the then-common habit of pointing almost exclusively to trouble spots outside his effective orbit. When he was in the South he concentrated on what was wrong with the North and the rest of the world. When he returned North he proceeded to direct his invective against the South.

One looks in vain for a hint of the need for the religion of love for neighbor. If he had been asked the question as to the place that love should occupy, he would probably have replied that love is something on which we dare not depend; that too few possess this love for neighbor; that we can expect to do no more than harness selfish impulses, redirect them, and sometimes thwart them.

I am not trying to create the impression that this pre-Civil War period was any worse than any period that preceded it. I do not think it was. The crisis merely exposed to prominence what had been there all the time. The same is true of the crisis in which we are now living.

The sole object of this little excursion is to emphasize that we have grown, spiritually as well as materially, since then; that when we turn our thoughts back in time, it should be merely to detect growth; growth that will gradually bring us up to a heaven on earth.

There is an irresistible force in the making. There is no immovable body. The irresistible force is the ultimate good. The pseudo-immovable body is the evil, but not ultimate.

Lieber's emphasis was on *forms;* William Graham Sumner of the post-Civil War period emphasized *facts.* Both erred in rationalizing their forms and facts to fit the conditions of the periods in which they lived.

Let it be emphasized here that we must recognize that men like Lieber and Sumner made real contributions to the upward climb of civilization. The world would have been worse off without them. Form is still better than chaos. Facts are still better than airy nothings.

I cannot leave Francis Lieber without paying tribute to the excellent portrait Frank Freidel paints of him in his biography. It is excellent because it lacks embellishments. There is no evidence of hero worship. As a man Lieber is not painted as being more or less than run-of-the-mill folks. Lieber is an example of the man—still very common—who submerges his convictions in the need for making a living for himself and his family; and brings them to the surface only when it appears safe. In his teens he had learned too well the lesson of what happens to a person who is too outspoken in his views.

The question of teacher strikes is now in the air. Our thinking should be clarified on this issue. When people say that teachers should not strike, they generally say that it is all right for labor to strike. The assumption is that striking is too low for a teacher. If that is so, then it is also too low for a laborer. One of the worst things we teachers can do is put ourselves on a pedestal. The Pharisees and modern Germans did that to themselves.

Some will say that when teachers strike they are striking against the government. What is the government? Is it something mystical or is it all the people? I believe we shall all agree that it is all the people. Are all the people weaker than a private employer?

198

The line should not be drawn between the government as an employer and private industry as an employer. Rather it should be drawn between strikes whose immediate effect is disastrous and those that do not lead to immediate disaster. A strike of policemen, firemen, public utility employees, etc., is immediately disastrous. Where strikes are prohibited, some agency with power to act must be set up to see to it that justice is done these employees. Legislation against teacher strikes is grossly unjust if it does not provide such machinery.

I hope that this little excursion into the workaday world will not be resented by philosophers. They need practice in getting down to grass roots.

From the beginning, philosophers have been looking for a solid foundation on which to build. It did not require the findings of modern science to convince them that such a foundation is not physical. For close to three thousand years, at least, they have been looking for a great truth on which to build. They have never succeeded, and never will succeed on the same tack, because the constant effort has been to define this base in the absolute sense. This effort sweeps them out into infinity, and no matter what they started with they look the same at the end.

Today most philosophers refuse to be left dangling in infinity. They try to be practical. They continue to study the virtues and stop short when inconsistencies start piling up. But they are still too prone to consider the great forces in life as being beyond human control, because against the backdrop of all creation, all human efforts seem infinitesimal.

Viewing the panorama with detachment is a preliminary step. Too many philosophers make it the last step. Following an appraisal of the situation, the next step is to plunge in at the right spot and come to grips with reality. Many philosophers would not "stoop" to anything so low. They do not have Robinson's "ardent detachment." Selfless immersion probably would better portray the picture of ardent detachment.

Philosophers must learn that they above all others should not run away from the practical problems of their day. Fundamentally, their troubles arise from their inability to evolve a proper philosophy from the many forces that are clamoring for attention. Philosophers can become the most cynical creatures when they try to become practical. I am thinking of the power-philosophers who were centered mostly in Germany and gave such aid and comfort to Hitler and his kind.

I am ever trying to analyze my own inner convictions on all matters through the years. I believe philosophers make too little use of critical self-analysis for the purpose of breathing life into their concepts.

I often bolster my own inner convictions by my observation of children and adults at the various levels of maturity. I do not take the trouble at all times of stating whether I draw my conclusions from my own past inner experience or from the observation of others. In most cases it is a combination of both.

So philosophers must not disdain a consideration of how the average person's mind operates. They must not say to psychology, "Come up here and enjoy our company." I am told that drunks also sometimes mistake up for down, and vice versa.

I am closing this chapter with two papers that I submitted in a graduate course in education. I consider it best to present them without any changes.

The last paper, on objectives, does not strictly belong to this chapter, but I am presenting it because of its relationship to the first paper. To many it may appear that this paper winds up the chapter on philosophy on too prosaic a level. Even at the end, philosophy is not far removed from the starting point.

Finally, these last two papers point directly to the chapter on education, which follows immediately.

A Philosophy of Secondary Education

The secondary school should be *interested* in every phase of the development of *all citizens* between the ages of eleven and nineteen. I have in mind the six-year junior-senior high school, with one year's leeway at each end.

The curriculum should embrace those activities for which the school is better fitted than any other agency; and should supplement the work of the other agencies, even taking over where the other agencies are lax.

The method should be that of constant experimentation. This experimentation should lean heavily on logic, ultimate goal, and pupil interest. The goal should be self-improvement for altruistic service. A very effective way of implanting this vision of altruism is for the school to give *freely* of all those things that make for the upbuilding of the pupil. In World War II the armed forces paid the whole expense, with pay, of training the men for the job for which they were supposed to be best fitted. There is much that we can learn from that system.

The staff should represent a wide range of special interests that are built around the central philosophy of the school. Each member of the staff should be vitally interested in at least one activity outside the school that would tend to make an impression on the consciousness of the community. He should be able to do this without being overworked. It should be emphasized in connection with this thought that a person who has a large share in the selecting of his activities is not easily overworked.

Thorough grounding in his teaching specialty is important; but it is not as important as a well-rounded personality. Such a person has a keen sense of the subsidiary relationship of his subject matter to the whole program of the school.

200

The secondary school should regard itself as being co-worker with the state and with society in general toward one ultimate goal and toward short-range goals that point to the ultimate goal. This ultimate goal, as previously mentioned, is altruistic social service.

This philosophy does not deny the existence of goals beyond this ultimate goal of secondary education. It does recognize that we should not let our philosophical imagination run away from our human limitations.

In the elementary field adjustment to society is stressed. In the secondary field the emphasis gradually shifts to making an impression on society. But both phases are always present at all levels. In higher education this second phase becomes predominant.

We need to do some serious thinking on the subject of integration. A naive past generation assumed that we integrated in the elementary field and differentiated in the secondary field. The work of integration is a lifetime job. No individual is ever perfectly integrated with society. Perfect integration means perfect love for neighbor.

It is impossible to formulate a philosophy of secondary education that is much different from a philosophy of elementary or of higher education simply because we are dealing with people who refuse to be compartmentalized; who are developing at different rates and in many directions; and who will not attain like statures.

Objectives of a Secondary School

The seventh and eighth graders should receive a well-rounded education such as cannot be given in the traditional elementary school. But it is not enough just to add a few courses and to give each pupil a few more teachers.

Great efforts must be made to keep teachers from shirking their individual responsibilities under the plea that each teacher has each pupil only a short time and can therefore not be held responsible for the pupil's shortcomings.

Each course should be aimed at exploring the individual pupil's interests and capabilities. But it must be recognized that the kind of education that the pupils still need is that which generally goes by the name of elementary education.

In the ninth grade only about the upper third should take algebra. There would, of course, be much leeway in borderline cases. There should be courses in commercial arithmetic and in general mathematics. The general mathematics course would be mostly elementary arithmetic.

Latin would be given, not on the basis of utility, but as a concession to traditional requirements that still persist.

In the field of English, there would be an end to going through the motions of teaching grammar to those who will never get it. The study of literature would be aimed toward giving them something that will carry over into life. I would drop Shakespeare into the ashcan.

Social studies should expend great efforts to implant the idea that democracy is not primarily a form, but a spirit. Entirely too much time is spent on the *form* of our government.

All courses should be built around the social studies. In school there should be much practical demonstration of how rules must be changed to meet changing conditions. The adjustment must be made in the spirit of altruism. This should be the very heart of secondary education.

One of the major tasks of the school should be to get the pupils to see that we rise together. Too many teachers do not see it. This requires faith. It is often not self-evident. But a proper evaluation of the past can give us this faith.

Strenuous efforts should be made to meet the challenge of the majority—which constitutes the average and below-average students—who will need little or no preparation for the tasks they will perform in making a living. In their case the concentration can be almost wholly on making a life.

We must adjust our attitude in the direction of this majority as being the group most in need of the cultural courses. Great care must be exercised that the cultural courses will not be ossifying courses.

Such courses will evolve if we have enough teachers of vision. Such teachers will have a sympathetic attitude toward this majority.

What about the pupils of superior ability? We need not be concerned about them because tradition and inertia will take care of them for a long time to come.

It must be emphasized that the first step in this program must be a change in the average teacher's attitude. Outward changes will be evolutionary. So, in general, will be the teacher's attitude.

This attitude—in its present stage—is well expressed by the parent who says that he does not want his son to do the lowly chores that he himself has to perform. If the lowly chores are the result of lack of financial means or educational opportunity, then of course he is right. Too often, however, his attitude is that all those problems will automatically be solved if his son spends enough time at school, takes the right courses, and applies himself.

The school has gradually arrived at the ridiculous attitude that *all* the students should prepare themselves for something considerably above the lowliest tasks, without regard as to how many of those exalted positions are available.

Let us attack with evangelistic zeal this mistaken attitude. Let us never make the mistake of making the one-talent person (against the ten-talent persons) feel that he is a failure simply because he has no vocational aim. He must be made to feel very keenly that his biggest task is building his life.

15. EDUCATION

Let us begin with an enigma. Why are the best educated people lagging so far behind the masses in forward-looking legislation? Many will deny that it is so. I believe historians will agree that the milestones of progress that we celebrate were generally forced on the educated few by the ignorant majority. But many of these selfsame historians are lining up with the reactionaries on current issues.

Their case is analogous to that of our industrialists who admit that industry committed many sins against the workers fifty years ago, but that these have now all been corrected and no new ones have been added. Fifty years from now they will see the injustices that are being perpetrated *now*.

When future historians will evaluate the achievements of the New Deal, for an example, they will be able to tell almost exactly, through the kind of public opinion polls that are now being conducted, where the educated people stood on each issue.

We say that democracy depends on education. Education is supposed to make for liberalism. And yet the least educated seem to be the most liberal. Why not try less education?

One is tempted to suggest less education—until one starts to contemplate the lot of the poor in illiterate countries. No, the trouble is not with education, but with something that generally accompanies education; special privilege. The best educated are generally those who possess the most special privilege. The climate of opinion that special privilege creates outweighs the power of education.

The underprivileged are really more conservative than the privileged. But they know what is good for them. Reform is aimed at righting injustices. That makes it possible for the poor to be selfish and still right. Theirs is generally not the altruistic attitude. It just happens that justice is in line with their selfish aims. That is why if they ever get to the top, they tend to become as reactionary as those whom they replaced.

The underprivileged generally have an inferiority complex. Too many of them agree with the privileged that the lowly lot of the poor is their own fault. Their more enlightened leaders often have trouble in getting their cooperation in the crusade for justice.

Fortunately, education also reaches even the lowest strata in society. Therein lies the hope of the underprivileged. This fact is a guard against the underprivileged majority being too complacent about injustices that can be corrected. The more education we dispense at the top, the more seeps down to the masses. It is now more than a seep, or even a trickle. The more intelligence the masses have, the more likely they are to attain their goals.

Do teachers belong to the special privilege groups? They may not have many of the special privileges, but they are there all right. They are there largely because they have not risen sufficiently above the original aim of education, which was to *preserve* the heritage of the past for the future.

203

They do too little nurturing. They would correct all errors of the present by going back to the discarded policies of the past. It is the task of teachers to absorb the idea that perhaps all "inalienable rights" were sometime in the past wrested from the privileged few. Then, having absorbed the idea, they must pass it on to others.

Education generally succeeds in getting us to see injustices where we are not personally adversely affected by their correction. But it too seldom succeeds in getting us to look after those cases where we are involved to our own advantage.

Teachers should make more use of our mania for impartial judgment concerning things in which we have no personal stake. After judgment has been passed in such a case, special efforts should be made to carry it to an analogous case in which we have a personal stake. The first step, of course, is for us teachers to school ourselves to this type of analogy.

Few teachers are educators. Most of them are trainers. Few college graduates are educated. Most of them are trained. At the opposite extreme, we occasionally find a comparatively illiterate person who is educated.

Robinson's main line seems to be that the mind tends to regard the rules of the game that we inherited as having a kind of divine sanction; that education tends to free the mind. This is true. The special privilege groups would be even more reactionary if they had no education.

But this kind of education is acquired outside the school more than inside. Teachers in general are primarily concerned with providing the tools of education. They do not yet do enough to unshackle the mind.

I shall never forget the male teachers of the old school who survived to my time. I refer to those men who owned a little farm and taught in the nearby rural school. Most of those that I remember had that well-tailored look; they conformed to a pattern. To them, education was something cut and dried. Their job was to preserve it and pass it on in its preserved state.

It is probably still true that the general public thinks of the teacher more as a preserver than as a creator. "You are a teacher and should not express an opinion," is an attitude that is still too prevalent. Today's teacher still has too much of that tailored look. MacCallister's "inducation" describes that growth, or rather change, that is in the wrong direction. It is possible to have training and teaching that results in more maladjustment than adjustment.

The chief ingredient of education is learning. Teaching is a by-product that has some value. We have too many teachers who have not learned, or who have learned too little. It might be a great help if we teachers were to form the habit of asking ourselves at the end of each day, "Well, what did we *learn* today?"

The creative teacher draws much more inspiration from contact with pupils than from other teachers. In a forest of teachers it is often difficult to see past the fossils. The attitude of the pupils is, "Show me." The fossil's attitude is, "Let me show you." The fossils like to teach more than learn. The creative teacher is always more interested in learning than in teaching.

I never cease marveling at the great gap between the teacher's supposedly simple instructions and the child's grasp, or lack of grasp, of them. Understanding the child mind is a lifelong task. We dare never let down. I believe that the child is meeting us more than half-way in this task. The fossils do not try to bridge the gap.

None of us can educate somebody else. We can only set the stage for making it easier for others to educate themselves. Education is a spiritual conditioning and reconditioning. It is a conditioning to the conviction that spiritual growth need not end with bodily growth.

Many teachers mistake habit-forming and fact-acquiring for education. This is why many of their pupils become better educated, in time, than they. They will *sense* at least, if not know, that education is living. And the education that is living can be very contagious. Here lies the teacher's— and everybody else's—big chance.

"Equals do not learn from equals." Fortunately, none of us are equal. There are always respects in which the lowliest pupil in the class can teach us something. We teachers, and adults in general, must learn to never quit striving to learn from children. There is something inherently wrong with the educational process that allows only one-way traffic. Along with the general onward flow, there is much interaction. After all, the children have much to do with the formulation of the curriculum. Our ideals that we hold for our children must be tempered by what and where they are and how far and where they can go, and want to go.

One of the hardest ideas to down is that education is book-learning exclusively. Practice in the art of getting along is also education. After all, isn't education just preparation for the business of living? Therefore, when this preparation can be direct, so much the better. School should be living as much as possible. If we do not accept this, we must also reject the philosophy that all of life is an educational process.

I once had a visitor in school who liked everything he saw except a pupil reading a newspaper. To him, education was exclusively what you gleaned from between the covers of a book.

205

What is education? It is effecting a change in our thought processes. It is forming new habits and ways of looking at things, and learning new techniques. It is learning things we never knew before. It is learning new relationships. It is developing skills. It is a striving for certainty where only a vague idea exists. It is probing fixed ideas. It is developing attitudes. It is all this and probably much more.

Giving the proper credit and blame is one of the requirements of education. A sequence does not necessarily constitute a cause and effect; nor do the parts necessarily constitute causes of the same effects, or effects of the same cause.

The practical consideration in connection with this is that we are too prone to overlook the multiplicity of causes that produces an effect, and that the effects are much more numerous than we are prone to realize. Our analysis is too much influenced by our prejudice or bias. In many cases it is just plain careless thinking. In other cases it constitutes an inability to evaluate complex factors.

Education is a physical, mental, and spiritual conditioning. It affects being, knowing, and feeling.

Education goes on the assumption that for us mortals, all truth is relative. What may be true or false for a child need not be true or false for us.

Most important of all, education with the religious approach implants a humble spirit.

The religious approach to education means that we recognize that well-enough today does not necessarily mean well-enough tomorrow. It develops that lean hungry look. Lean means stripped for the quest. Hungry means we shall never reach perfection this side of the grave.

The religious approach should lead to the realization that the best reward for work well done is bigger things to do. The truly educated person thinks of his heritage as a growing, expanding thing.

The truly educated person is always on the alert lest he take too much credit to himself. I heard a college instructor say that he does not see why any teacher should have any disciplinary problems. The implication was very plain: that if all teachers were like him the schools would have no discipline problems.

A lay listener asked me afterward what I thought of that statement. My reply was that he never had to try to teach pupils who did not want to go to school .The speaker made the mistake of taking a wishful thought for an accomplishment, and of thinking that his experience in college had covered all phases of the problems of education.

I believe that a long stride in the right direction would be made if teachers took most of their courses in teaching methods while they are teaching, and that they should periodically take, or teach, the various methods courses throughout their whole teaching life.

The point will be raised that teachers need this knowledge of methods before they start teaching. They certainly do. But they are not getting it even if they take the courses. Methods courses should help solve *felt* classroom problems. And embryonic teachers have no such problems.

The methods courses build a halo about teaching that is rapidly dispelled during the first year of teaching. If the teacher has faith and continues to strive, a new halo will gradually appear, and this halo should stay and grow with the years.

The religious approach demands that we impart to the pupils some of the faith that we have, or should have, in education. They should realize that the world in which they live was built up by education; that they can enjoy vicariously its blessings through education. But the abiding joys come from the knowledge that they personally are contributing something to this advance. The law of love assigns to each one of them a task that he can perform.

One of the objectives of education is the building up of genuine self-respect. This is achieved through a frank appraisal of both assets and shortcomings, and by building a life that recognizes its limitations. This is a self-respect that needs no veneer. Putting pupils on edge does not build self-respect; easing tensions does.

The habit of probing and facing shortcomings has made many of us feel that we are today living in the most miserable age. But it is a real question whether this feeling is any stronger than it has been in any preceding generation.

A more basic reason is that most of us have to grow into, or past, middle age before we begin to appreciate how much misery there is in the world. It is true that an adult should have fewer worries than a child. But does he?

A child generally regards his worries as problems that will be solved in the process of growing up. The average adult can not see anything bright ahead. To him, doom lies ahead. To a child, salvation lies ahead.

Teachers must realize that one of their main tasks is that of integrating the products of specialization for the benefit of the pupil. It consists of more than relating the previously unknown to the known. It also finds new relationships between knowns.

The greatest danger is that the educator will overestimate the ability and capacity of the learner. Biting off more than can be chewed often results in chewing nothing at all. It again adds up to the task of keeping one eye on the do-able task at hand and the other in the general direction of the main objective. Lack of objective results in dawdling.

We can learn much from the great teachers of history. They all used illustrations, concrete examples, to illuminate their abstractions. I am not thinking now of people whose profession was teaching. Perhaps the greatest teachers have not been professional teachers. Even grown-ups need concrete examples.

Let it be emphasized that much of the life and teachings of Jesus could be introduced into the curriculum of the school; and that it would be in complete harmony with Judaistic teachings.

What about time released from school hours for religious instruction by the church? Most important, it is based on the assumption that the schools do not teach religion. What we should say is that the schools do not teach theology. Most important is the question whether the teacher has the religious attitude, and whether his attitude is transferred to the pupils.

It must be emphasized that many preachers dispense more pharisaism than religion. Many of them breathe hatred for those who do not agree with them. The churches and preachers should be more concerned about what they are doing to or with the children, and adults, during the short time that they do have them.

The religious approach to education demands that we analyze the steps to a program that will take care of our need for a sense of mission in life. It is the opposite of a sense of futility and frustration.

The first step is well understood—taking an interest in something outside oneself. The mistake is in not gradually widening the circle of interest. Altruism becomes selfishness if it is not allowed to expand.

Let us use here a few illustrations of an expanding altruism. It evolves the problem of who is *my* neighbor. Certainly it includes those whose interests are closely akin to mine. But if I stop here I am not being neighborly. I must include in my thoughts those whose interests often run counter to mine. Being neighborly is gradually coming to an understanding of the viewpoints of such people. A great help is a proper evaluation of history; a keener understanding of the struggles of those who went before.

Some secret organizations have a special pitfall to guard against. When their members must make a decision that affects one of their own number and an outsider on a matter that affects those outside their organization, they too often feel that their own member should be given priority. This is unreligious. Clannishness is not neighborliness. But mutual helpfulness that does not do violence to the rights of others does not come under the ban.

Even those of us who think of the whole world as our neighbor have not expanded to the full, and never will. We never achieve a complete integration with all the problems of all the world. We never get through the task of viewing the scene from many focal points outside our special interests. But this is not a hopeless task; the scenery along the way can be very inviting. The way to, and of, salvation is pleasant!

A continuing task of education, whether it be in the church, school, or life, is to learn, and help others to learn, this art of ever-expanding neighborliness.

A step in the right direction would be a contest to give Jesus' parables a modern setting. As one instance, what is the modern counterpart of the woman who swept the whole house for a lost coin, and then called in all the neighbors to rejoice with her? Or what is a modern counterpart of the Good Shepherd? By doing this we would be treading in the footsteps of Jesus. We would be doing it as he did it; using illustrations from the pulsating life about us.

Another step in the right direction consists in making the proper use of those things that we learn about those who live outside our orbit. The customary way is to pat ourselves on the back and say that we have risen above the shortcomings of such people. The right way is to study the local situation to determine what forms spirits similar to theirs assume in our midst. In most cases we shall be able to say that we have done much to overcome the spirit, if it is evil; but we are too prone to assume that in our midst the evil spirit in question is dead.

An evil spirit likes nothing better than being considered dead. This is the condition under which it thrives.

Let it be emphasized it is essential that we believe we are gradually mastering evil spirits; otherwise we should be living without hope.

Another well-known step in this religious approach to education is self-improvement for greater service. The second part is too often forgotten. Self-improvement palls in time if it is not put to work.

The religious approach is the candid approach. We teachers can take our pupils much more into our confidence than most of us realize. Too many of us take the attitude that all methods for maintaining control in

209

the classroom should be kept a dark secret from the pupils.

Many of us teachers feel that all things about which pupils are sensitive should never be discussed in front of the class. Our attitude is induced largely by our observation of the effects of an *improper* airing We have often observed the devastating effect that followed the ridiculing of the pupils' shortcomings; their low I.Q.'s, for instance.

The ideal solution is found in middle ground. A candid, objective discussion of pupils' shortcomings can do a great deal of good. In most cases it is not necessary to put the finger on any pupil. They make their own applications. I am thinking now of shortcomings that cannot be corrected. This is just another way of saying to the pupils that we are trying hard not to expect the impossible from them.

In the dark closet of every pupil's mind are many skeletons that would vanish if the light of day could be brought to bear on them. Teachers should be on the lookout for such skeletons in the closet. It all adds up to a recognition of the need for regarding personal limitations in a rational light. And it leads to a focus on the things that can be done.

Some people regard form and technique as being all-important. They should never be considered except in the light of attitude. Many thoughtful Americans consider Jefferson our greatest American. Jefferson is remembered for his attitudes, not for his techniques.

We older teachers remember when the daily lesson plan was the vogue. The theory seemed to be that if you carefully card-indexed all you taught the child, then nothing would be missed. It overlooked the question of readiness on the part of the child; the child's remarkable capacity for forgetting what he had learned; that learning is a cumulative process; the need for integration; and the vast differences in the interests and abilities of the various pupils in the same class.

At present we are considering the question of whether we should consider the citizenship mark in making up the honor roll. I believe that the more a person thinks about it, the more he will be convinced that citizenship should be considered. Teachers as well as adults are still thinking subconsciously of education as being something that is extracted from between the covers of a book. We are also, for the first time, considering the question of whether the subjects other than the "cultural" subjects should count in determining the honor roll.

The official action on both these questions was in the affirmative. But since that decision was made the citizenship mark has been dropped—at the same time that a nearby school is starting to place more emphasis on it.

The religious approach calls for giving credit where credit is due. We teachers should keenly recognize that most education does not come from teachers or the school. The school merely adds fuel and direction to the fuel and direction that education already has. We are educated by others; others are educated by us. Natural growth is an educator in the sense that it increases our capacity for learning. Education is growth. The school but helps to direct this growth.

I am thinking of a faulty line of reasoning that follows lack of recognition of this principle. It is the argument, sometimes heard, that if the school term were lengthened from nine months to ten months, then the schools would accomplish in nine years what they are now doing in ten. Degree of maturity is a factor that dares not be overlooked.

I have stated that historians are better at evaluating the past than in evaluating the current scene. Even this statement must be made with much reservation. The problem of the past is probably even greater than the contemporary one. Thus historians see *those phases* of the problem that seem to have bearing on the current scene. But if anything suffers, it is the present, not the past, which is gone.

What we probably need first of all is scholars who will not oversimplify problems and solutions of the past. Such over-simplification leads to oversimplification of the present problem and solution.

Education is preparation for social competency. What we need is a better technique for following a movement through from its historical beginnings to the present, with the idea of making the proper applications today. When we come on the contemporary scene, even among renowned scholars, it becomes extremely difficult to see the whole problem. They see but a segment of it; and nearly always the segment that they see is determined by their selfish interests.

In the teaching of democracy, rules, regulations, and laws must be visualized as serving the needs of the individuals who make up the democracy. Veneration for law must be based on the fact that it is man-made, under spiritual guidance, for men. Too many teachers do not recognize that laws are plastic, and always potentially in the formative stage.

In my earlier years as a teacher, I took the attitude that once a rule had been laid down to the pupils the next step was its enforcement and the punishment of all infringements. As it began to dawn on me that we grown-ups are constantly forgetting—and deliberately violating—rules, I gradually grew more tolerant toward violations that were not willful; and discipline improved apace.

211

I realize that for a beginning teacher this is dangerous ground—so dangerous that many teachers seldom venture on it. But it must be explored if the teacher is to become an understanding teacher.

It is strongly urged that wide application *outside* the classroom be given this thought. It is a phase of bending without breaking. A tree's greatest strength is in the direction of its bent. A strong man—not physically—has learned to bend.

"Experience is the best teacher." This, of course, means first-hand experience. Much ill can result from this statement. Experience is often too expensive. All safety education aims to substitute vicarious experience for direct experience. Naturally, experience must often be resorted to, but always with careful consideration of possible consequences and a consideration of whether a better method is available. In other words, experience as a teacher must be carefully chaperoned. Civilization is built on vicarious experiences. Education's task is to give past experience assimilable form.

The school does too little to consolidate its gains. It encourages greenhorns to rehash that which has been thoroughly covered by experts. It does this in the name of impartiality and freedom.

Here are two illustrations.

Our teachers' associations encourage the local teachers to study their local salary situations from the ground up. They generally end up on the ground.

When a high school gets ready for evaluation by an outside agency, it must build a philosophy of education for its own school from the ground up. It generally gets off the ground by surreptitiously copying a pre-digested philosophy from some outside source.

In the former case, they end up on the ground because they have too great a personal financial stake in the outcome of their deliberations. In the latter case their interest is only academic.

Most of the things that go into a salary schedule are pretty well agreed to by experts. Where there is disagreement, it would be easy to delineate the scope of the disagreement. This should be outlined and given to the local teachers as the framework within which the local salary schedule should be adopted. Exploring outside this framework is not to be discouraged; but any definite action outside this framework should be taken only after careful consideration of all ascertainable factors, and then only in moderate degree.

We should have available philosophies for the various types of high schools, prepared by experts after consultation with all types of teachers

212

found in the respective schools. The local committee should take the philosophy that most nearly fits its school and study it and the local situation to see if alterations would result in a closer fit. That is all. Energies thus saved could be applied to practical problems of teaching and administration.

Teachers have learned imperfectly the lesson of how civilization advances. It advances by substituting new forms for old; or, better still, by enlarging the old forms in the right direction ,and gradually closing up from behind. They make very poor use of vicarious experience—and all in the name of progressivism!

When I move along swimmingly at my job of teaching, I am prone to think that there is nothing to it—that anyone can be a good teacher. But when I see evidences of poor teaching, I begin to realize how much there is to good teaching. Once we have reached an objective, we are prone to overlook the many obstacles that we had to overcome to get there and we become impatient with others for not progressing faster than we did. We must continually be on the alert so that we do not lose sight of the devious paths that must be followed by the uninitiated; and if we lose it, we must rediscover it.

The early Christian leaders in education had an insight into the problems of education that leaves little to be explored by us moderns. They set up standards that we have not yet reached. If we were to judge the education of the past by the writings of its deepest thinkers and noblest souls, we would decide that education is slipping back.

But if we follow a reporter on actual conditions in the average classroom of that period, we get a different picture. The educational ideals were not being put into practice! This fact gives further point to Jesus' stand that the state of the human heart is the supremely important thing.

So it makes a great deal of difference whether we judge education today by the writings of the leading theorists, or whether we judge it by observing teachers at work with the pupils.

When teachers go back to classes in college, they like to brag about how they got out of doing the assignment and about how little work they did to pass. Let us not be too hard on our pupils for being no better than we.

We used to think that the harmonious development of all our faculties called for concentration on our poorest facilities. We now place the emphasis on our special faculties. The field theory of the conditioned response way of learning helps us realize that our best faculties are not developed at the expense of the other faculties; but rather that the other faculties are helped. In other words, there is transfer of training.

213

The theory of the transfer of training must be accepted if the complexities of life are to be met. Transfer is the very essence of the religious approach. It is closely allied to integration. But transfer of training, of course, must never be substituted for direct action when direct action is feasible. It should be a by-product, not a goal. In our learning it is best to lead with our best, not our worst. After all, isn't the learning process an attack on ignorance and prejudice?

Similarly, for each task we should lead with the best *person* available. The question is sometimes asked, "Shall the white man rule, or shall the Negro rule?" The proper, and practical answer is "Neither; each individual, regardless of color, should wield the influence that is his by native endowment and by personal industry."

How often do we hear adults tell pupils to study hard so that they will not have to work hard later! They are assuming that concentration on their studies will qualify almost any student for a white-collar job. Viewing pupils as a group, we should teach them instead to assume a philosophical attitude toward the niche that nature has probably cut out for them. Let us be easy on others and hard on ourselves.

One of the obligations of education is too teach us to recognize limitations and consequently not to bump our heads against stone walls. Stone walls don't "give" or take much except the leavings. There is too much debris piled up against stone walls that education should teach us to by-pass or hurdle.

I am thinking primarily of the stone walls of the pupils' limitations. We still spend too much time trying to teach children things they are simply too immature to grasp and, higher up, things they will never have the capacity to grasp. As one instance, why have we not come to an agreement as to what proportion of the pupils should never be taught grammar? All investigations show that some simply cannot grasp it. Every time we bump our heads, or the pupils' heads, we are doing something much worse than wasting the taxpayers' money. Fortunately both body and spirit have wonderful powers of recuperation.

We cannot recognize too clearly that many teachers are pursuing policies that tend to build up the pupils' inferiority complexes. Many pupils must leave school to rise above them. Too little effort is made to make pupils conscious of their abilities. Adults in general are just as guilty as teachers; in fact more so. Teachers need more training that will tend to raise them above this human frailty.

The first step toward the recognition of abilities should be the recogni-

214

tion of limitations. Limitations are boundaries. Even freedom without boundaries as meaningless. At present, too much emphasis is placed on breaking down limitations that cannot be broken down; or that can be broken down only at too great a cost. Education must pay more attention to relative costs.

We dare not leave the stone wall without recognizing that many stone walls are figments of the imagination. Every stone wall must be carefully and comprehensively probed to see if it is real and if it has weak spots. In fact, our continuing self-imposed task should be the probing of stone walls that stand in our way. Whether we should climb a mountain or go around it depends on our destination; and the size and nature of the mountain.

One of the functions of education is to deflate the egos of some. But there is probably no one who does not need to build up his ego, or self-confidence, in some phase of his personality. Education must be constantly on the alert to find areas within which the pupils can be built up. This is teaching pupils to help themselves.

This should not mean that the teacher should set up a blueprint for each individual pupil. Rather, the result is achieved through a changed attitude on the part of the teacher. This attitude is that the teacher must be harder on himself than on his pupils. Pupils are great imitators. This attitude will constrain pupils to set up for themselves tasks that they would not perform if they were imposed from without.

The main objective of the junior high school movement has been the finding of the pupils' strong points. The junior high school organization can be an improvement over the system that it superseded; but in many cases it is not. Too much dependence is often placed on the organization and too little on the new spirit. Before the re-organization, the seventh and eighth grades were generally taught by one or two or three teachers who felt a keener responsibility than do the many teachers of one pupil in the new setup. Besides, there is a greater tendency to ignore the tools of learning.

When I hear junior high school teachers talking about the poor preparation of the pupils who come to them, I feel like suggesting that we had better be more concerned about how much they are absorbing during the three years that they are with us.

Hitch your wagon to a star! But do not make the star your only objective. The road you choose must be dotted with minor objectives that have worth and interest independently of their relation to the star.

215

I have often told my pupils that if they have several tasks to perform, they should do the most difficult task fiirst. This is better than never getting to the difficult task. A better method often is to do the most *interesting* first with the idea of working up enthusiasm for the tasks that are to follow. This focuses attention on the task at hand and not on the clock. This is a sample of transfer of interest.

There was a time when I dreaded checking pupils' papers. While I was checking, my thoughts were on the end of the task, and how disagreeable the task appeared! Now I focus my thoughts on the pupil whose paper I am checking; I think in terms of what is right and wrong with my teaching technique; and I forget that I am engaged in a task.

Deliberate attempts should be made to get the child to center his attention on the task and not on its end. There definitely is such a thing as thinking too much about a goal, and too little about the interesting scenery along the way.

I do not believe in the school in which the children choose their own major activities. Certainly their interests must be considered, especially when we consider the method of approach to the problem that has been selected for study.

I have seen classes at work that pride themselves in their progressive spirit. In most cases it appeared that many fundamental tools were being neglected. I believe that the intangibles were neglected even more.

The successful teacher can take the things that he, and society, think should be taught and present them in such a way as to set up goals that give immediate satisfactions. That is all children ask for. The teacher sets up the goal and shows the children the beautiful scenery along the way. The successful teacher recognizes that even he becomes bored if there is little change in the routine. He recognizes the need for stopping, resting, gamboling.

Most of us are miserable in the midst of our pleasures. We are miserable because our thoughts are dwelling on the onerous tasks that are to follow. And we shall continue miserable until we learn to find interest in the scenery all along the path of life that it is our lot to travel.

As our misery is gradually trasformed into pleasure, we discover that our lot is much more plastic than we had even dreamed of hoping.

There are two kinds of automobile drivers. The one strains toward the goal. His nerves are worn to a frazzle by impeding obstacles. And when he gets there he is still miserable.

The other kind takes time to enjoy the scenery along the way. He is

216

not irritated by impeding factors. Instead he takes advantage of them to learn more from the situation at hand. He still has the play instinct. The child lives today, not tomorrow. So should we.

The average boy wants to be Ted Williams. This would not be the case if he did not find the scenery along the way very entertaining. He is living today, but not blind to the distant goal.

Enthusiasm for the task at hand can cover a multitude of shortcomings. The enthusiastic teacher can completely alter his technique without an appreciable immediate change in his effectiveness; provided he retains his enthusiasm. Technique is important, but enthusiasm is more important. I am thinking, of course, of enduring enthusiasm; enthusiasm that is resting on solid foundations.

I once had the experience of hearing a state supervisor praise to the skies the least popular and least effective teacher in the school system because the techniques of teaching that he outlined for the benefit of the supervisor were *letter* perfect.

I recognize the problem of the state supervisor; but is there no way for a state supervisor to evaluate spirit and enthusiasm?

Evaluating high schools is all the rage now. It consists in having a committee of outside teachers and administrators come to a high school to evaluate it on the basis of a rather fixed pattern.

This is preceded by a self-evaluation by the school which is almost invariably based on what the faculty thinks will make a favorable impression on the visiting committee. So they mechanize the school for the benefit of the visiting committee and for their own benefit in the added prestige that a favorable report will give them.

It is recognized all around that a school can be efficient while lacking the accepted patterns, while another school may have all the patterns and be inefficient; and the committees try to make allowance for it, but too often they do not succeed.

The immediate result often is a less efficient school. Forms and techniques will have been set up that are harmful, worthless, or at least not worth the effort spent on them.

However, the ultimate result is undoubtedly beneficial. Many a teacher merely moved from one rut to another; but some did more. And perhaps none will be as complacent as they were before.

At the beginning the school mostly conformed. But this is generally followed by more creative thinking than was ever engaged in in the past. It all adds up to another halting step forward and upward.

217

One way to remove ourselves as teachers from the niche into which the public has placed us is to resolve that our teaching, direct preparation, and work incidental to it shall take up between forty and forty-five hours a week, the remainder of the time to be devoted to living as citizens interested in community affairs. There we should find our field of greatest service.

But when we make contact with the public, we teachers must get off our high horse. We must get away from the attitude that our judgment on current public issues is superior to that of John Q. Public. We have a tendency to feel that we are the possessors of a spiritual heritage that in general is denied the public. A teacher once said to me, "We know what the public thinks; but what stand should *we teachers take?*"

My answer was that we teachers are not a group apart; that if we, in the light of history, stacked up our judgment on current problems against that of the public, we teachers, like the philosophers and college presidents, would emerge second best.

Why is the average teacher so unsure of himself outside the school? It is because he is very much a despot in the classroom. The chief characteristic of a despot is lack of proper consideration for those under him. And a despot in a democratic society is like a fish out of water. The veneer of bravado that is so evident in the classroom melts under public scrutiny. It is newly applied every morning.

What errors are teachers prone to fall into when they present a case or give an address? They generally present too much evidence. They have the philosophers' conception of impartiality. They too often fail to realize that unequals should be called unequal. They too often fail to draw conclusions, affecting instead the philosophical attitude of detachment.

Ninety percent of their speeches often are preamble, five percent is body, and five percent is conclusion. They find it difficult to plunge into a thing. They seem to be afraid that they might be considered ridiculous.

Here are experiences that I packed into one day at a teacher's convention. First came the core curriculm. That consists in incorporating several cores — like English. history, and geography — into one.

Good judgment was shown by the speaker in not forcing the new cores on unwilling teachers. It became plain, however, that he was beginning to think of core as an end, not *a* means to an end. He assumed that any successful amalgamation of two cores is always better than keeping the cores separate. He should have been concerned with the question of whether the same kind of interest on the part of the teacher in the separate cores might produce even more satisfactory results.

I do not believe that the new core curricula have as yet been properly evaluated. It is always difficult to determine how much of the improvement is due to renewed interest by the teacher. The same renewed interest in the traditional subject might have achieved results just as satisfactory. And I believe that it is just as easy to stir up enthusiasm in the smaller cores.

The object of the larger cores, of course, is to achieve a unity between the smaller cores in the pupils' thinking, that they had not achieved before. I personally believe that there is distinct danger of sacrificing depth for breadth. We must consider the limits of the pupils' horizons. We must again remind ourselves that a thing that is logically very sound may psychologically be very unsound.

I am personally of the opinion that we would teach English more effectively if we were to eliminate it as a separate subject. Teachers would no longer be able to blame the pupils' shortcomings on the English teacher. All teachers would, of course, have to have a clear conception of what their duties are regarding the teaching of English. The various types of literature could be assigned to the various subject fields.

The next speaker presented "life adjustment" education. Officially he was the head of an instructional problems section. They were still problems when he got through. He did nothing of a constructive nature but utter generalized statements about which no one could argue.

He said that no teacher should launch his program without having the Board of Education behind him. The trouble was that he did not present his program; and that he did not seem to realize that all education is in varying degrees life-adjustment education.

The remarks that followed showed that the audience as a whole shared my disgust with the speaker's lack of program. Questions that followed showed that many of his figures were faulty; and that he did not understand the significance of some of the figures that he used.

The moderator came much closer to the truth when he said that the school that made good readers, spellers, writers, calculators, and speakers out of the pupils could do almost anything else and have the public with it. He made it plain that by good he merely meant not being glaringly deficient.

There was also a speaker on "democratic action" education whom I had heard before. He at least presented a program. But it was merely the project method parading under another banner.

The last two speakers teamed up for a dissertation on the consolidation and reorganization of the secondary schools. They were addressing

219

administrators. I was perhaps the only black sheep in the audience. I am only a teacher.

At least seventy-five percent of each speaker's talk was preamble—about background with which all were thoroughly acquainted. Finally both came to the point in which the administrators—and I—were interested, said a few words; and stopped.

What does it all add up to? Too much preamble, too much skirting, too little plunging in, too much "philosophical" detachment, too much logic, too little psychology that is based on the pupils' manifest interests. For what is found in a teachers' convention is but a reflection of the spirit—or lack of it—that is found in the classroom; and in the teachers' contact with the outside world.

Most of them do not realize that the audience is more interested in the question of where the speaker stands, and what he would do, than in the presentation of a great deal of evidence.

Fortunate is the teacher who can sift from a mass of factors involved in a problem, the few that have the strongest bearing on the question at issue. Even this does not guarantee that he will be followed by the audience. Edward Bellamy thought that in *Equality* he could present such a fair, clean-cut case that every intelligent man could not help accepting it. He did not reckon with the extreme inertia of the average human mind. He did not reckon with the habit people have of disposing of compelling arguments with, "Yes—, but . . ."

The average high school student has an idealistic conception of our legislators. The average adult is too cynical or callous. Students should understand this cynical attitude so that they will be on their guard when they are temped to become cynical. For what is the cynical attitude if not that if I do not look out for Number One, no one else will? It is an unreligious attitude.

Pupils must learn to be on the alert when they grow up, so that public servants will perform their tasks without waste. The best preparation for alertness is to have mastered the art of conservation themselves.

The schools should lay great stress on true conservation, which consists in putting persons and things to the best possible use; or building them up for future service.

There is much waste in every war. I am now thinking only of that waste that reduces our fighting efficiency. But war itself is waste. It is an accumulation of the wastes of peace. In an all-out war there is less waste than in peace.

Jesus often drew lessons from the devotion of unprincipled persons to their nefarious schemes. So also peace can learn from war. The job of education is to get us to analyze the causes of the wastes of peace and then start on the tedious task of eliminating them. It is a life-time job. All we can hope to do in our generation is to eliminate enough of these wastes so that the residue will not add up to another world war. True education gives a religious bent to our impulses.

The schools must give much thought to relative values. In incorporating new ideas or techniques, great care must be exercised that the incorporating will not be at the expense of more important things.

For years, while I was teaching in the grades, I was agitating the idea that all subjects that involved reading and retention—like history and geography—should be treated primarily as reading lessons. I was, of course, thinking of the reading lessons as including all that is included in a comprehensive reading program.

The idea is excellent; but I allowed it to carry me too far. In my state, the reading of at least ten verses from the Bible is required at the beginning of each school day. I decided to make a reading lesson of that, too. Since the reading must be without comment, this could be nothing but oral reading—reading for expression. Now, most pupils do not read with sufficient expression to hold the interest of their fellow pupils. The result is often a Bible reading that meets legal requirements and nothing more.

Teachers should select their Bible readings carefully—not hurriedly at the last minute—and have a clear knowledge of the contents. This is necessary for reading that will carry over.

There are, of course, teachers who read with less expression than many of their pupils. The important consideration is that the method used must be based on the need for getting the maximum out of the lesson.

This is further an illustration of how teachers often fall pitifully short of the very things that they expect of their pupils—careful preparation. Instead their preparation is often very slipshod.

What's wrong with our schools? Somebody outside the school system tests some children on local government and is appalled at their ignorance. Then he raises the cry, "The schools should teach more local government." Others test the pupils in other subjects and are all appalled at the pupils' ignorance. Combining all their demands into one statement, it amounts to this: "The schools should teach more reading, spelling, composition, grammar, writing, arithmetic (oral and written), history and civics (local, state, national, and world), geography, health, physiology, speech, character, etc." This is no exaggeration. What is the answer?

221

We are agreed that the products of our schools know little American history, little about local government, little about our federal government. The main reason is that we are giving the schools a job that should be a life-time job. Training for citizenship is a life-time job.

A big part of the answer to the question, "What's wrong with the schools?" is, "Not as much as we are prome to think." What would happen if we conducted a searching poll of church members about their religious beliefs, doubts, and ignorance?

When we test adults, including teachers—the product of the schools of the preceding generation—we are again duly appalled at their ignorance. The product of the schools of the past was at best no better than the present product. We must remember that in those days we did not have such copious tests that are designed to display ignorance. We face facts more frankly today.

To begin with, we should never say that the schools should teach more of anything without giving thought to the question of what less important thing is to be eliminated. My own answer is that we should really teach more simple things and quit going through the motions of teaching more complicated things that the pupils will not grasp.

We are glibly assuming that all the pupils know things that even the brightest do not know. We are constantly using words that are "Greek" to even the brightest pupils. Every teacher must be constantly vigilant to these pitfalls.

I have often been appalled when I considered how much more immature my pupils appear to my eyes when I meet them outside the classroom, in the workaday world, than when they are lined up in front of me in the classroom. I believe the outside view is the truer view. Here we see them in connection with the complex world in which we live. In the classroom we tend to manufacture a world for them.

The secondary schools are much concerned about the problem of the kind of education to give the pupil who is of the non-academic type. Those schools that have done nothing to correct the condition are not much behind those schools that have tried to solve the problem by segregation and by setting up new courses of study.

I am convinced that the main trouble lies in the mind of the average teacher. These pupils are stigmatized by the average teacher, and he often goes out of his way to make his feelings known to them. In the mind of the average teacher, the pupil of low I. Q. is a problem pupil. When such pupils are concentrated in one group, *such a teacher* intensifies the problem; but for the right kind of teacher, the problem is simplified.

I deliberately used the word segregation instead of homogeneous grouping, because in the mind of the average teacher they are segregated. They are "put out of the way" instead of being launched in the direction of the kind of preparation that will best fit them for their role in the complex social order.

It is now recognized that the expansion of the practical arts program is not the answer to this problem of the school's misfits. I call this group misfits with misgivings. It would be better to call the *school* a misfit. Most of these pupils will fill unskilled positions. The justification for keeping them in the secondary schools must be found in the general, or cultural, program. Can it be done?

Eventually it will be done or provision will be made for the pupils to leave school at an earlier age. The school's objective must be to teach pupils how to make a life *with the talents at their disposal.*

The problem can be simply stated. The answer is not simple. It begins with cultural courses close enough to their interests to elicit a spontaneous response from them. The teachers themselves must know how to live. The grand objective must be kept in mind, but the road to it must be dotted with many more points of interest than it now has.

The big question should not be how much of the road is covered, but how thoroughly it is being covered up to the stopping point. Integration must be mostly with what preceded, and with life. At present too much effort is expended toward integration with a projected future that in many cases is unattainable.

The religious approach demands that we formulate cultural courses that are geared to the interests and capacities of the children at all levels of intelligence. This is the crying need today. Still more crying is the need for teachers who have the vision for this.

When I went to high school, I conceived the cultured courses as being something cut and dried that was handed down, not up, from the past. I do not recall any effort on the part of the faculty members to make me think otherwise.

The most cultural pastime in the world is the investigation of the spirit of the social sciences; and then the furnishing of a body—a changing and changeable body—for the spirit. This, and not the "cultural" courses of the past, furnishes real culture.

The surest way to bring the dead and quiet past to life is to learn to recognize that there is life—change—in the present.

So the truest cultural courses are those that help the pupil along and up the road, however slow the pace, of getting the feel of his neighbor's feelings, getting along with himself, and with his own spirit. This is a pragmatic way of saying "getting along with God."

As the pupil absorbs this spirit, he tends to conceive of this world as something that is moving from chaos to order, and not vice versa. And the school can make the greatest contribution when it recognizes, and puts its belief into practice, that its function in relation to the average and below-average student is to be almost exclusively concerned with what the future worker will do when he is not putting in his forty hours a week. There are still 128 hours left.

I realize what a tremendous task it will be to build up a course such as I visualize. My concern here is to get ourselves to see the need.

We must learn to be the kind of child psychologist that we have never been before. We must learn to find the pupil's level and then learn not to move up at too fast a pace. Too often we come down to the pupil's level, point out to him the top of the skyscraper, and then say, "Jump."

We do not learn to build a house by looking at a completed one. Teachers, and others, seldom recognize the mental conditioning that was necessary to make some of the simplest concepts part of their own being. It is this fact that makes so many of us adults so impatient with the child world.

The general courses in manual dexterity are not ruled out. They can be a great help in building up a pupil's self-respect and confidence. But their limitations must be recognized.

Provision must still be made for those who have a special aptitude in the practical arts. We must give all encouragement to those pupils who have the ambition and initiative to rise above their normal level. But the cultural courses must still be the core. They must be of such a nature that they will tend to help build up the pupils' self-respect.

I am indebted to the authors of the *Harvard Report* for my observation to the effect that whereas misfit pupils used to leave school and achieve respectability by earning a living, now they stay in school and, with the teacher's hearty cooperation, eventually leave school with a beautiful inferiority complex. The schools are not yet ready to take care of all kinds of pupils to the age of eighteen.

During this transitional period, we teachers must work overtime reconditioning our attitude toward these pupils. Parents must work overtime reconciling themselves to the real limitations of their children. They should aim for the altruistic attitude that every position should be filled by the one best qualified for it; and that the most apt must be trained or educated for it.

Within the family variances in abilities and kinds of abilities are clearly, and often entirely too clearly, recognized. The necessary next step is to recognize our neighbor's children as part of a bigger family.

The mother of the Comptons recalls that when they were growing up she was asked, "What are your children going to be when they grow up?" Her reply was, "Why, I haven't thought about it." She was more concerned about the immediate task of building lives. Even in the case of such as these, the greatest task is building lives.

I am very much concerned at present with problem of how the problem of choosing a life vocation should be presented to the child. I do not believe in portraying any occupation as being holier than another. It causes the holders of the less holy occupations to feel that they don't count. It must be emphasized over and over again that the most eloquent sermon anyone can preach is the example of the kind of life he is leading—and that can be done in any kind of life work.

In choosing a life work, what should be considered? Many things. We should not expect *others* to choose a poor-paying position in preference to a better-paying one on the ground that the low-paying position is the more honorable or affords the greater opportunity for service. Rather, our efforts should be directed toward rewarding positions according to service rendered and amount of preparation required.

So long as society is so constituted that the greater part of our energies go toward making a living for ourselves and for others, so long must we give major consideration to financial remuneration. Pupils should be encouraged to face this problem candidly.

The pupils' special interests and aptitudes are of paramount importance. Consideration must be given to the question of whether a field of activity is expanding or contracting; whether many or few are preparing for a particular field. Location of the proposed field is an important consideration.

The final decision should not be made by taking a pencil and jotting down various weights for each factor. Rather, it resolves into a problem of the student's preference after a careful consideration of all factors.

And we must remember that for the majority of the pupils there is little choice. The jobs they will fill will call for little training. They will take the job that appears the most available and agreeable at the time. For them, in particular, the problem is to teach them to live the fullest possible

225

lives within their capacities. We must recognize the stone walls of definite limitations.

Teachers are often unintentionally cruel to pupils in their references to blind-alley jobs. If these teachers were to classify all the jobs in their community, they would place over half of them in the blind-alley category. It should be as plain as day from this that they are telling their pupils in effect—if the pupils are an unclassified group—that more than half of them will fill blind-alley jobs.

No job should be called blind-alley without reference to the capacities of the persons who are being considered for it. If the job rates as high in the job scale as the worker rates in the worker scale, in the light of his capacity, then that job is not blind-alley for that person.

Two years ago I took a course in high school evaluation. During that course, I made the remark that I got less guidance from the chapter on guidance than from any other chapter in the book. I still believe that there was more truth than smartness in the remark.

Recently I listened to a high school principal who spoke about the guidance program in his school. Prior to his promotion he had been the guidance supervisor in the same school. He made the remark that sometimes they succeeded in steering a below-average pupil into a job that was not blind-alley. Plainly he took the attitude that the others had not profited from the guidance program. This, I believe, is typical of the attitude of the great majority of our guidance supervisors.

I insist that the main task of the guidance program is to steer the thinking of the below-average pupils away from concern as to what they are going to do for a living, and toward concern with what they are going to do with their lives.

It is dangerous for secondary school teachers to point to a trouble spot outside their field. But it is a well-recognized fact that most pupils don't become maladjusted in the secondary schools. They are maladjusted when they get there. Maladjustment is a continuous growth that begins in the home and gradually becomes more acute up through the grades. Each succeeding grade adds its quota of pupils who for the first time are recognized as being maladjusted. It must, of course, be recognized that maladjusted pupils sometimes become adjusted.

"An ounce of prevention is worth a pound of cure," is an understatement. It is agreed that the behavior pattern of the child is well-set by the time he reaches school age. I believe that almost everybody will agree, on reflection, that the most fateful years of a person's life are the first five. If everyone keenly recognized this, it would be a great stride forward.

We cannot *prevent* the irreligious attitude in children. They are born with it and it is nurtured until the child begins to acquire a sense of right and wrong. This irreligious attitude is simply selfishness. In his natural state the child thinks of no one's welfare but his own. The child must be *cured*.

We must treat with sympathy children's outlandish notions. Education begins at this point. It does not necessarily consist in showing the child how foolish his notions are. Rather it consists in opening up new vistas for the child. The child will do the rest. The vistas must not be too far-fetched.

A child who is properly conditioned by his parents can withstand a great deal of poor teacher example. We have an unfortunate corollary to this. The child who is improperly conditioned can withstand a great deal of good teacher example. The parent's biggest task is prevention; the teacher's main task is cure where there has not been prevention. Both are necessary. When a child gets a false start, we can never be sure that it is too late to effect a cure.

It is too bad that even the "experts" are so far apart on the subject of bringing up children. I hope that I can add something to which all can agree. The major part of a parent's problem of bringing up his child is mastered if he has mastered the problem of bringing up himself. In thinking of himself, does he think of his duties first; and in thinking of his child, does he think of his child's rights first?

If I were asked, "How do you bring up your children?" I would reply, "I don't, I try to bring up myself." This does not rule out correction and direction. It merely points the emphasis. Almost every parent tries to teach his child unselfishness. When he does not succeed, it is generally because he has not taught himself.

The reason that this truth is not recognized more generally is that we have too many examples of children growing up with a great deal of freedom; whose parents give little or no thought to the influence that they exert by their example. Worse yet, most parents seem to think that they are brought up already. Bringing up ourselves is a never-ending task. Even grown-ups do not grow spiritually like weeds; that is, without nurturing.

If children have the example of parents who believe in piling burdens on themselves and not on their children, they will tend to do to themselves in the process of growing up that which worked so successfully with their parents.

227

Children must not learn to become cruel taskmasters when they grow up. The best guarantee against this is a good example by the teacher and parent.

I am not building up the other people's character by making them do my work for me. This is aimed particularly at parents. Perhaps the most important phase of education is the instilling of proper attitudes into the adult population. "Teach children unselfishness." This is a common headline; but a better one would be, "Set children an example of unselfishness."

Teachers should make it a habit never to assign a task without being convinced that it has validity. If teachers make this a habit, there will be no need for explaining to children the reasons that are hard for immature minds to grasp. The teacher will acquire the reputation of knowing what he wants and knowing how best to achieve it.

We teachers would consider that administrator or supervisor a tyrant who expected the impossible of *us* as we so often expect of our pupils. We teachers need religion.

Our relations with children would immediately improve for the better if we repeatedly asked ourselves the question, "Now how would we act toward this child if he were as big as we are?"

I recall two instances of boys of high school age engaging in public mischief. In each case a member of the Board of Education made the remark that we teachers should tell them not to do it. In both cases, the argument was based on the assumption that if we teachers *told* the pupils not to do a certain thing, then they would not do it. If that were true, then there would be no problem of juvenile delinquency.

Teachers have the responsibilities of parents, and then some. They must face the problem of what to do with children who are already spoiled. No child must be considered beyond reclamation. They need the truly religious approach. They often need to take the attitude, "Forgive these children, my neighbors, for they know not what they do." This attitude must be one of true humility.

Principals in high schools have sometimes asked teachers to take certain classes and do anything with them and teach them anything so long as they kept order. Few teachers have accepted such a challenge. Some who accepted it have failed. Others have succeeded.

No fault can be found with the principal who issued such a challenge when all the circumstances are considered. But it certainly is an appalling confession of how much we teachers, and our schools, still lack.

What would you do if you were assigned such a task? There are at

228

least two approaches to this problem that may work. One is to take hold of the class as though nothing unusual had happened and try hard to discover their interests and dispel their resentments.

A method that I prefer is frank statement to the pupils of the actual conditions. If the teacher convinces the pupils that he is really trying to promote their interests, and that he does not say nasty things about them behind their backs, he may get a favorable response.

Failure on the part of the teachers does not necessarily mean that he has the wrong attitude. Technique also counts for much. It may also mean that the pupils have reached a point where they are beyond reclamation. This is a stark fact that must be recognized.

Should parents be held responsible for the delinquency of juveniles? The answer is no, if by that we mean that every parent should be held responsible for every wrong committed by his children. We can take this stand and still believe that there is more parental delinquency than juvenile delinquency.

I do not like to get in touch with the parents if a pupil begins to fall off in his school work. The results are generally bad. The reason undoubtedly is that the parent in most cases knows less than the teacher as to how the situation should be corrected. There is the further fact that since the child is a school problem, he is probably a home problem too. Making parents responsible for the punishment and correction of delinquents is giving them a job for which they have already proved themselves unfit.

This is an argument for considering each case on an individual basis. It is a warning to guard against trying to make the catchword, parental delinquency, a catchall for a great ill.

Why do children live as in a world apart? It is largely because we adults have consigned them to such a world. We must vividly realize our shortcomings in not being able to recognize that children are entitled to as much consideration as adults. We must realize as we never realized before that childish needs are just as real as adult needs; that we must be as polite to children as to our official superiors.

Some of us teachers often marvel that pupils are as good as they are, considering what they have to put up with. The pupils know that most of the teachers ridicule them for their low I. Q.'s, their unfortunate backgrounds, and their ideals.

Right here it should be emphasized that there is a vast difference between smiling indulgently at childish ideals, and ridiculing them.

There is great need for getting down to earth about the simple little things that children can do better than they are doing them. Teachers recognize the problem, but too often try solve it by yelling and not by demonstration and help.

"Playing down" to people whom we consider our inferiors seldom works. In the first place, we should not consider them our inferiors. In the second place, we are putting on a show of pretending to be less than we really think we are. One of the secrets of Franklin D. Roosevelt's phenomenal success in dealing with people was the fact that he never played down to them. Playing down is unnecessary if we *come down*.

The malcontents in school, and in society, perform a useful function. They are a guarantee that we teachers, and society, will not become too complacent. These tactless youngsters, and oldsters, should impress us with the need for the exercise of much tact on our part. Tact is essentially a question of how I am going to do a thing that I have decided should be done. It is not a question of *what* shall be done. It involves a study of the psychology of the person involved.

Henry Wallace is a puzzling figure to many thinking Americans. They do not dismiss him with a wave of the hand. Therefore I shall try to analyze him.

Henry Wallace is better on the approach than on the follow-through. His approach apparently is that the established nations were very unfair to post-tsarist Russia in its early stages. These nations are the possessors of many special privileges that were acquired in the past by methods that are no longer sanctioned. Therefore they are denied Russia, which got a late start. So much for the approach, which is excellent. It is the religious approach.

His follow-through appears to be based on the assumption that as soon as we start to be fair to Russia, Russia will be fair to us.

Let us drop Russia temporarily and see if we can find a fair analogy in the field of juvenile delinquency.

Most parents are never confronted with a major juvenile delinquency problem. I refer to the kind that is represented by the lowest one percent in the behavior scale. And most of them think that they know the solution. They recognize, as nearly everybody recognizes. that in the great majority of cases of juvenile delinquency, the basis is an unfair deal that the child received. These misguided people feel that as soon as these problem children are confronted by an understanding and sympathetic person, they will immediately react favorably to kind treatment.

Those of us who have had first-hand experience with this problem know that such problem children are suspicious of all expressions of sympath and understanding. The road to a cure is rocky indeed.

One of the most difficult things for a beginning teacher to become adjusted to, particularly if that teacher has been brought up in an atmosphere of cooperation, is the pupil who will not cooperate, listen to reason, or explain his stand. Such a pupil is full of resentments piled up from the past. Such a pupil has a feeling that he will never be understood.

There is an occasional teacher who gets along better with extreme problem cases than with normal pupils. He gets that way by catering to these problem pupils, at the expense of the normal pupils. The overall effect of his influence is that he contributes more to the problem than to the solution. The case of such a teacher is somewhat analogous to that of the public official who gets along wonderfully with the crooks in the community.

Under tsarist domination, and since, the Russians have acquired the attitude that it is safer to be very suspicious of all expressions of kindly interest. They as a nation are like the juvenile delinquent. We must expect a *slow* change for the better. Wallace seems to think that Russia has already acquired this new attitude.

We as a nation are contributing more to the problem than to the solution if we cater to Russia at the expense of the other nations. Here by all means we must not get away from the religious approach, and the follow-through.

It seems that the most difficult and onerous subject to teach is English. I do not have the answer as to what should constitute the English course in high school. Certainly there is too much grammar for the below-average pupils. Most of the fiction is beyond their interest and experience. Certain it is that the content should bring them closer to home than it does at present.

If all English teachers were pragmatically-minded, there would be an instant improvement in the outcomes. Certain it is that the general public has more faith in their efficiency than the teachers themselves.

It seems fitting here to consider why our educational system does not make readers out of our people. Undoubtedly an important reason is that what they had in school was too far outside the range of their experience. The various types of book clubs that have evolved are undoubtedly a step in the right direction.

Reading the newspapers regularly is not enough. We must occasionally read summaries of big movements, in book form, to acquire and to keep our perspective. Every person should make the reading of books one of his hobbies. There should be a system; but there should be no hesitancy about breaking off into new directions if interest points the way.

I believe that the great majority of persons who can read can make the reading of good books a habit—a habit that they will enjoy and find very uplifting. But the needs of every individual will not completely fit into any one pattern. It must be made easy for him to expand in the direction that suits his bent.

We generally do not instil the reading habit by beginning with the old classics. The starting points should be, almost invariably, authors of the present. We must have a good idea where we now are to come to an appreciation of what the past has done for us.

For instance, I recall that in my immature days, I often became disgusted with the views expressed in old established classics. I was not sufficiently conditioned to the heritage that was theirs to appreciate what they had contributed to what.

Let me make definite recommendations for making better readers. It is for a new kind of bookstore. The store would start with nothing except all available book catalogues. The customer would be allowed to order any book in print. He would make a ten percent deposit when ordering. He would pay the remaining ninety percent when receiving the book. He would return the book within a month and get a refund of eighty five percent of the purchase price.

The book would then be placed on the shelf for the next customer. The next customer would pay only ninety percent of the original price of the book and get a refund of seventy-five percent. The tenth person to borrow the book would keep it. Any borrower could keep any book at any time by not returning it for a refund. The books would contain the names of the persons who read them with room for comment, favorable and unfavorable.

There should also gradually be built up a free-book shelf consisting of books fully paid for that are added to the list.

If no one would be willing to take the risk of organizing such a store, or club, it could be underwritten by a group of interested citizens, or a service club.

Why all this? Readers become thinkers; unless they never change their reading fare. This method would encourage exploration. Readers, if given sufficient opportunity and incentive, will explore new fields. Too often they don't know which way to turn.

I recall vividly the first story I read as a boy that had no villain in it. Before that time I had become very tired of the villains in the stories and had begun to wonder whether it would be possible to write a story without one.

So readers generally will find, when they look for something new, if they look long enough, that someone before them looked for the same thing that they looked for, and found it; or created it! The implication should be plain: Perhaps *we* can create!

The end of all this would be a citizenry of old people with the habit and a technique for getting what they want. How much misery old people endure because they never formed the reading habit! A person can become poor company for himself if he does not occasionally refresh his thinking by contact with the thoughts of others.

The Board of Education needs religion. It must recognize that the teachers are not hired to impose the Board's views on the pupils. We must at the same time recognize that the Board also has its obligations, or else there would be no need for it. In fact, an unusual amount of tolerance is required of Board members. They must guard against the two extremes of being tyrants on the one hand and mere rubber stamps on the other.

They have a responsibility, with the superintendent, for looking into the beliefs—religious, social, economic, etc.—of their teachers. Perhaps about the only safe thing that can be said here is that they should be on guard against the teacher who is more interested in tearing down than in building up—the cynical teacher.

Perhaps every school system has its quota of teachers who have a cynical attitude toward orthodox religion. The superintendent has the responsibility of talking to the whole group of teachers on this subject. The object should not be to change the beliefs of the teachers; but to impress on them—particularly on the young teachers—that their views are not necessarily the right views. and that if they are interested in their own spiritual *growth* they will not be so quick to play with the beliefs of those who are less mature than they. Here in particular they need to be reminded that a little learning can be a very dangerous thing.

We must be exceedingly wary on the question of barring teachers with dangerous ideas. In practice it too often means the exclusion of all ideas but our own.

Jesus' ideas were considered dangerous. Innumerable other illustrations could be added. The great danger is that so often we take the attitude that all this belongs to the past; that today with our superior knowledge, we can infallibly spot a person with dangerous ideas. And this is exactly what every age has thought.

This illustrates how ridiculous is the suggestion that persons with dangerous ideas should be excluded from teaching. What are dangerous ideas? Those that are contrary to those held by the Board of Education or superintendent. Many Boards would consider me dangerous. Most Boards are conservative.

The best plan is to let nature take its course and hope that teaching will draw its share of the liberals, and that liberals will remain liberal.

Let us take a further look at the teacher. Teachers have the reputation of being the most gullible of people. As a result some have set up a defense mechanism that swings them too far in the opposite direction.

I believe I am indebted to Santayana for this illustration:

There was a sheep that was considerably more intelligent than the other sheep in the flock. It did not follow blindly. It always lingered behind to profit from the experiences of those that went before.

One day the sheep had to cross a ravine that was spanned by a narrow plank. As this sheep watched the crossing, it noticed that many of them fell in on the right side.

After all the other sheep had crossed—or tried to cross—this sheep proceeded to cross very carefully and fell in on the left side.

The teacher with *a little* learning is alert to the danger on *one* side. He must be alerted to the need for being on guard against danger on the other side; and also against manufacturing dangers in his mind.

They must remember that it is still better to trust too much than to suspect too much. They suspect too much that pupils do not want to learn. They suspect too much that it is better for them not to express an opinion on a controversial issue. They are very brave—in front of their pupils.

The average audience is too gullible. A speaker presents a message. The audience nods in approval. A week later another speaker presents a message that is in many respects diametrically opposed to the first speaker's. The same audience again nods in approval. It can almost be said that they nod in their sleep; or under a hypnotic spell. The hypnotic spell issues from the feeling that the speaker, as such, is the repository of some divine inspiration. The audience should realize that they also have, and should exercise, the power to think creatively.

Now here comes a speaker who starts with, "What are we headed for? I am going to make some bold statements. I don't care whether or not you agree with me." This, naturally, is a condensation.

He, of course, was not telling the truth. He *did* care whether or not people agreed with him. He knew from experience that more than ninety percent of them would agree with him.

Here are some of his statements: Our country was built up by businessmen, not by politicans. How presumptuous for Chancellor Hutchins and Ely Culbertson to think that they can make a contribution to world peace! How wonderful is business!—and how corrupt is government! How democratic is business, and how tending toward socialism and communism is government!

These are the kinds of utterances that the unthinking listener applauds. It is things like these that lend stress to the statement that few people are thinkers.

I recall the general reaction of an audience to a Chinese speaker. He was asked many questions on China. He invariably took the attitude that his faction in China was always all right and the opposing faction always all wrong. And the audience took the attitude that he must be right because he observed conditions first-hand. All we have to do to clarify this muddy line of reasoning is to consider how we Americans can look at the same conditions and be at opposite poles in our interpretation of them. A person who views from a distance often shows better judgment than the one who has his nose close to the grindstone.

We come close to a problem when we are doing our bit; but we must repeatedly step back for an overview of the whole situation. This is life, and living, and education.

It is because of this that I have singled out certain writers whose views are in many respects—in my opinion, at least—diametrically opposed to mine. I want to make sure that the reader will clearly see these views. Besides, this sometimes leads to understanding where only misunderstanding existed before.

There is danger of curtailment of free speech through monopoly in the newspaper, magazine, and radio field. This gloom is pierced by the fact that Franklin D. Roosevelt's strongest support came from the cities, where most newspapers and periodicals were against him. Harry S. Truman's victory in 1948 demonstrated that the monopoly is still ineffective.

16. WORLD PEACE

For several years before I actually started this book, I was mulling over the prospects of producing a book with a new sustained line of thinking that would make a real contribution to world peace. All that precedes in this book has this as *an* ultimate goal. We might add that the atomic bomb made it *the* ultimate goal. But we dare not fold our arms and say, "The atomic bomb will make *others* work for world peace." It must make *us* work for world peace, unless we are already working from loftier motives.

When I was a boy, people were more panicky about smallpox, diphtheria, cancer, and witchcraft than they are today about the atomic bomb. There never was a time when people were not panicky about something. Two of the main feeders of panic are ignorance and superstition. In the case of the bomb, we can be more realistic. And there is a more obvious link between the atomic bomb and possible world catastrophe.

World peace is not achieved by a frontal attack. It is something that gradually descends on us as we go about doing the little things that are big things in the aggregate. We must have a crusading faith that these little things count. Like the bluebird of happiness, world peace is satisfied with the crumbs that are left as we go about being mutually helpful.

We are all individuals. We all count. Our attitudes and actions count. All of us are doing our bit for world peace or for World War III.

We are all potentially creative individuals. Doing something more effectively or putting it to better use for humanity's sake is being creative.

The opposite is nihilism. It is doing something less effectively or putting it to purely selfish use. Democracy does *not* teach that all our selfish efforts add up to the best interests of all concerned.

The kind of democracy that we as a nation practice in our contacts with other nations is very much conditioned by the kind of democracy that we practice as individuals. The nation can also influence the individuals.

In our international dealings we are beset by one consuming thought: "What can we do for our world neighbors that will prevent another world war?"

The thought should be instead: "What can we do for our world neighbors that will be good for them?" This thought is the very *spirit* of democracy. This essential democracy will live to the extent that it permeates the hearts of the doers. In its exercise we shall be making our greatest possible contribution to world peace.

The attaining of world peace and the forestalling of another world war are not identical objectives. At present we do not have world peace; and we are not in a new world war.

When the likelihood that one nation will make war on another nation will be as remote as is the likelihood that one of the states of the United States will make war on another of the states, then shall we be able to say that world peace has arrived.

Too many of us Americans take the attitude that if the rest of the world would be like us then world peace would be assured—just as so many of us churchgoers take the attitude that if everybody went to church as we do, then everything would be all right. We think it is the other nations that are grasping while we are being overindulgent.

And then we take the contradictory stand that the material help that we have given to the rest of the world has been with the attitude that we are doing it to save our own skins; that we are really helping ourselves when we grant this aid. And we are right, but it is the wrong approach to the problem.

We should not give aid primarily to assure world peace or for our personal gain, but rather because the nations are entitled to it. The best way to assure world peace is to forget about it in dealing with other nations and to think only in terms of how we can give them the help to which they are entitled.

We must stand up for our principles. But we must remember that they are not fixed. They can be bent without breaking. So we must learn to bend without breaking; to recognize that other nations often have principles that they cherish and that are often in conflict with ours.

We must recognize that many a supposed basic principle is resting on the very insecure foundation of special privilege. We must also recognize that making our neighbors' need and interests the basic criterion has the effect of putting all "basic" principles to the acid test of workability.

The early founders of the church knew the art of bending without breaking. It is the quality that made it possible for the church to survive. Jesus gave no skeleton outline of what kind of organization his followers were to build up. He posited attitudes and left the rest to events and the guidance of the divine spirit. They set up forms to take care of current needs, and changed them in keeping with changing needs.

Where does the church fit into the picture of world peace? It doesn't, if it will not recognize that other theologies seek and receive the guidance of the divine spirit. We can recognize the truths in other religions without in any way sacrificing any of Jesus' basic teachings on human relationships.

237

If there is one thing that should became increasingly evident about world conditions today it is that it is not *forms* that are causing out misunderstandings today and it is not forms primarily that will clarify conditions. The conditions are caused by an evil spirit. This evil spirit is partially the result of the accumulation of many special privileges from the past to certain large nations. The evil spirit gets a hold on the haves as well as on the have-nots.

Still we dare not overlook the fact that there is much interaction between form and attitude. Proper forms tend to induce proper attitudes and vice versa. This is very evident in the work and deliberations of the UN.

The countries that are of recent origin have been short-changed on heritage. To make matters worse, they are novices in the art of making their desires known to the rest of the world.

Many of the older countries have also been short-changed, but they have been so conditioned to many of these evil heritages that they do not recognize them as such. We Americans must be extremely careful that we do not allow our many special privileges to blind us to justice; and that we tie every special privilege in with an obligation.

It appears that in the work of the United Nations, more real statesmen are emerging from smaller nations than can be found in the ranks of those who represent the physically mighty nations. The representatives of these big nations are generally so busy harboring special privilege that they have little time left for statesmanship.

In our own country we should thank God for the numerical might of the little fellow; United Nations should be equally thankful for the numerical might of the little nations.

While we continue the probing and solving of these problems of special privilege by a combination of education and force, it is imperative that we roll up our sleeves and get up to work on the problems that we must solve if we hope to come to an understanding with the rest of the world.

The problem of the relationships between Russia and the rest of the civilized world is of such moment that special and specific attention must be accorded it.

One approach can be found in a careful consideration, in a practical way, of the difference between inherent rights and special privileges. A consideration of this problem would show that many of the things that we call inherent rights are called special privileges by the Russians

But this problem is so vast and complex that we dare not let it be our only concern. Pending agreement on the problem, we must set ourselves the task of leaning over backward in our effort to be fair to Russia. But having done so, we must also know when to be firm. This attitude is necessary because Russia has little experience in self-government; and we have given them much reason, during their darkest hours, to be suspicious of us.

We need the rough outline of an anatomy of world peace from which each individual can shape his own anatomy of world peace. We must be keenly aware that we are continually, as individuals, contributing to world peace and to chaos. This awareness must lead to an emphasis on the things that lead to peace..

We must cultivate more peace of mind within our own individual selves before we can be sure of permanent world peace; and that peace of mind comes from projecting our interests into the problems of our neighbors. In general, we can say that peace of mind comes from a sense of having made a worth-while effort.

If we would achieve world peace we must believe in its possibility. And we cannot believe by just willing to believe. Belief is based on something more substantial than that. We must begin with our own inner selves. Are we at peace with the all-pervasive spiritual world? This is just like saying, "Do we really love our neighbors?" But its very simplicity tends to make us overlook the devious paths we must tread to achieve genuine love for neighbor. Love is both a goal and a tool; we never achieve it fully.

It was not a handful of evil-minded men who brought on the two world wars. It was a multitude of "we's." The decision on another world war is also in the hands of the multitude of "we's."

The UN is indispensable. So are we. The UN delegates, in making their decisions, tend to react as they did back home when they were private citizens, as most of us will always be. If they had all been different as private citizens, they would not be the same kind of delegates that they are today.

We can *build* up an *attitude* that will lead us to believe in the possibility of *earning* world peace. The best foundation for this attitude is the sense that we ourselves are contributing something toward it.

Many have been deterred from doing good because the field is so vast and seemingly inexhaustible. It seems to be like trying to fill a bottomless hole. Those of us who have that attitude must restrict our horizon; temporarily, at least.

Each individual's anatomy of world peace is a separate mansion. Its dimensions are in a state of flux in keeping with the individual's growth. The general trend is expansion, but there may be contraction for the purpose of achieving a weightier concentration.

If we as a nation will start thinking about the rights of other nations, then the other nations will start thinking of our rights. After all, the other nations envy our position, and will therefore come more than half-way to meet us.

World peace, like happiness and peace, gets its start from within. It feeds on selfless service. Are we as a nation contributing our share of this *selfless* service? Let us give thought to the widow's mite. We are not the widow.

The best kind of help is the help that helps people to help themselves. This is our greatest social responsibility. An effort to discharge this responsibility runs head-on into the problem of special privilege. How a large segment of our population could persist for a whole generation or more in the belief that we could forever keep on selling to the world more than we were willing to buy from them can be explained by nothing except shortsighted self-interest. Every effort to protect a special privilege is an effort to prevent another person, or nation, or other section of the country, from helping himself.

The rich tend to portray themselves as benefactors of the poor at the same time that they seek to increase their special privileges. We are the rich among nations and prone to the same danger.

Every real confession of sin is accompanied by a recognition of a real sin or sinful condition. We are not doing enough by merely saying that we are all partly responsible for the conditions that bring on wars. We must be able to put our fingers on things that we can correct.

We must confess that we often do not use the upper hand wisely. In the pre-Civil War period the North held the upper hand over the South. It did not use it wisely. To this day the South holds the upper hand over the Negro. He who uses the upper hand wisely is always striving to make others independent of it.

The pre-Civil War period can be summarized as being too much occupied with the shortcomings of others—too much concerned with our rights and other people's duties. There was too little evaluation of the contemporary scene at home, as Jefferson always recommended.

Economic royalists from the North shed copious tears over the southern slaves, while many of their workers had to exist under conditions worse than slavery.

What is the biggest thing that the Civil War settled? Lincoln in his "Gettysburg Address" says that the people of the North and the South were engaged in a war to "determine." The war did not determine anything ex-

240

cept that the North was more powerful on the field of battle than the South. It did not solve the Negro problem. It may even be questioned whether it made an *approach* to the solution of the problem. We know that elsewhere in the world slaves were gradually being freed without recourse to arms, and it would have happened here.

This thought is injected here primarily because so many conservatives of today have made Lincoln's words their Bible; something that must not be questioned. Everyone's words should be questioned and weighed.

All theologians must reappraise their views to see if they are centered in their neighbors' good. Are their views contributing to world peace?

There is much talk these days about the need for removing trade barriers, political barriers, economic barriers, social barriers, and natural barriers. This is excellent. But why do we nearly always stop short before the momentous of all; theological *barriers?*

The theologians may counter that God never changes and they will not try to remake Him. We religionists must then remind them that even theologians change *their conceptions* of God when the pressure becomes sufficiently strong. At least that is what they have done in the past.

In considering reforms, we dare not ignore human nature. The Abolitionist movement started in the South. When it spread to the North and the North started to preach to the South, the South put its defense mechanism into operation. It is interesting to speculate on what a difference it would have made if the North had allowed the South to evolve its own Abolition movement.

The lessons most of us think we learned from the Civil War demonstrate that our attitude must change basically if we are to achieve world peace. We must learn to give others more chance to reform themselves.

If we in our zeal call on the spirit of Jesus for justification of our attitudes, we must remember that he made all his applications in the light of conditions as they existed in his day.

It is not of record that slavery stirred Jesus' indignation. He merely recognized that an outward act does not necessarily change an attitude. If the attitude is not changed, one reform merely leads to another great evil. Garrison's and Brown's attitudes were, "Crush them, and never mind their attitudes."

One of the most difficult retarding forces to cope with is cynicism, the attitude that questions all the motives of all our leaders. We shall not promote world peace by treating the word diplomat with scorn. Diplomats are also necessary. Besides good will there must be techniques. Our task is primarily prevention—preventing the attitudes that cause war. Diplomacy's

241

main task is repairing the damage that has already been done. Both are necessary.

At the same time, the laggards among the leaders must be prodded on by the force of an enlightened public opinion. The best prod consists in letting them know that we give them credit for the good intentions that they have.

In the present condition of the world, it cannot be emphasized too often that our greatest present hope for the future lies in the fact that we are not complacent. We no longer take the attitude that our way is the only way. We are keenly aware of the enormity of the task that confronts the world today. There is no definite blueprint to guide us and this holds for our pet theologies. We must remember this when we are tempted to snipe from the rear.

I just finished a letter to the parents of the pupils in the local schools. I ended with this sentence, "Let our common stake be education for the kind of citizenship that will insure world peace." That is as specific as I could be, because we local teachers are not at all agreed as to the nature of this education. Some of us think that the best way to insure world peace is to spend all our nervous energy in denouncing communism.

Al nations must take the attitude that the greatest danger is at home, where they can do something about it. Nothing is gained by being obsessed by the thought of what other should do.

Let us set ourselves the task of leading our national leaders to a realization of the fact that world peace is never achieved by a frontal attack; it comes on us unawares as we go about serving the needs of other nations. It is the spirit of democracy, regardless of name, that will usher in world peace.

Democracy does not chase after world peace. Instead it chases after world justice. When democracy possesses enough of us, then will world peace catch up with us as we pause to lend a hand to those on whom fortune has smiled less indulgently than on us. In so doing we shall be dispensing, not charity, but justice.

As we strive upward without losing sympathetic contact with our neighbors we shall discover that, like the bluebird of happiness, world peace is gradually overtaking us.

Peace comes to the heart through altruism. The prerequisite for world peace is more peaceful hearts—hearts of faith; trustful hearts.

Let us close this chapter and book by recapitulating. It seems safe to say that when Jesus was weighted down by the problems of this world, he found solace in the company of children. They trusted him and he trusted them.

What was the source of this mutual trust? In his dealings with the children he had the upper hand. He did not use the upper hand as a club or big stick. He was dealing with *people* who ultimately were potentially as great as he.

He did not try to build up their character by getting them to do his work for him. Each individual deserves the chance to discover—or create—his own mission in life.

What is our attitude when we have, or think we have, the upper hand? A satisfactory answer to this question will insure world peace—provided enough of us can give a satisfactory answer.

It is perhaps impossible to find a person who does not have the upper hand in some of his relationships with other people. There is his chance to make his own contribution to world peace.

As a nation we have the upper hand. And we are dealing with nations that are composed of individuals that *right now* are as great as we. Do the other nations cherish our company? It is largely our own fault if we are treated as a rich uncle. Some people who have the upper hand are esteemed as true friends by the lesser fry.

This is not over-simplying the problem of world peace—if we recognize the devious paths that must be traveled to come to so simple a faith.

BIBLIOGRAPHY

All the following books have made a contribution to the writing of this volume. In some cases I have completely forgotten all about the contents of the books; but they are included because at the time that I read them, I recognized a definite contribution that they had made to my thinking.

A few are included of which I do not approve. They are included because of the hold that their authors have on a considerable segment of the reading public. In all such cases my disapproval is found somewhere in this volume.

All authors and titles mentioned in the book that are not listed in this bibliography are taken from *Science, Philosophy and Religion—A Symposium*.

Adams, James Truslow. *The Living Jefferson.* New York: C. Scribner's Sons, 1936.

The Autobiography of Lincoln Steffens. New York: Harcourt Brace and Company, 1931.

Bellamy, Edward. *Equality.* New York: D. Appleton and Company, 1899.

Blanshard, et al. *Philosophy in American Education.* New York: Harper and Brothers, 1945.

Bridgman, Percy Williams. *The Intelligent Individual and Society.* New York: The Macmillan Company, 1938.

Brightman, Edgar S. *A Philosophy of Religion.* New York: Prentice-Hall, Inc., 1940.

Browne, Lewis. *This Believing World.* New York: The Macmillan Company, 1926.

Brubacher, John S. *A History of the Problems of Education.* New York: McGraw Hill, 1947.

Bryson, et al. *Conflicts of Power in Modern Culture.* New York: Harper and Brothers, 1947.

Burlinghame, Roger. *Of Making Many Books.* New York: C. Scribner's Sons, 1946.

Carrel, Alexis. *Man, the Unknown.* New York: Harper and Brothers, 1935.

Carver, Thomas Nixon. *Essays in Social Justice.* Cambridge: Harvard University Press, 1915.

Coe, George Albert. *Social Theory of Religious Education.* New York: C. Scribner's Sons, 1918.

Cripps, Sir Stafford. *Towards Christian Democracy.* London: F. Hubner and Company, 1946.

Durant, William James. *The Story of Philosophy.* New York: Simon and Schuster, 1926.

Einstein, Lewis. *Historical Change.* Cambridge: Cambridge University Press, 1946.

Eisenhower, Dwight D. *Crusade in Europe.* New York: Doubleday and Company, Inc., 1948.

Finkelstein, Brown and Ross. *The Religions of Democracy.* New York: Devin-Adair Company, 1946.

Frank, Glenn. *Thunder and Dawn.* New York: The Macmillan Company, 1932.

Frank, S. L. *God with Us.* London: J. Cape, 1946.

Freidel, Frank. *Francis Lieber.* Baton Rouge: Louisiana State University Press, 1947.

General Education in a Free Society. Cambridge: Harvard University Press, 1946.

Hartz, Louis. *Economic Policy and Democratic Thought.* Cambridge: Harvard University Press, 1948.

Hook, Sidney. *John Dewey, An Intellectual Portrait.* New York: John Day Company, 1939.

Kerschner, Frederick D. *Pioneers of Christian Thought.* New York: Bobbs-Merrill Company, 1930.

Lerner, Max. *Ideas are Weapons.* New York: The Viking Press, 1939.

————. *Public Journal.* New York: The Viking Press, 1945.

Liebman, Joshua Loth. *Peace of Mind.* New York: Simon and Schuster, 1946.

Link, Henry C. *Return to Religion.* New York: The Macmillan Company, 1936.

Lippmann, Walter. *A Preface to Morals.* New York: The Macmillan Company, 1929.

Ludwig, Emil. *The Nile.* New York: The Viking Press, 1937.

Madison, Charles Allan. *Critics and Crusaders.* New York: Henry Holt and Company, 1947.

McCallister, W. J. *The Growth of Freedom in Education.* London: Constable and Company, Ltd., 1931.

Orton, William Aylott. *The Liberal Tradition.* New Haven: Yale University Press, 1945.

Parkes, Henry Bamford. *The American Experience.* New York: Alfred A. Knopf, 1947.

Patterson, Howard S. *Readings in the History of Economic Thought.* New York: McGraw-Hill Book Company, 1932.

Pyle, Ernie. *Home Country.* New York: William Sloane Associates, 1947.

Religious Liberals Reply. By seven authors. Boston: The Beacon Press, 1947.

Robinson, James Harvey. *The Mind in the Making.* New York: Harper and Brothers, 1921.

Roosevelt, Franklin D. *Looking Forward.* New York: The John Day Company, 1933.

Science, Philosophy, and Religion—A Symposium. New York: Conference on Science, Philosophy, and Religion, 1941.

Shotwell, James T. *Essays in Intellectual History.* New York: Harper and Brothers, 1929.

Sumner, William Graham. *The Challenge of Facts and Other Essays.* New Haven: Yale University Press, 1914.

Symington, Thomas A. *Religious Liberals and Conservatives*. New York: Columbia University Press, 1935.

Thomas, Norman. *Appeal to the Nations*. New York: Henry Holt and Company, 1947.

Voorhis, Horace Jeremiah. *Confessions of a Congressman*. New York: Doubleday and Company, Inc., 1947.

Wallace, Henry. *The Century of the Common Man*. New York: Reynal and Hitchcock, 1943.

Warren, Robert Penn. *All the King's Men*. New York: Harcourt, Brace and Company, 1946.

Wells, H. G. *The Outline of History*. Garden City: Garden City Publishing Company, 1929.

Woodward, Hugh McCurdy. *Humanity's Greatest Need*. New York: George Putnam's Sons, 1932.